Mastering Amiga
AMOS

Phil South

Bruce Smith Books

Mastering Amiga AMOS

© Phil South
ISBN: 1-873308-12-4
First Edition: First Printing: October 1992

Editor: Mark Webb
Typesetting: Bruce Smith Books Limited
Series Cover Design: Ross Alderson

Bruce Smith Books is an imprint of Bruce Smith Books Limited.

Published by:
Bruce Smith Books Limited, Smug Oak Green Business Centre,
Lye Lane, Bricket Wood, Herts, AL2 3UG.
Telephone: (0923) 894355 – Fax: (0923) 894366.

Registered in England No. 2695164.
Registered Office: 51 Quarry Street, Guildford, Surrey, GU1 3UA.

Printed and bound in the UK by Ashford Colour Press, Gosport.

The Author

Phil South is a freelance writer and journalist, who started writing for a living in 1984, when he realised he couldn't actually stand working for anyone but himself. He says his popular columns in computer and other magazines are much harder to write than they are to read. Apart form being a writer he's also a heavy duty film buff, and owns a huge collection of ex-rental and sell-through videos. In his spare time he runs the White Goods Support Group, helping people to rid themselves of the insatiable desire to add more automatic washers, driers, cleaners and toaster ovens to their homes.

Phil lives in Somerset with his wife Stacey, a mouse called Ralph, and a dishwasher. (Oops!)

Contents

Appendix

Preface

There was a period of time when nobody but the most talented and mathematically trained people could program a powerful computer like the Amiga. All that changed with the release of AMOS.

AMOS has been out for about five years now, and in that time it's become a standard way for most normal human beings to program their Amiga in ways previously out of their grasp. AMOS is loosely based on the old BASIC programming language, but AMOS is carefully slanted towards the use of graphics and sound to make the best use of your Amiga.

You may have used a BASIC program before and not stuck at it because it was too difficult to get gratifying results. You won't have that problem with AMOS. You might have tried to learn a BASIC program before but given up because it was too complex. AMOS is simple. Don't think that you can never program in BASIC, as if you're too old or too young or too stupid to take something like this on. That's rubbish! If you can read or write or draw a stick man you can program in AMOS, and once you have the basics down, you'll never believe how easy the rest of it comes flooding along. You won't believe the pleasure you can get from programming, solving problems and creating your own software.

The reasons I'm doing this book are twofold, threefold if you count doing it for the money, which being a new father I have to consider. That aside the motivation behind it is all too simple:

1) to instruct you in how to use AMOS as a moderate beginner and

2) popularise the use of AMOS for things that you may not think of using it for, ie for other things as well as games.

AMOS is a remarkably flexible and easy to use programming tool, and like any kind of programming language it's only with *use* that it actually starts to make sense. You have to use the program before you can get any idea of how it does what it does, and why you'd want to do it, whatever it might be. What kinds of programs would you like to own? Are the ones you can buy not really what you were looking for? Well why not write your own software? Programming isn't about dry learning from books, it's about experience, and with a new programming language the quicker you get that experience the better.

So this book is packed with examples for you to type in and try out. There is one very good way to embed things into your memory, and that is to *do.* Type in short programs and run them, debug them and re-use them in your own programs. In the words of some really smart old dead guy *When you see, you know. When you do, you understand.* Fiendishly clever, these Chinese.

One important point I would draw your attention to is that although you can probably take to AMOS right off the bat, it's not going to hurt you to have experience of AmigaBasic (or any other BASIC) before you begin. Obviously if you have no idea about programming or BASIC itself then it might be an idea to read an excellent AmigaBasic guide book, or better still the brilliant *Illustrating Basic* by Donald Alcock, before you embark upon AMOS. It's not really my mission to teach you BASIC here, or the principles of programming. Although as a by product, teaching you AMOS may be just the thing you need to learn BASIC. (Take a deep breath and read that last sentence again before you ignore it!)

Having said that, I've done my best to create a book that's all things to all men, but as usual this is quite difficult. The tutorials are fairly lightweight at the start of each chapter, and much heavier at the end, so each chapter builds up to a climax by which time you should have an idea what I'm blathering on about. I've put in as much detail about what programming is, how it works and why you should do it, as I can. Frankly the rest is up to you, sunbeam.

Tech Talk

The raw text for this book was written on a combination of Protext 5.5 on an Amiga 2000, Word 4 on an Apple Macintosh IIsi, Windows Write on a Commodore LT286 laptop, and the Editor program on an Atari Portfolio. I like to be able to write on a number of things, as this keeps me fresh, and not only that but if I use any of the portables I can sit in the garden sunning myself while I work, like I am at the moment!

The AMOS programs were saved as text from AMOS itself, and pasted into my word processor at the time, so the code has not been changed in any way from the time it was running perfectly on AMOS. (If any typos creep in during the process of making the book, I blame Bruce but then again he'll blame me so I guess we're even! Only kidding.)

The raw text was all converted using my old (but worth its weight in gold) Readysoft Λ-Max II Mac Emulator on the Amiga and then saved to a Mac disk, and then transferred to Word 4 on the Mac IIsi, reformatted, spell checked and prettied up, and finally saved to disk and sent to Bruce who did all the typesetting on his Mac. (Phew.) The pictures were grabbed using a Datel Action Replay II inside my Amiga 2000, chopped over to Mac disk using the process described above, and finally converted to Mac format by Bruce using Adobe Photoshop 2.0.

The AMOS version used for this book was version 1.34, and if you know what's good for you you'll use that version too! Although any version of AMOS from Easy AMOS through to Amos Pro will do.

Many Thanks

Thanks are due to Bruce Smith for asking me to do this book and for selling my first one so well, Stacey and Harriet (my wife and daughter) for putting up with me writing another book so soon after the last one, and also many thanks to Europress Software for all their help in solving technical problems, giving out information and upgrades, and generally being into the project from the start. Thanks also to Aaron Fothergill, Richard Vanner, Peter Hickman and Sandra Sharkey for all their help on technical matters and things which I didn't know about. Thanks be to everyone.

Lastly, on a sombre note this book is dedicated to the memory of the late Kevin Hall, ace writer, AMOS conference moderator on CIX, and all round good egg who died young and for no reason at all. Words really are far too inadequate. See you later, Kev.

Phil South, Somerset, October 1992

Without Whom

This book has been driven by my own intense desire to get it finished in time, a thing which would not have happened without the help of my AMOS friends all over the country.

First and foremost for help and encouragement I'd cite Peter Hickman as the best friend a writer of an AMOS book could have, for his free advice and monumental knowledge of AMOS and all its ins and outs. He's also contributed as much to the furtherment of AMOS as a programming tool than almost anyone else I can think of besides Aaron, Len and Anne and Sandra. Thanks Pete, I owe you more than one.

Aaron Fothergill also contributed in no mean terms to the way the book turned out, and many thanks are due to him also for keeping me up to date on the workings of the AMOS Club and latest versions of CText, SpriteX and TOME.

Thanks also to Len and Anne Tucker of Totally AMOS and latterly of the AMOS PD Library for their constant support of the column and this book.

And thanks are definitely due to Sandra Sharkey for creating both the AMOS PD Library and Deja Vu Software, and bringing AMOS kicking and screaming into the 90s.

And finally posthumous thanks to Kevin Hall for all his advice early on in the making of this book, and for the help he would have given had he not been taken from us so young.

Cheers everyone. Go and buy yourself a big drink.

1:
Introduction
to AMOS

If you bought your Amiga wanting to create your own programs rather than just enjoying other people's creations, it must be very frustrating for you to discover how hard it is to create something on a modern computer. You are in luck, however, because in the 1990s AMOS has taken away all that difficult learning from you, and given you an easy method of creating slick and professional looking and sounding programs in very little time. You can load in sounds and graphics and have them all at your disposal through simple BASIC language commands, enabling you to create not just game programs, but also utilities, applications and even operating systems, of a kind. All kinds of games and programs can be made and compiled into machine code for placing in the Public Domain or selling to the world, and all for very little outlay. Your biggest asset is the one between your ears.

AMOS has been a long time in the making, and although now it's the engine of choice for anyone wishing to develop a program without the need for machine code or C, it's taken a while to get to that stage. Although it began life on the Atari ST, it's found a home on the Amiga, being the more powerful computer. Ever since the creator of AMOS, Francois

Lionet, first began to create AMOS, he fell in love with the Amiga's beautiful graphics and sound, and he's been very loyal to the machine ever since.

AMOS Genesis

Francois was working as a vetenary surgeon in his native France, and programming on his Atari ST in his spare time, when he came up with the forerunner of AMOS, an ST program called STOS.

The program grew out of a need for an easy way of creating games on the ST, the earliest 16 bit mass market computer. The ST had good graphics, tolerable sound, and was streets ahead of the competition. (The Amiga wasn't really around much yet, I hasten to add.) But programming it meant either tapping in code in the form of assembly language, or C, and compiling it. This was a very specialised job, and not really possible for beginners to computers to learn easily. BASIC was easy to learn, but lacked any real punch in the sound and graphics department, which was what was needed for games on a 16 bit computer. So Francois set himself the task of trying to write a version of BASIC which had all the power of machine code but in a simple to use language.

The first lines of code were written in December 1986, and the French version of STOS was released to an unsuspecting French public on November of 1987. They were so unsuspecting in fact that in Francois' own words it was a *"Total flop, we only had around 50 sales!"*

In the Spring of 1988 however a chance contact with Europress (then Mandarin) Software's Richard Vanner secured a deal for the UK release of STOS. A lot more work was done on the program to make it faster and more attractive, and in the Autumn of 1988 the program was released with all the hype and coverage usually reserved for a game program.

The program was an almost immediate success, and prompted the creation of the STOS Compiler in February 1989 to fill the need for still more speed and power. Once a program had been written in STOS, it could then be compiled into fast machine code, making any program you wrote in STOS as fast and as powerful as if you'd coded it from scratch.

STOS gained a lot of followers all over Europe, and envious glances from the new Amiga camp. The Amiga was a newer computer, had more powerful features but had no such easy way of getting to all its important little places like its superb stereo sound and 4096 colour graphics. This was soon to change forever.

After STOS

The original STOS program was crude by modern standards, it had line numbers (like all old fashioned BASICs) and all the direct mode commands were entered without a line number on the same screen. Modern compilers and interpreters had a lot more going for them in the interface stakes, and this was something that had to be addressed if STOS was going to move on in any way.

Francois knew there had to be a next step, and it wasn't long before it happened. *"The ST version was over"* he told me. *"The Amiga is rising in popularity all over the World, so I thought it was time to program the Amiga version of STOS. As soon as I discovered the Amiga, I realised that AMOS, as the Amiga version of STOS would be called, would have to be totally re-written to make use of the enormous power of the Amiga. I also wanted to make AMOS a more modern computer language, without line numbers and with a good editor."*

Programming on the new version started in April 1989, then stopped again abruptly in March 1990 when Francois was called up by the French Army for his National Service. AMOS was nowhere near finished, and so he took his Amiga and PC with him to Boot Camp, and programmed in his room after hours. *"I still managed to work,"* he says, *"but what a stress!"* In the end he had to move out his computer equipment to a place near his mother's house, and this meant that in his time off he could work in peace and quite. AMOS was duly finished after 14 months, and version 1.1 was released in June 1990.

In September of that same year Francois upgraded the system based on customer feedback, and version 1.21 was released into the Public Domain. Upgrade disks were PD for convenience, and for security reasons they updated the previous system rather than being a new stand alone program. But the upgrades were free to all users, and this was one of the great strengths of the system which still prevails to this day.

But everyone was waiting for the AMOS Compiler. Some people are on record as saying it couldn't be done, and if it could be done it wouldn't be very good. But as usual Francois proved them wrong and in September 1990 he began work on this mammoth task. Not only must the compiler compile AMOS programs into machine code, but the resultant code had to be runable from the CLI, the Workbench or from within AMOS. The program was to have a front end, for ease of use, or just a plain CLI runnable version for codeheads who can't relate to front ends! In between starting the compiler project and finishing it, Francois also made substantial upgrades and fixes to the system in version 1.23, released in December 1990, and in March 1991 released a French version of AMOS, and finished his National Service (with a big sigh of relief).

Suitably recovered from his stint in the military, Francois put the finishing touches to AMOS Compiler and made a new version of AMOS to support it, version 1.3, which were both released eventually in June 1991.

Meanwhile working away in seclusion Voodoo Software were at work on a secret project for AMOS, which emerged as AMOS 3D in July 1991. This was a bolt on extension to the language which enabled users to create 3D vector graphics objects and animate them at speed within AMOS programs. The program is the first such commercial product on the market, soon followed by a few more limited imitators PD and commercial programs. At the same time AMOS 3D was knocking them dead, work began on Easy AMOS, a beginners product aimed at first time programmers and children. The project seemed like a doddle at first but actually took over 8 months to complete.

Easy AMOS was finally complete in February 1992, and as well as this a newer version of AMOS was released, version 1.34, and a new version of the compiler too. Easy AMOS was released in April 1992, and was followed in May by the long awaited release of AMOS in German.

Despite being five years old, AMOS continues to go from strength to strength, and as the program develops and changes, so too do the uses and possibilities for the program in the future.

The next step is a version of AMOS for the IBM PC called PCOS, and of course AMOS Professional, taking AMOS into the 90s and beyond.

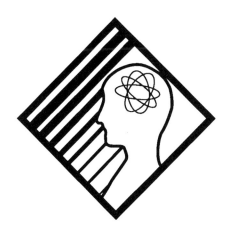

2:
Basic
Principles

AMOS is a programming language, but like most languages it takes a little time to learn it. You have to get to know a little bit of the lingo at a time, a bit like learning a foreign language in the real world. If you want to learn French really well, go and plonk yourself with a guide book in the middle of Paris for a month or three. You'll be using the language all the time, so you'll get really good at it in a really short time. You'll start by learning a few phrases that you need all the time, and add new words as you go along as you need them. Some of these will only crop up from time to time, but other words you'll need every day, every time you need to speak to anyone.

The same is true of learning a computer language like AMOS. Once you have a few phrases (what we call *keywords*) down pat, you'll be able to venture forth on your own. After that you need to know the *syntax*. In a spoken language the syntax is the grammar, or how the words are put together to get the right effect. In computer languages like AMOS, the commands or keywords must be used in the right order and context to work properly, or to have the right effect. Once you have a vocabulary of AMOS keywords and a knowledge of the right syntax in which to use those words, you can build on the keywords you know and use them with confidence, learning by experience.

But the most important thing to know about is that learning AMOS should be fun. Enjoy yourself, because this isn't a test that you're going to pass or fail. You're learning because you want to.

How AMOS Works

The whole point about AMOS is that it is an *Extended BASIC*. That is to say if a normal BASIC was a 1964 Ford Cortina, a 1992 Porsche would be an Extended BASIC. AMOS is just like a normal BASIC except that it's been optimised in certain ways, tuned up to work faster and do far more than any normal BASIC.

AMOS uses a few tricks to get the most power out of your Amiga. Firstly sounds and graphics are stored in memory banks inside your Amiga's memory. These are special areas of memory which AMOS allocates to store these things, and calls them up from memory when needed. This is a lot faster than loading graphics or sounds from disk, as you can imagine. The main reason for doing this is speed. Once you've loaded a screen into memory, for example, you can flip it up onto the screen in less than a second, rather than about four seconds from disk. Sounds too are stored in memory, like music and sound effects. They can be used on demand without loading from disk. And the beauty of this system is that the sounds and graphics you load into the memory banks are saved invisibly to disk with your program code, so when you load and run a program you're getting a darn sight more than just the raw text that makes up the program. All the saved memory banks load into memory as well, so the program has a lot of hidden allies waiting in the wings, supplying more power.

Another trick that AMOS uses, is the very fast optimised commands. Optimised means that the command has been written so as to be as fast as it can be. No AMOS command is running at less than peak efficiency. This means that even a simple program runs much faster than a program in a normal BASIC. Secondly AMOS has another simpler computer language which can be used inside AMOS programs, and this is AMAL. AMAL stands for AMOS Animation Language which is a special set of animation and movement routines which are not only automatically compiled before running, they also operate simultaneously on a number of AMAL *channels*. This is *multitasking* at its best, and AMOS is the first true multitasking BASIC for the Amiga. (Note for tech heads: it multitasks AMAL, but you can't run AMOS as well as another program in memory.)

Because AMAL can take over the animation and movement of items on the screen, as in a game for example where the sprites must all move at once, the rest of the AMOS commands can be saved for slower processes in the program, like loading screens or files, turning sounds on and off, that kind of thing.

So there are memory banks, optimised commands and AMAL, but at the centre of AMOS there's the editor and Direct Mode and these two windows are where everything happens.

The Editor

When you first start the program you get presented with the editor screen. Figure 2.1 shows you the initial state of the editor, with the rows of buttons along the top of the screen. (The credits as pictured here vanish when you press the mouse button.) The program has disabled the Amiga's normal windowing system, Intuition, or at least the Workbench side of it, and so there are no Amiga back and front gadgets on the window, neither are there any menus along the title bar. (There's no title bar in fact!) What you have instead is a pair of rows of buttons along the top of the screen.

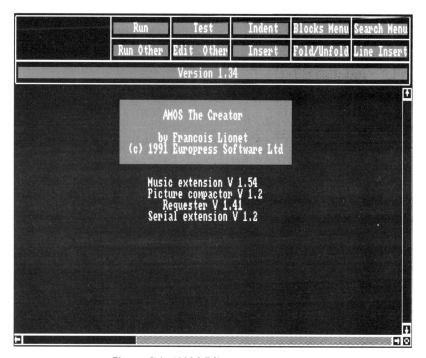

Figure 2.1. AMOS Editor startup screen.

Press the right button and the titles of these buttons change, to the rows in Figure 2.2. These are your basic AMOS editor commands.

		Load	Save	Save As	Merge	Merge Ascii
		Ac.New/Load	Load Others	New Others	New	Quit

▮   L-1   C-1   Text-53246   Chip-799856 Fast-1068752 Edit:

Figure 2.2. Alternate editor menu.

AMOS Editor Commands

The commands are activated by a clever bit of button twiddling. Click on one of the buttons and the command is activated. Press and hold the right button, and click on a button, and the new command (revealed by pressing the right button) will be activated. For example, clicking on the button on the top left will run a program, but holding down the right button and clicking on the same button will load a program. You can also use the Shift key on your keyboard to get the other menu up instead of using the right button. Here's what all the commands do, starting from top left and ending at bottom right:

Run

Obviously this runs the current program. You can also press F1 to achieve the same result. The program is first tested for any syntax errors and then it is run, until an error occurs that is. If you get an error of any kind (see Appendix B for more details) then the program will stop with an error message at the bottom of the screen, giving you a fair idea of what went wrong and where.

Test

This command tests the program without running it. If you have written any obvious syntax errors into your program, these can be weeded out here. These will generally include any unintentional mistakes like using an AMOS keyword as a variable name, like A$=Load. If your variable is correctly named, it will always appear in capitals, but if you've used a keyword by mistake, it will start with a capital letter and the rest of the word will be lower case.

Indent

Indents all the lines (like the lines within a loop) which are better off indented in the program to show the program structure. This just neatens up your program and makes it easier to read, rather than affecting its function.

Blocks Menu

This takes you into the Blocks menu, replacing all the main menu command buttons with new commands for marking, cutting and pasting sections of your programs.

Search Menu

This takes you to the Search menu, where you can apply search/replace type commands to your program.

Run Other

This runs an accessory program, or another AMOS program in memory. You can run as many AMOS programs as you have room for in memory.

Overwrite

Hit this to change the text editing mode from Insert to Overwrite. Insert means that all letters already on the screen will move to accommodate any you type at the start. In overwrite the letters will write over those already on the screen.

Fold/Unfold

Procedures can be folded to take up less space and show the true structure of your program.

Line Insert

This inserts an extra blank line in your program if there's something you forgot to put in.

System Menu

Now when you press the right mouse button (or Shift key) you are looking at another menu, called the System Menu. Here is what you can see on this menu:

Load

This brings up a requester for the loading of programs into memory ready for running.

Save

This brings up the same requester for saving your freshly written program from memory onto disk for safe-keeping.

Save As

If you already have the program on disk but want to save it as a different name, you can do so like this.

Merge

This adds a program on disk into the current listing on screen at the point you have placed the cursor. This is brilliant for bolting together separate PROCs or even sections of other programs, to make a whole functioning program.

Merge ASCII

This is the way you can load ASCII files, usually programs from other forms of BASIC, for conversion to AMOS. If you've obtained an AMOS program from a bulletin board, or a listing from a magazine, you can load it in this way. This even means you can use another sort of editor to create your program (if the AMOS editor isn't to your taste) and then load it into AMOS later as ASCII text!

Ac.New/Load

This clears the space reserved for Accessory programs and loads a new one from the disk. It does this automatically, taking the first program it finds with the .acc extension.

Load Others

This enables you to load a specific accessory program from disk, selecting it from the usual requester.

New Others

This enables you to erase one or all of the acc programs you have loaded from memory.

New

This blanks the memory of all AMOS code, meaning you can load in a fresh program. This command also clears any memory banks you have operating, so be sure you either save them out as .abk files or save the main AMOS program and these with them.

Quit

This stops AMOS and sends you back to the Workbench.

Blocks Menu

Some of the buttons on the initial menu page will take you to another set of buttons which do other things. Like the Blocks Menu where you can mark blocks of code for cutting and pasting:

Block Start

This marks the beginning of the block. (You can also mark blocks using the right mouse button.)

Block End

This similarly marks the end of the block. (Don't forget the right mouse button can be used instead! Nah, nobody's memory is that short.)

Block Cut

Once you've marked a block you can cut it out using this command.

Block Paste

Once you've cut a block it sits there in the buffer until you want to paste the code in the block somewhere else in the program. You may not want to, but you can if you like.

Block Move

This moves the marked block to the location of the cursor. So you'd mark a block, move the cursor to where you want the code in the marked block to move to, and then hit Block Move.

Block Store

This is what you'd call Copy in any other program. The block you've marked is copied into memory and can be pasted in the current program (or one of the other AMOS programs in memory) using the Paste Block command.

Block Hide

This clears the block marks, in case you've highlighted the wrong bit and want to start again.

Block Save

This saves off the marked section of code onto disk, so you can borrow bits of code from other programs and assemble them all on disk. Later you can use Merge to bring them all together as one program.

Save ASCII

This is the way you generate ASCII code from your AMOS programs, should you want to that is. AMOS code is not readable by anything else but AMOS, but if you wanted to save off an AMOS program for printing out or loading into a DTP program (like I have in this book for example), you would highlight the code you want to save, and save it as text using this command.

Block Print

This prints the currently selected block out to your printer, if you have one! There is one keyboard command which you won't find on a button and that's Select All. This selects the whole program for saving as ASCII text or for printing, and you do this by holding Ctrl-A. Obviously if you Select All by pressing Ctrl-A and then print, you can print out everything rather than just a small section.

Search Menu

Then finally we have the Search Menu, where all the search/replace commands are:

Find

This searches from the cursor position down your file for a certain word, which is handy if you write big programs and can't remember where you've left something.

Find Next

This repeats the Find command using the same word you typed in before using Find.

Find Top

Exactly the same as Find, but this time it starts from the top of your file.

Replace

This works in concert with Find to replace the found word with the correct word, of your choosing. You are asked if you want to replace the word or not.

Replace All

Same as Replace, except it just changes all occurrences without your consent. Use this with caution.

Low<>Up

This button changes the case sensitivity of your word search. Leave it like it is and it will treat upper case letters like *A* differently from lower case ones like *a*. If you click on this it toggles to say Low=Up, which means that all cases are treated equal.

Open All

If you have folded all the PROCedures in your program, this will open them all up again. Handy if you want to print out the whole program and want to make sure you don't get any stray closed PROCs.

Close All

Same as above but this time all the PROCs in your program are closed all at once, making the listings shorter and more manageable, and also saving on memory.

Set Text B.

Stands for SET TEXT BUFFER, and this means the amount of room you have in the editor for your programs. This is preset for you in the config program, and this is handy if you need to expand the amount of space you need for any reason.

Set Tab

This simply allows you to set the amount of spaces the Tab key will move the cursor. Rather than tab all over the place to make your listings interesting, why not use the Indent button?

Make an effort to learn all the keyboard short-cuts for the various menu items. To help you Table 2.1 contains a list of all the keyboard short cuts in AMOS.

Menu	Option	Hotkey
General	Run	F1
	Test	F2
	Indent	F3
	Blocks Menu	F4 (or Ctrl key)
	Search Menu	F5 (or Alt key)
	Run Other	F6
	Edit Other	F7
	Overwrite	F8
	Fold/Unfold	F9
	Line Insert	F10 (or Ctrl-I)
System Menu	Load	Shift-F1
	Save	Shift-F2
	Save As	Shift-F3
	Merge	Shift-F4
	Merge ASCII	Shift-F5
	Ac.New/Load	Shift-F6
	Load Others	Shift-F7
	New Others	Shift-F8
	New	Shift-F9
	Quit	Shift-F10
Blocks Menu	Block Start	Ctrl-B (or Ctrl-F1)
	Block End	Ctrl-E (or Ctrl-F6)
	Block Cut	Ctrl-C (or Ctrl-F2)
	Block Paste	Ctrl-P (or Ctrl-F7)
	Block Move	Ctrl-M (or Ctrl-F3)

Table 2.1. AMOS Editor keyboard short-cuts.

Menu	Option	Hot key
Blocks Menu	Block Store	Ctrl-S (or Ctrl-F8)
	Block Hide	Ctrl-H (or Ctrl-F4)
	Block Save	Ctrl-F9
	Save ASCII	Ctrl-F5
	Block Print	Ctrl-F10
	To select all	Ctrl-A
Search Menu	Find	Ctrl-F (or Alt-F1)
	Find Next	Ctrl-N (or Alt-F2)
	Find Top	Alt-F3
	Replace	Ctrl-R (or Alt-F4)
	Replace All	Alt-F5
	Low<>Up	Alt-F6
	Open All	Alt-F7
	Close All	Alt-F8
	Set Text B	Alt-F9
	Set Tab	Ctrl-Tab (or Alt-F10)

Table 2.1. AMOS Editor keyboard short-cuts.

Using the Mouse

The mouse is used in the AMOS Editor for a number of tasks, much like in a word processor. Use of the right mouse button in the editor, for example.

When I first used AMOS I had a problem with the file requester. I couldn't initially figure out how to look at another disk drive (or assigned path or device) without waiting till the computer had read the disk and then laboriously typing the name in by hand. But using the right mouse button makes it a lot simpler.

If you click the right mouse button in an AMOS requester, you get a list of current devices, drives, RAM: etc. Just click on the one you want and bob is very much your uncle. Simple really, but I never saw this in the manual. I just don't read the things, a by product of being a computer writer and not believing that a manual could tell me anything useful. What a cynic! I really should read manuals more you know because, unlike so many others, the AMOS manual is very good, and although it may take a while and a bit of delving to find what you're looking for, the information is in there somewhere if you look for it.

Anyway in order to bring up the drive and device selections you must press the right button. Then once you've selected your disk and directory, simply click on the SetDir button, and this directory will pop up every time. It's so simple even Ralph my pet mouse could do it. Okay, so his paws are a bit too small to move the Amiga mouse, but I was only joking and you get the gist.

The second way of using the right button is for selecting text in the program, as I've said just a short while ago in the bit about Blocks. In a normal word processor or text editor, you can use the left mouse button to stroke a highlight around the text you want to mark, and cut, paste and copy it around the current and other documents. In AMOS the right button performs this function. Try it. Load a program, then put the pointer on the first character of the listing. Press the right button and move the mouse down. Brilliant eh? Now you can cut and paste this section, even save it off as ASCII text using the Block Menu's ASCII Save option.

Direct Mode

As well as the main editor, there is a separate screen for direct mode. In a normal BASIC editor with line numbers, any line which is not started with a line number is deemed not part of the program, and so is executed immediately. All manner of things can be done like this, from testing out lines you're not sure will work, to loading and saving programs.

In AMOS these direct mode commands are tapped into a sort of modified Command Line Interface. You can list the contents of disks, load screens, and even load and save .abk files into memory banks. ABK Files are a special memory bank format used by AMOS, and if you have a file ending with .abk, then it's an AMOS memory bank. To load them in in direct mode you simply say:

```
Load "whatever it is.abk"
```

and the file will hop into AMOS in the correct memory bank for whatever the information is. It finds its own way you don't have to tell it where to go!

A memory bank is where AMOS stores all its sprite, screen and sound information. You can even use a memory bank as a temporary workspace to store information until you need it.

There are 15 memory banks, and they're laid out as in Table 2.2.

Memory Bank	Contents
1	Sprites
2	Icons
3	Music
4	Amal
5	* data
6	* data
7	* data
8	* data
9	* data
10	* data
11	* data
12	* data
13	* data
14	* data
15	* data

Table 2.2. AMOS's 15 memory banks.

The first four banks always have those sorts of data in them, number 1 always being for moving screen objects or *sprites*; number 2 always being for blocks of graphic data for background, or what they call *icons* in AMOS; number 3 is always music (.abk versions of tracker files); and finally number 4 is always reserved for AMAL files. All the other banks can be used for samples, compressed screens, and any other type of data you want to store in your AMOS program. When you save the AMOS file, then all these banks of data are saved with it. You can of course also save the banks on their own as .abk files, if you want to use the same files for other programs. You can also steal other people's .abk files this way!

Compressing Graphics

You may wonder why a lot of the graphics you see in AMOS programs aren't accessible from disk. Sometimes you will run an AMOS program and you'll get a screen of graphics which you can't find as a file on the disk. The reason is that these graphics are compressed or *packed* into a memory bank, taking up less room and being accessible instantly rather than loading from disk.

To compress screens you use the Spack (or *Screen Pack*) command, and what it does is compress IFF screens (or portions of screens) into banks of memory. Once in a bank of memory, the screens are saved with the program and can be unpacked onto the screen with the Unpack command. Here is an excellent example of how to Unpack a series of packed screens (quick fanfare for your first AMOS program):

```
Close Editor
Hide On
Music 1
A=4
Repeat
Unpack A To 0
If A=4 Then Wait 400
If A>4 and A<13 Then Wait 250
If A=13 Then Wait 300
Fade 3
Wait 30
Inc A
If A=14 Then A=4
Until Mouse Key=1
End
```

To get the screens into a memory bank you need to write a small AMOS program to pack the screens into a bank, like so:

```
F$=Fsel$("*","","Load a picture")
Load Iff F$,0
Spack 0 To 1
Print "The length of your new bank is ";Length(1);"
bytes"
Wait Key
Screen Close 0
Unpack 1 To 0
```

Now if you go to direct mode and type Listbank you will get a listing of the current graphics bank. Don't worry about what all this means for the time being, just type it in and save it. Notice how AMOS knows that keywords should have a capital letter at the beginning and be lower case otherwise, and that all variables are changed to upper case, no matter how you type them in?

Why should you use Spack and Unpack? Well, one of the most memory intensive bits of code you can include in your programs is a graphics screen, and although you can read and write IFF style graphics, you can fit more in if you use compressed AMOS graphics. That way you can approach the kind of graphics quality in commercially produced software, as the only way they can fit a huge game and graphics into memory is to crunch the graphics down a lot.

Chapter 15 has more details about Spack, and information on ways of saving and loading sections of a screen or even a brush. Brushes load into the screen at the top left corner so to save a brush all you have to do is set the Spack command to compact only the top left square of the screen. Then once you've unpacked the graphic you can plonk it anywhere on the screen. This could be a series of mouth portions of someone's face, where rather than redrawing the whole head each time the character's mouth moves. You can just unpack a new mouth and stamp it over the bottom of the head.

The Config Program

To set up the basic configuration of your AMOS system, you must load and run the CONFIG.AMOS program on your disk. This tells you what extensions (like TOME and Compiler) you have loaded and generally sets the system up. This is better described in the chapters concerning each extension, but for now Ill just say that to run the config program, load it into AMOS and click on run. You'll be prompted as to what you have to do.

AMOS Compiler and AMOS 3-D

We'll go into these in more detail in Chapter 16 and 17, but for now let me tell you about how these extensions work. An extension in AMOS is a bit of code which is attached to the program to drive certain new functions and commands. The compiler adds the ability to compile an AMOS program in machine code. The resultant program can be run like any other Amiga program, via the Shell or the Workbench. Compiled programs will run on their own without any further interference from AMOS, so your AMOS program can be thought of as the source code (the original uncompiled code) for the finished program. Anyone using your compiled AMOS program will know you used AMOS, it won't look shabby like some BASIC programs, and it'll run fast and sweet time after time.

AMOS 3D is a different Morphy Richards of Pilchards altogether. Once this extension is installed you can animate 3D objects in your AMOS programs. The objects are created in a special Object Modeller (called OM for short) and then the objects are loaded into an AMOS program for use. The objects can be moved around over

IFF pictures, along with sprites and other types of graphics in pretty much the same way as any other AMOS graphics and screen objects.

Using compiler and 3D you can create literally *any* kind of program you desire, from a utility to a 3D game simply, quickly and professionally.

TOME

Finally, and once again we'll go into this in more detail in Chapter 20, there is AMOS TOME. This is the Total AMOS Map Editor. It's designed for the creation of large maps for games, where the backgrounds have to be carefully constructed, consistent and be far larger than the normal Amiga screen. TOME not only edits the maps, but supplies you with the commands you need to move them around within your AMOS programs. Like 3D, all programs with TOME in them can be compiled.

So that's AMOS

This is how AMOS works and what you need to know in order to get the best out of it. All that remains for me now is to cover all the fine detail, the bits in between the facts, so you can do some of your own AMOSing. Turn the page and let's get started.

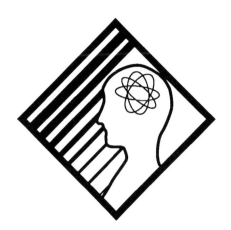

3:
Program
Structures

So now you know how to use the editor, the thing you will want to do is start programming, but hold on to your need for gratification for a minute. Before you start programming you must figure out what it is you want from your program. Okay so what you really want to do is mess about with AMOS and find out what it can do. That's fine, go right ahead. Run through the chapter on AMOS commands and what they do, and see what happens. You can test out any command you like to see what it really does, but some commands don't work without a little bit of preparation. For example, you can't load a picture unless you've got a picture on disk ready to load! You may want to load and run some music, but you'll have to have prepared some music to load, and so on and so forth.

Once you've toshed about with AMOS and got it all out of your system, you'll finally come back to this book and want to know how to do it all properly.

Dem Bones, Dem Bones

The way your program is laid out on the screen, what goes where, is called the *structure* of your program. AMOS programs have a similar structure to other types of BASIC, and the worst thing about trying to explain the best way to lay out a program is that there is no real *best* way.

You can write the program in one big lump, with lines of code calling other lines of code back and forth, and this is what I would call the linear approach. The other major way of doing it is by using subprograms and procedures (*Procs*), where you have a main program and this drives all the other parts of the program, which can be added and subtracted without harming the structure too much. This is what I'd call a more modular approach, and it is this way that I think is the best. In fact as you work your way through this book you'll come across routines that can be included in your programs, and if you follow the modular approach these will be a lot easier to insert into your own programs.

Proc and Roll

Procedures are at the very heart of what makes AMOS so powerful as a development programming language. In fact all well structured versions of the BASIC language have a Procedure system of some kind, and in this case AMOS is not exceptional. But if you've come from a lesser BASIC to AMOS, you might not really know what you're missing if you don't use them.

Using Procs is easy. Imagine a Proc as a command you've added to AMOS which does something you would like a programming command to do. If every function a program does is a Proc, you can write each segment of the program separately and test them one at a time, then finally combine everything into one big program. Instead of debugging the whole program you are ironing out any glitches along the way, and so you don't run into problems later on.

So before you can use a Proc, first you have to define it, and this can be done anywhere in the program, using the:

        Procedure <name>

command. This could be placed at the beginning or the end of the program code, but it doesn't matter as AMOS can find a Proc definition as long as it's there. If it's not there AMOS will tell you so. After the Proc is defined, it can be called, and you do this either with:

        Proc <name>

or just the name of the Proc. So as I said before the new Proc is almost like a new AMOS command that you've written yourself, and once defined you can use the Proc any time you like in the program just like any other AMOS command, simply by typing in a line of code.

To demonstrate this principle take this very short demo program:

```
Proc OYEZ
'
Procedure OYEZ
   Print "Phil South! And why not?"
End Proc
```

The procedure in this case is a simple routine to print the "Phil South! And why Not?" string in the Print command. Every time you use Proc's title, in this case OYEZ, in the program, you get the same result as if you'd typed the Print line inside the Proc. Most of the time you'll use the name of the Proc without typing the Proc part of the call, like so:

```
OYEZ
'
Procedure OYEZ
   Print "Phil South! And why not?"
End Proc
```

Of course the routine inside the Proc definition can be more than just a single command, even a whole little program to itself if you like, and this is the big idea. In a program you have a Proc for each bit of the program which you then call from a main loop. For example you could have a program like this:

```
MAIN:
'
CHECK_COLISION
MOVIT
SHOT
'
Goto MAIN
'
Procedure CHECK_COLISION
Procedure MOVIT
Procedure SHOT
```

which is an idea for a simple game program. As long as the Proc defs are in the program somewhere, the Procs will work. They don't have to be in the actual flow of the program, inside a loop or something. These are like DATA statements, which can be read anywhere in the program by the READ command.

Looking at the Procs in the last example you may think I've forgotten to include anything inside the Proc defs, but this is not the case. The Procs have been *folded.* You see the real groovy thing about Procs is you can fold them up into one single line to make your listings more readable. (Folding is done using the Fold/Unfold command in the AMOS command menu.) When you activate this command it toggles the folding on and off for the procedure at the point you've inserted your cursor. Toggling means you press it once and it folds the Proc, press again and it unfolds it. When you've folded the Proc, there is only a single line left, this is how our simple example would look:

OYEZ

'

Procedure OYEZ

It works just the same as it did, but the trick is that you just don't have to look at all the annoying details.

Even better, there is a special Proc locking program called Lock.AMOS on your AMOS disk, which locks the Procs in your program meaning that anyone else who gets hold of the disk cannot unfold your Procs and examine the code. Nice if you spend a lot of time coming up with neatly coded Procs which you use in all your own programs, and it means that prying eyes cannot steal your code. Of course you can also compile the program to keep out code stealers, but we'll get to that later on. But let's not be too paranoid. If you think you're such a good coder, how is anyone going to copy your style? Be better, not just good.

Once you've finished a Proc you can even save it off on its own like a separate program, like so:

SCREENSAVEPROC.AMOS

for a Proc called (for the sake of argument) ScreenSave, for instance. You don't have to save Procs with the same name as the Proc, but it helps to identify them on the disk if you do.

So your routines for all the day to day business in your programs like opening screens, loading .abk files and all that other mundane stuff, can all be saved off to disk as folded and locked Procs. All you do to build a program from these disconnected modules is to Merge them with the current program.

So every time you write a program, you start by creating a different module for each stage of the program, and then just bolt them together. It's a nice way to work as the job is neatly broken down into manageable bits, and also you may have some very nice routines you can reuse, just by reloading them!

What's Up, Procs?

Procedures are one of the most important things to get to grips with in AMOS, apart from AMAL that is. So it's important you use them properly. Remember to declare variables you want to share with the rest of the program, or they will be *local.* Like so:

```
SNOUT=10 : SNOOT=15 : SNOUT$="Phil"
Procedure SNOUTY
   Shared SNOUT, SNOOT, SNOUT$
   Print SNOUT, SNOOT, SNOUT$
End Proc
```

If you forget to do this you'll get an error.

When you develop a program you often use a different disk from the final disk, and then have to alter the program to run from df0: If the program can't find any of the .abk files it needs, the program won't work and it sometimes takes ages to weed out all the problem lines. To prevent this, always get into the habit of working from a disk with the same name as the finished program disk, and put a:

```
Dir$="GameDiskName:"
```

at the start of each program. This automatically CDs to the disk in question and means that all disk calls will go to this disk.

Going Loopy

AMOS has a number of looping structures which enable you to do repetitive tasks (all programs involve repetitive tasks!) either over and over until the end of time, or over and over until certain conditions are satisfied. The looping structures I'm talking about are While Wend, Repeat Until, and Do Loop

The first two are superficially similar, but the difference between While Wend and Repeat Until is that While Wend repeats a section of code while a condition is true. For example:

```
X=0
While X<10
```

```
      Inc X

      Print X

Wend

Print "finished"
```

so while x is less than 10, the program runs. When the number x reaches 10 or over, then the loop is terminated and the next line of code is run, in this case *finished* is printed to the screen.

Repeat Until is the exact reverse of this, as this function waits until the condition is true before it stops, like so:

```
X=0

Repeat

   Inc X

   Print X

Until X>10
```

So until x is greater than 10 the thing keeps going round.

There are other ways of getting loops, and some are unconditional, which means they don't test anything but they just keep going round and round until the cows come home. Do Loop is one of these, like a sort of close loop form of Goto. Do Loop is used if you want a part of the program to go around and around forever. If you want to leave a Do Loop, apart from using Control C to break out of the program, you can insert an Exit command, like so:

```
X=0

Do

   Inc X

   Print X

   If Mouse Key=1 Then Exit

Loop
```

This pops out of the loop if you hold down a mouse button. I prefer the more elegant loops myself, as Do Loop is a bit crude, but it has its uses.

Exit can also be made to test something itself, if you use Exit If. To test a condition of a variable using Exit If you do it like this:

```
X=0

Do
```

```
    Inc X

    Print X

    Exit If X>10

  Loop
```

Obviously these are very simple examples, and most of your control statements will be more complex than this, but it gives you an idea of the reasons why you would and wouldn't use a certain statement.

Various Variables

Some types of variable come into their own when you start using Procs. The main things you'll encounter are local and global variables.

The main difference is that a local variable (variables in Procs are local by default) is independent of the rest of the program, and only comes into force when the program is running inside the Proc itself. So inside the Proc A might be equal to 10, but outside the Proc it equals nothing, nada, zilch. Plain zero.

A global variable can be set however, and this means that the variable is equal to whatever it is set to all through the program, inside a Proc and outside.

So a local variable is the default for variables in AMOS, where a variable inside a Proc is independent from the rest of the program. Like this example:

```
    X=20 : Y=50

    TRYIT

    Print X,Y

    Procedure TRYIT

      Print X,Y

    End Proc
```

So not only can variables used inside the Procs be different from ones used outside the Procs but you can't carry over any variables into a Proc unless you make them global. So for example if you define arrays with DIM, you must watch out if you're going to use them in a Proc, especially if that Proc has been imported from some other program. Make a habit of defining such things as global variables if you think you may need to use them in Procs later.

If you want to turn a list of variables into global variables then you use the Global keyword to define the list. Like so:

```
X=20 : Y=50
Global X,Y
TRYIT
Print X,Y
Procedure TRYIT
   Print X,Y
End Proc
```

Global variables can be accessed from anywhere inside the program, even inside Procs.

If you want to access a list of variables global from inside a Proc, you must define them with Shared. Like so:

```
X=20 : Y=50
TRYIT
Print X,Y
Procedure TRYIT
   Shared X,Y
   Print X,Y
End Proc
```

The Proc can now tap into the variables X and Y, and read and write to them, whereas other Procs cannot.

Are You Def?

Another neat Proc trick is the use of *parameter definitions*. This is a kind of reverse trick, where you pass a specific list of variables complete with their contents to a Proc as you define it, like this:

```
Procedure NIT[A$,X,Y]
```

The variables are loaded directly from the main part of the program, and the Proc can be called in two ways. Either you pass another variable to the Proc which has a value you wish to pass to the new variables in the Proc. Like this:

```
N$="Phil" : A=45 : B=3
NIT[N$,A,B]
```

Or you can add the precise values you want to fill these variables:

```
NIT["Phil",45,3]
```

This is one of the best ways to pass values from a main chunk of code directly to a Proc.

Daddy Pop

Just before we leave Procs for the moment, a quick word about Pop Proc is in order. The only way you can exit a Proc without going all the way through it to End Proc is by employing the Pop Proc command. You'd use it as a part of a conditional branch command like this:

```
PITIT
Print "Proc Popped"
'
Procedure PITIT
Input A$
If A$="yes" Then Pop Proc
Print "The Proc NOT Popped!"
End
End Proc
```

This program shows you how to Pop out of a Proc without going to the end. The end of the Proc here is the end of the program. If you type *yes* into the prompt, you pop out of the Proc and you get the line *Proc Popped* printed to the screen. If you type *no* (or indeed anything except *yes*, because this is a very crude program) then you drop through the conditional branch and hit the line which prints up *Proc NOT Popped!*, with that little exclamation mark just for emphasis.

Cooking with AMAL

Another important part of program structure is AMAL. The thing of it is, that games programmed in AMOS using AMAL are better than those that don't use it. The trade off here is that AMAL programs are harder to get going, so for beginners I'd leave out the AMAL until you've got a full grasp of AMOS first.

But once you do use AMAL there are two ways to put it in your programs. The first and most frequently used method is to insert an AMAL program into the AMOS program, a line at a time like this example:

```
A$="line of AMAL"

A$=A$+"another line of AMAL"
```

Each line of the code adds the current line to the variable A$, and then executes it as if it were one line. Another way of utilising AMAL is to use the AMAL Editor program, which enables you to write your AMAL programs as a number of channels and save them in a block as a .abk file. After you've saved this to disk you can reload it to an AMOS memory bank and access it invisibly from within an AMOS program. The AMAL commands are saved with the program and so they are invisible to the casual user, and faster because they are accessed from memory rather than being loaded inside a program or from disk.

This is all I'll say about AMAL for the time being. If you want to know more you can find out all about AMAL in Chapters 10 and 11.

Music and Graphics

The thing which separates AMOS from all other BASIC interpreters is the ability to play music and sound effects from a bank rather than having to load a module of music and play it from disk. The music can be created in any number of *tracker* programs like Soundtracker, Noisetracker, MED, Game Music Creator or something like that, and then either converted into an .abk file and read into a memory bank or played in some other clever way, using a stream of new utilities which are coming out almost daily.

Once a music module is in a memory bank it can be played at any time in the program by typing in:

```
Music 1
```

which plays the first tune stored in the Music memory bank (bank 3 always). To stop the music you just add:

```
Music Off
```

to your program and the tune stops. This is a much more modern way of treating music (and the same goes for graphics) in a programming language, as a separate thing from the code which it drives.

As I say, the same goes for graphics. Any icon banks or IFF screens in your game can be loaded and saved using banks rather than loading or saving the files from disk. The files are always in memory in a specially compressed format, until required, at which time they uncompress and play or show on screen (whichever is appropriate).

Saving and loading banks can be done within a program at the start, or to save time they can be loaded in direct mode and saved with the program for instant access when the program is loaded again.

More Variable than Not

And finally you'll need to know about the various types of variable. We've looked at shared and locals, but individual types, no. There are a number of different types of variable and these fall into two ready categories, alphanumeric and numeric. Alphanumeric are always given a $ sign to denote the fact that they contain words or letters, *strings* as they are called in the trade. Ordinary numeric variables are simply letters or numbers. So:

```
A$="Bob's Bottom"
```

is a alphanumeric variable, and:

```
Z=3
```

is numeric. The variable names can be more meaningful, but be careful you don't give a variable name which is also a reserved command name in AMOS, like ADD, COLOUR or MENU. AMOS is fairly clever about this sort of thing, and will tell you that you've made a mistake. The best way around this is to say the word and write it down phonetically, like MUSIK instead of Music or FWEE for Free. This come naturally after a while.

Other types of variable are to denote different kinds of variables within those groups. *Integers* are variables with nothing attached, like Z in the example I gave a second ago. Integers are whole numbers without any fractions, like 3 or 4, but not 3.142. Anything with a decimal point in it is a floating point number and you call these *real numbers*. Integer maths works faster than floating point, but floating point is more accurate. To denote that a variable is a floating point number, you must append it with a hash symbol, or #. Like so:

```
P#=3.1245
```

```
NUMBER#=45.62
```

This is a type of notation used with few other BASICs, so it's worth bearing this in mind if you intend typing in programs written in another sort of BASIC.

The only other types of notation you have to know are for binary and hexadecimal numbers, which are not variables as such but they are used when assigning numbers (constants) to variables. These types of numbers are written thus:

Binary   %11111111

Hex $FF

Decimal   255

to distinguish them from normal types of numbers.

And that's it. I know it's been tough to wade through all this basic stuff, but you'll feel the benefit of a little recap like these last two chapters when we start grinding some real programs. That's pretty much all you need to know to get you going. Now we begin the tortuous journey through AMOS, hoping to visit all its important little places along the way.

4:
Graphics

Using AMOS you can combine IFF graphics created with a drawing package to produce dazzling on-screen displays, but there is another side to AMOS, the ability to produce graphics by programming rather than drawing. We'll get onto Sprites and Bobs and Screens soon enough. For now let us content ourselves with looking at the drawing routines in AMOS, plus some very neat rainbow effects you can get using a few tricks of the graphics coprocessor, or *Copper* as it is called.

Painting with Maths

Using a graphics package on the Amiga is a very easy thing to do, as you know. You simply boot it up and draw using the mouse. This is a very convenient way of producing the kind of graphics you see in most game programs, but what about another kind of computer graphics, where the emphasis is on the computer part of the phrase. Graphics that are drawn by the computer are born of the time when the only kind of computer graphics you could get were characters on a sheet of paper rolling out of a teletype terminal. You could imitate what you wanted to depict using letters, and many games were just a letter H chasing an asterisk across the screen. (And a lot of fun it was too, I might add. At the time, at least.)

Then plotters came about, and you could not only type a page of text on your regular printer, you could output flowing drawings onto paper using various different coloured pens. The lines the computer drew on the paper were smooth and curved, and these lines were said to be *plotted* rather than bashed out line by line like you would on a normal printer.

With the advent of computer terminals with video monitors, the plotted graphics were drawn to the screen, but the word plotting had stuck, and so the pixels on the screen took the place of the pens on the paper, and *computer graphics* as we know it was born. Things have moved on since then and graphics means something different to what it did ten years ago, but you can still get some very useful effects out of your screen by drawing rather than painting.

Drawing on the Screen

Why would you want to draw on the screen using AMOS rather than a mouse and a paint program? Well for embellishment of your excellent AMOS programs, that's why. Like this sort of thing:

```
Rem ** Snoutbox1.AMOS **

Rem

Curs Off : Flash Off : Cls 0

Paper 0

Box 0,0 To 319,100

Box 2,2 To 317,98

Locate ,4 : Centre "Title Box for AMOS programs"

Locate ,6 : Centre "by Phil South"

Locate ,12 : Centre " Snoutware (c)1992 "
```

This is a nice quick and easy way of creating a title for your programs. It draws a couple of boxes, with a 2 pixel gap between them, and it then positions a few lines of text, with the last line overlapping the box at the bottom. You can simply type your program name and your name into the Centre print strings, and Robert is your uncle. I put a space on either end of the Snoutware line, just to crop a bit of the box off at each end.

You can go further still with this kind of thing, like how about this:

```
Rem ** Snoutbox2.AMOS **

Rem

Curs Off : Flash Off : Cls 0
```

```
Paper 6

Ink 2 : Bar 0,0 To 319,100

Ink 6 : Bar 2,2 To 317,98

Locate ,4 : Centre "Title Box for AMOS programs"

Locate ,6 : Centre "by Phil South"

Locate ,10 : Pen 0 : Centre " Snoutware (c)1992 "
```

This time instead of using the box we've used a bar, with one bar being smaller than the other to make a nice border. If you wanted to get really flash, you could make it 3D like so:

```
Rem ** Snoutbox3.AMOS **

Rem

Curs Off : Flash Off : Cls 0

Paper 7

Ink 2 : Bar 0,0 To 319,100

Ink 8 : Bar 2,2 To 319,100

Ink 7 : Bar 2,2 To 317,98

Locate ,4 : Centre "Title Box for AMOS programs"

Locate ,6 : Centre "by Phil South"

Locate ,10 : Pen 0 : Centre " Snoutware (c)1992 "
```

You just make one bar form the highlight on the top and left, and another bar for the shadow bottom and right. Draw one bar from 0,0 to 319,100, then the next one over that from 2,2 down to 319,100. Finally the last one in a medium shade over both the others leaving a two pixel gap all around the outside to show the highlights and shadows. Simple *bas relief* effect, but it's never done Workbench 2.0 any harm! We'll come back to this effect in a minute.

Figure 4.1. Snoutbox3.AMOS in action.

You can also sprinkle patterns about, for example in another visit to my introduction bar we can do this:

```
Rem ** Snoutbox4.AMOS **
Rem
Curs Off : Flash Off : Cls 0
Paper 7
Ink 2 : Bar 0,0 To 319,100
Ink 8 : Bar 2,2 To 319,100
Set Pattern 5 : Ink 8,7 : Bar 2,2 To 317,98
Locate ,4 : Centre "Title Box for AMOS programs"
Locate ,6 : Centre "by Phil South"
Locate ,10 : Pen 0 : Centre " Snoutware (c)1992 "
```

and this is the most sophisticated version yet. In order to get the patterns, you must have the MOUSE.ABK file loaded into a bank, as this contains all the patterns. You'll find it in your AMOS_SYSTEM drawer on the AMOS disk. Notice how I set the ink and paper colours to suit the background that the pattern is going on. This now looks very cool. If you wanted to edit the patterns at all, you can do so in any sprite editor, like SpriteX for example.

To go beyond the preset patterns, you can use a pattern number less than zero, and even have animating patterns! Try this one for size:

```
Rem * Patternmania.AMOS *
Rem
Load "spritefile.abk"
Flash Off
Get Sprite Palette
Ink 15,0
Do
    For N=1 To 22
        Set Pattern -N
        Wait Vbl
        Bar 0,0 To 319,199
    Next
Loop
```

The *spritefile.abk* mentioned isn't in your memory banks, you'll have to load a file in direct mode to try this on. Anything except the octopus.abk should do. Something from Sprite600 perhaps? Anyway, once you've bashed the program in, run it, and you'll see the effect. Careful jiggling with the size of the sprites can give you some very exotic and mesmerising moving patterns.

Pretty Polys

Plotting and line drawing are another thing entirely. You can use plotting single pixels to do anything from starfields to fractals to ray traced images, all you need are the algorithms. You can plot the trajectory of a rocket or plot a graph depicting how many times your girlfriend has stood you up. (It's painful to reflect on such things I know.)

To do 3D bas relief effects you could simply draw a series of coloured lines on the top and sides of a bar (filled box). You can do similar tricks with filled polygons, using the Polygon and Polyline commands, like so:

```
Rem * Polybox1.AMOS *

Rem

Curs Off : Flash Off : Cls 0

Paper 7 : Ink 7

Polygon 0,20 To 20,0 To 299,0 To 319,20 To 319,80 To
299,100 To 20,100 To 0,80 To 0,20

Ink 2

Polyline 0,20 To 20,0 To 299,0 To 298,1 To 20,1 To 1,20

Ink 8

Polyline 319,20 To 319,80 To 299,100 To 20,100 To 21,99
To 299,99 To 318,80 To 318,20

Locate ,4 : Centre "Polygon Title for AMOS programs"

Locate ,6 : Centre "by Phil South"

Locate ,10 : Centre " Snoutware (c)1992 "
```

And this can be used for any and all combinations of the above.

```
Polygon Title for AMOS programs
         by Phil South


      Snoutware (c)1992
```

Figure 4.2. Polybox1.AMOS.

Using patterns is good too:

```
Rem * Polybox2.AMOS *

Rem

Curs Off : Flash Off : Cls 0

Paper 7 : Ink 7,8 : Set Pattern 8

Polygon 0,20 To 20,0 To 299,0 To 319,20 To 319,80 To
299,100 To 20,100 To 0,80 To 0,20

Ink 2

Polyline 0,20 To 20,0 To 299,0 To 298,1 To 20,1 To 1,20

Ink 8

Polyline 319,20 To 319,80 To 299,100 To 20,100 To 21,99
To 299,99 To 318,80 To 318,20

Locate ,4 : Centre "Pattern Polygon for AMOS programs"

Locate ,6 : Centre "by Phil South"

Locate ,10 : Centre " Snoutware (c)1992 "
```

giving you a range of ways to create more interesting text screens with the barest minimum of coding.

Warp-Factor 2

On the subject of plotting single dots to the screen you can go mad plotting fractals and such (although this is best done line by line as we'll tackle later on) but one of the most popular uses of single points on a screen must be starfields. Starfields are the kind of thing you see in Star Trek on the main viewer, when Captain Kirk (or Pickard for that matter) says *Put it on the main viewer...* What you usually see is the stars zipping past and some big alien ship threatening the Enterprise. Well, we can't do an alien ship (well we could as a Bob I suppose) but what I can do very quickly is show you the starfield.

```
Rem * Starfield.AMOS *
Rem
Screen Open 0,320,200,16,Lowres
Curs Off : Flash Off
Cls 0
Double Buffer
Hide
CX=Screen Width/2 : CY=Screen Height/2
Update Off
Autoback 0
STARS=20
Dim X(STARS),Y(STARS)
Dim X_STEP(STARS),Y_STEP(STARS)
Dim C(STARS)
For ST=0 To STARS
    Gosub INIT_STEP
    PHASE=Rnd(CY)/16
    X(ST)=PHASE*X_STEP(ST)
    Y(ST)=PHASE*Y_STEP(ST)
    C(ST)=Rnd(14)+1
Next ST
Do
    Cls 0
    For ST=0 To STARS
        Gosub MOVE
    Next ST
    Screen Swap
Loop
End
'
INIT_STEP:
X_STEP(ST)=8-Rnd(16)
Y_STEP(ST)=8-Rnd(16)
```

```
Return
'

MOVE:
Add X(ST),X_STEP(ST)
Add Y(ST),Y_STEP(ST)
X=X(ST)
Add X,CX
Y=Y(ST)
Add Y,CY
If X<0 or X>Screen Width or Y<0 or Y>Screen Height
   Gosub INIT_STEP
   X(ST)=0
   Y(ST)=0
End If
Plot X,Y,2
Return
```

Pretty isn't it. I can sit and watch this one for hours. Of course you can adjust the flow of stars to be affected by joystick input, which gives a feeling of movement through space. All you have to do is alter MOVE to accept input from the stick using the JOY command. Then you pass this data to the algorithm in MOVE to shift the plot points of the stars up or down depending on the direction. Or how about doing a side view so the stars go by as if you're looking out of a side window of a space ship?

Req the Place

Using the same principles as we did before in the title box you can also create 3D Workbench 2 style requesters, with a bit of judicious boxing and drawing, and one very clever procedure:

```
Rem * 3D_Req.AMOS *
Rem
Default
Paper 0 : Pen 2 : Cls : Curs Off
REQ[" A 3D Requester"," Neat eh? ","Continue",""]
Print "Please press S to Stop"
Z=0
```

```
MAIN
'

Procedure MAIN
    Shared Z
    Do
        K$=Upper$(Inkey$)
        If K$="S" Then REQ["You S for Stop","Did
        you?","Okay!","Cancel"]
        If Mouse Key=2 Then REQ["You hit the Right Mouse
        Button","Did you?","Yes","Cancel"]
        If Z=1 Then REQ["Okay Quit, see if I
        care","","So...","Long!"] : End
        If Z=2 Then Z=0
    Loop
End Proc
'

Procedure REQ[T1$,T2$,B1$,B2$]
    Shared Z
    Screen Open 7,640,60,4,Hires
    Screen Display 7,130,110,,
    Limit Mouse 215,110 To 350,155
    Show
    Flash Off
    Paper 0 : Cls : Curs Off
    Palette $0,$444,$777,$FFF
    Reserve Zone 2
    If Len(T1$)>33 Then T1$=Left$(T1$,33)
    If Len(T2$)>33 Then T2$=Left$(T2$,33)
    If Len(B1$)>8 Then B1$=Left$(B1$,8)
    If Len(B2$)>8 Then B2$=Left$(B2$,8)
    Ink 1 : Bar 170,0 To 470,52
    Ink 3 : Bar 171,1 To 470,59
    Ink 2 : Bar 171,1 To 468,58
    Ink 0 : Box 180,10 To 458,30
```

```
Ink 3 : Draw 180,30 To 458,30
Ink 3 : Draw 458,30 To 458,10
If  Len(B1$)>0
    Ink 3 : Box 200,37 To 270,52
    Ink 0 : Draw 200,52 To 270,52
    Ink 0 : Draw 270,52 To 270,37
End If
If  Len(B2$)>0
    Ink 3 : Box 360,37 To 430,52
    Ink 0 : Draw 360,52 To 430,52
    Ink 0 : Draw 430,52 To 430,37
End If
Ink 0,2
Text 184,19,T1$
Text 184,27,T2$
Text 204,47,B1$
Text 364,47,B2$
If Len(B1$)>0 Then Set Zone 1,200,37 To 270,52
If Len(B2$)>0 Then Set Zone 2,360,37 To 430,52
Do
    Z=Mouse Zone
    If Z=1 and Mouse Key=1 Then Ink 0 : Box 200,37 To
270,52 : Ink 3 : Draw 200,52 To 270,52 : Ink 3 : Draw
270,52 To 270,37 : Bell 70 : Wait 10 : Screen Close 7 :
Limit Mouse : Pop Proc
    If Z=2 and Mouse Key=1 Then Ink 0 : Box 360,37 To
430,52 : Ink 3 : Draw 360,52 To 430,52 : Ink 3 : Draw
430,52 To 430,37 : Bell 40 : Wait 10 : Screen Close 7 :
Limit Mouse : Pop Proc
    Loop
End Proc
```

A great little hunk of code, and thanks to Chris Hurst for the original idea. There you go, Chris, as promised you're world famous!

There are many other uses of lines and boxes, but what do you do if you want still more colour from your screen? You can laboriously paste lines on the screen, or you can get technical and resort to the graphics coprocessor, or Copper.

Over the Rainbow

Ever wondered how the experts construct those amazing rainbow Copper patterns in their programs? Well, they are very clever, but they didn't get that way without a little help from AMOS. Now you can be very clever too.

One of the most interesting pieces of software to come out of the AMOS PD Library was the *Rainbow Warrior* program by Spadge (aka my old mate Martyn Brown of *Newsflash* fame). This program lets you construct and save rainbow Copper patterns for use in your programs, and it uses mouse moves to let you draw them on screen. After you've drawn the rainbow of your choice, you can then save it to disk in a variety of useful formats, like AMOS program code, K-Seka and Devpac assembly language, and raw code.

The program itself is written in AMOS, and it saves its AMOS code in ASCII format. To use the code you must Merge ASCII. The code from a sample output looks a lot like this:

```
Rem

Rem * Created with RAINBOW WARRIOR - Amos Copper Generator *

Rem * Yup, you can blame good ol' Spadge for this one... *

Rem

Set Rainbow 0,0, 280,"","",""

Rainbow 0,0, 0, 280

Colour Back 0

Restore RDATA

For C=0 To 279 : Read CVA : Rain(0,C)=CVA

Next C : View

RDATA:

Data $0,$0,$0,$0,$0,$0,$0,$0

Data $0,$0,$0,$0,$0,$0,$0,$0

Data $0,$0,$0,$0,$0,$0,$0,$0

Data $0,$0,$0,$0,$0,$0,$0,$0

Data $0,$0,$0,$0,$0,$0,$0,$0
```

```
Data $0,$0,$0,$0,$0,$0,$0,$0
Data $0,$0,$0,$0,$0,$0,$200,$300
Data $400,$500,$600,$700,$800,$900,$A00,$D00
Data $C00,$B00,$A00,$900,$800,$700,$600,$500
Data $400,$0,$0,$0,$0,$0,$0,$0
Data $0,$110,$220,$330,$440,$550,$660,$770
Data $880,$990,$AA0,$BB0,$CC0,$DD0,$EE0,$FF0
Data $FF0,$EE0,$DD0,$CC0,$BB0,$AA0,$990,$880
Data $770,$660,$550,$440,$330,$220,$0,$0
Data $0,$0,$0,$0,$0,$0,$0,$0
Data $0,$0,$0,$0,$0,$0,$0,$0
Data $0,$0,$0,$0,$0,$0,$0,$0
Data $0,$0,$3,$4,$5,$6,$7,$8
Data $9,$A,$B,$C,$D,$E,$F,$F
Data $E,$D,$C,$B,$A,$9,$8,$7
Data $6,$5,$4,$3,$0,$0,$0,$0
Data $0,$0,$0,$0,$0,$0,$0,$0
Data $0,$0,$0,$0,$0,$0,$0,$0
Data $0,$0,$0,$0,$0,$0,$0,$0
Data $0,$0,$0,$0,$0,$0,$0,$0
Data $0,$0,$0,$0,$0,$0,$0,$0
Data $0,$0,$0,$0,$0,$0,$0,$0
Data $0,$0,$0,$0,$0,$0,$0,$0
Data $0,$0,$0,$0,$0,$0,$0,$0
Data $0,$0,$0,$0,$0,$0,$0,$0
Data $0,$0,$0,$0,$0,$0,$0,$0
Data $0,$0,$0,$0,$0,$0,$0,$0
Data $0,$0,$0,$0,$0,$0,$0,$0
Data $0,$0,$0,$0,$0,$0,$0,$0
Data $0,$0,$0,$0,$0,$0,$0,$0
Rem
```

```
Rem * Alter the values in the RAINBOW and SET RAINBOW *
Rem * to position and control the rainbows. See the *
Rem * manual to check on Y positioning, Length and *
Rem * which colour it is to effect.. Have fun! *
```

You can tap all this in to see what happens, if you like.

You have to add a few things to the code as it's meant to be within a program, so it expects certain things. If you just run the code, it'll print a duff rectangle screen over the nice bars. The best thing to do is open a screen before you go into the bars routine, using something like:

```
Screen Open 0,320,256,32,Lowres
```

and maybe even a Wait Key before the RDATA label, and you'll see the difference. Alternatively you could change the Colour Back 0 command for Cls 0 for the same effect. This gives you a good idea of the sort of thing you can generate with Rainbow Warrior *very* easily. In fact there are even some other more powerful utilities around now to do a similar job, so why not ask AMOS PDL or Deja Vu for a sample of what's possible. Or even do it yourself!

Ello Ello Ello

As we found out, Copper routines give you lovely rainbow colour effects, like smooth graduated skies or seascapes or just rainbow colours behind your text. To learn how to put a Rainbow behind text you have to try out the following program:

```
Rem * RainbowText.AMOS *
Rem
Cls 0 : Curs Off : Hide
Gosub BOZE
For X=0 To 10
Pen 1 : Paper 0 : Print "Rainbow Text!!! Rainbow
Text!!!"
Next X
Wait Key
'
BOZE:
Set Rainbow 0,1,280,"","",""
Rainbow 0,0,0,280
```

```
      Colour Back 0
      Restore BOZEDATA
      For C=0 To 98 : Read CVA : Rain(0,C)=CVA
      Next C : View
      Return
      Rem
      Rem * Data for the rainbows *
      Rem
      BOZEDATA:
      Data $FFF
      Data $EEE,$DDD,$CCC,$BBB,$AAA,$999,$888,$777
      Data $666,$555,$444,$333,$222,$300,$200,$300
      Data $400,$500,$600,$700,$800,$900,$A00,$B00
      Data $C00,$D00,$E00,$F00,$F00,$E00,$D00,$C00
      Data $B00,$A00,$900,$800,$700,$600,$500,$400
      Data $300,$200
      Data $330,$440,$550,$660,$770,$880,$990,$AA0
      Data $BB0,$CC0,$DD0,$EE0,$FF0,$FF0,$EE0,$DD0
      Data $CC0,$BB0,$AA0,$990,$880,$770,$660,$550
      Data $440,$330,$220,$101,$202,$303,$404,$505
      Data $606,$707,$808,$909,$A0A,$B0B,$C0C,$D0D
      Data $E0E,$F0F,$F0F,$E0E,$D0D,$C0C,$B0B,$A0A
      Data $909,$808,$707,$606,$505,$404,$303,$202
```

and as you can see when you run it, all the rainbows now show through the text. The:

```
      Cls 0
```

covers the screen with colour 0, and:

```
      Curs Off
```

and:

```
      Hide
```

blank out the cursor and arrow pointer for our demonstration.

Obviously the Gosub activates the stripes, but here's the impressive bit. Set Pen to the background colour black, and paper to the foreground colour, and look what happens when the loop fills the screen with text Rainbow text!!! Try using this technique for hi-score tables or even just text in any program you really *don't* want people to miss.

Now you are a computer graphics expert. You can dress up your screens like a Christmas tree, and *nobody* can ignore them.

Footnote

Phew, what a program intensive chapter that was. Don't just type in all the programs in one go or you'll get very tired and make mistakes. Take a regular break and save as you go along, it can't do any harm and it'll ensure you don't lose any work. *It can happen* so be warned and take it easy. Right, onto the next bit.

5:
Windows,
Text and
Menus

The Amiga is a WIMP system, as you doubtless know. The original concept of a computer interface containing Windows, Icons, Mouse and Pointers was developed by Xerox at Palo Alto Research Centre. I once interviewed Dan Silva the author of *Deluxe Paint*, who used to work there, and he said that most of the stuff they invent there will rarely be used, it's so far in advance of what we have now that it's practically science fiction. No wonder it took so long for WIMP interfaces, or Graphic User Interfaces as the suits prefer to call them, to catch on in the real world.

When the Amiga was made in 1985 GUIs were all the rage, so the very forward-looking designers incorporated a mouse and a GUI (*gooey*) called Workbench in the new machine. AmigaBASIC's way of accessing the windows and menus was adequate but limited. It's only with AMOS that we can unleash the real power of windows and menus.

Clean Windows

If what you have in mind for your AMOS program isn't a game but more of what you'd call a utility or productivity program, then you'll have to get a grip on the windowing aspects of AMOS. A plain window with pull-down menus may seem a little bit dull, although there are ways you can spice them up, but it's totally functional. A window is basically an independent little area of text and graphics on the screen. We'll go into how to make things a little bit more interesting later on, but for now we'll look at how to create simple window based programs.

To open a window on the screen you must employ the WIND OPEN command, like so:

```
Wind Open 1,10,10,50,10
```

This for example would open us a window onto the screen called window 1, which would have its top left corner at screen location 10,10 and would be 50 characters wide by 10 deep. The practical upshot of all this is that you can have a couple or more windows on the screen all of which have their own text running, like this example:

```
Rem * Two Windows.AMOS *

Rem

Screen Open 0,640,200,16,Hires

Cls 0

Flash Off

Paper 7 : Wind Open 1,0,0,40,20 : Print "Here is a win-
dow..."

Paper 4 : Wind Open 2,320,0,40,20 : Print "So this is a
window, eh?"

Wait Key

Window 1 : Paper 7 : Print "And I can print..."

Wait Key

Window 2 : Paper 4 : Print "...to any one I choose..."

Wait Key

Window 1 : Paper 7 : Print "...just by saying Window
x..."

Wait Key

Window 2 : Paper 4 : Print "...and typing whatever I
want..."

Wait Key

Window 1 : Paper 7 : Print "...and up it pops in each..."

Wait Key

Window 2 : Paper 4 : Print "...window I specify!!!"

Wait Key
```

Each time you hit a key in this program, the next bit of text jumps up onto the screen specified. Obviously you can take this to extremes, but only if you don't really care if people can read the text on the screen because there are so many windows!

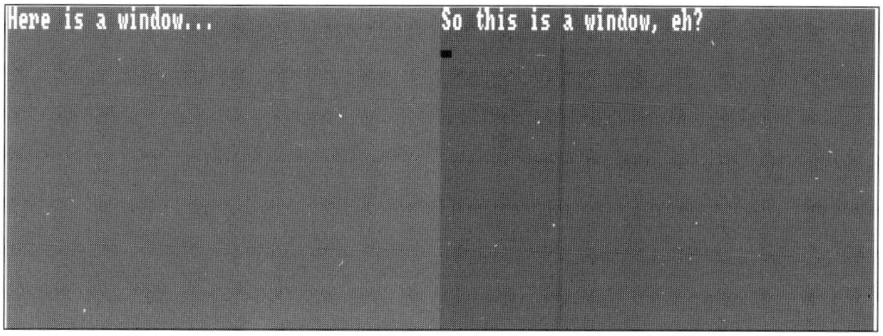

Figure 5.1. TwoWindows.AMOS.

Although the windows you get in AMOS aren't the same as the kind of thing you are used to in AmigaDOS, they still have a range of styles and shapes, and can be made to act like real windows with the minimum of tweaking. For example you can resize them, and even add gadgets like Intuition handles, but all this must be done manually as Intuition is not loaded when AMOS is running, alas. Resizing is a good example so let's look at that.

```
Rem * Resizing Window.AMOS *
Rem
Screen Open 0,640,256,16,Hires
Paper 0 : Cls 0
Wind Save
Reserve Zone 1
Wind Open 1,10,50,20,20,1
Border ,0,4
Title Top " Resize me, babe "
Set Zone 1,10,50 To 10+160,50+160
Do
    If Mouse Key=1 and Mouse Zone=1
        GX1=10 : GY1=50 : RESIZE
        Reset Zone 1 : Set Zone 1,GX1,GY1 To GX2,GY2
        SX=(GX2-GX1)/8 : SY=(GY2-GY1)/8
        Wind Size SX,SY
    End If
```

```
Print "AMOS: the only way to fly. ";
Loop
Procedure RESIZE
   Shared GX1,GX2,GY1,GY2
   Gr Writing 2
   Repeat
      If Mouse Key=1
         GX2=X Screen(X Mouse) : GY2=Y Screen(Y Mouse)
         OGX=GX2 : OGY=GY2
         While Mouse Key=1
            Box GX1,GY1 To GX2,GY2
            GX2=X Screen(X Mouse) : GY2=Y Screen(Y Mouse)
            Box GX1,GY1 To GX2,GY2
         Wend
         Box GX1,GY1 To OGX,OGY
         Box GX1,GY1 To GX2,GY2 : GOTCHA=True
         If GX1>GX2 : T=GX1 : GX1=GX2 : GX2=T : End If
         If GY1>GY2 : T=GY1 : GY1=GY2 : GY2=T : End If
      End If
   Until GOTCHA
   Gr Writing 1
End Proc
```

This little program is a neat trick. A window appears on the screen and you can pull at the bottom righthand corner and click the left mouse button. The window can then be resized to any size on the screen, and when you let go the window snaps to that shape. And better yet, being an AMOS window the text line flows ever upwards refitting itself to the new window size each time you pull it into a different shape with the mouse.

In order to grab anything on the screen (unlike the very convenient Intuition code which does it all for you) you have to draw a window, and then describe a Zone around it to sense the presence of a mouse click. Then once you've sensed it you have to see where it moves, and then resize the window with WIND SIZE.

So in this program we first open a hi-res screen and set the colours (blah blah) as normal. Then we activate WIND SAVE, which means our windows are smart and don't screw up anything we might have on the screen below it. This is really groovy because it means you can open a window over a game screen for example, like an IFF file, and nothing on the screen will be erased when you close the window.

Next we RESERVE ZONE, which is what you do every time you are about to SET ZONE. What this means is that if you:

Reserve Zone 1

you are basically saying *look, I'm going to define a zone later on in the program, so allocate some memory for it and I'll get back to you.*

Now we set up all the characteristics of the window we'll be defining, in this case Window 1 is a 20x20 character window, whose top left corner is positioned at location 10,50 on the screen. After that we set the BORDER and TITLE TOP functions to describe a little bit more about the window, like the title text, in this case the less than serious *Resize me, babe*, and the colours of the border.

The next bit is the interesting part. Next we open up the Zone we promised earlier. It covers the area taken up by the window, and does this by specifying the Zone number, in this case 1, and the coords of the top left and bottom right corners of the Zone. (Bottom right is set here by lazily multiplying the top left figures by 160, that is to say 8*20, 8 being the number of pixels in a character, and 20 being the width of the window.)

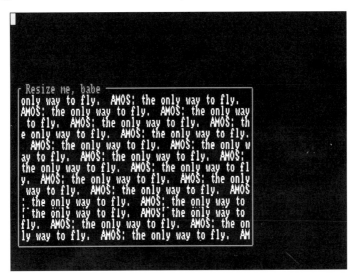

Figure 5.2. ResizeWindows.AMOS.

Then we're into the main loop of the program. This checks for the MOUSE KEY and MOUSE ZONE functions to see if the mouse is within the Zone and if it has the left mouse button pressed down. If it does then the PROC called RESIZE is activated.

The PROC then does all the work, creating a *rubber band effect* to show you where the sides of the window are, altering the variables containing the window coords, and checking to see if the mouse button has been released yet with the WHILE WEND loop. Once the button is released, the window is redrawn to the new size. Once the new coords have been stored, the old Zone is cancelled and redrawn to the new size, and it's all ready to start again.

By the way don't shrink the window too small or you'll bug out of the program with a *Window Too Small* error. The reason is that the windows need their border space, and if it can't accommodate them it can't draw the window, and boink, it flops out with an error message. You could of course guard against this with an error trapping routine which says *if the window is too small then redraw at the smallest size*. I'll let that little project fester in your mind for a while and move on to the next thing which makes AMOS windows such fun, and that is *sliders*.

Slide, Charlie Brown

As well as windows you can also add sliders to your screens, like the ones you see on regular Amiga screens, like so:

```
Rem * Slider bars.AMOS *
Rem
Screen Open 0,640,256,16,Hires
Flash Off : Curs Off : Double Buffer : Cls 0
Paper 0 : Pen 4
Set Slider 2,4,11,12,4,5,6,9
Reserve Zone 2
Set Zone 1,0,175 To 319,195
HSLIDE[10] : Screen Swap : Wait Vbl : HSLIDE[10]
Set Zone 2,0,0 To 25,170
VSLIDE[10] : Screen Swap : Wait Vbl : VSLIDE[10]
Autoback 0
Do
   If Mouse Zone=1 and Mouse Key
      X=X Screen(X Mouse)
      If X<>XM and Mouse Key=1 : XM=X : End If
   End If
```

```
   If Mouse Zone=2 and Mouse Key

      Y=Y Screen(Y Mouse)

      If Y<>YM and Mouse Key=1 : YM=Y : End If

   End If

   Locate 5,0 : Print "X slider=";X;" " : Locate 22,0 :
Print "Y SLIDER=";Y;" "

   VSLIDE[Y] : HSLIDE[X]

   Screen Swap : Wait Vbl

   Locate 5,0 : Print "X slider=";X;" " : Locate 22,0 :
Print "Y SLIDER=";Y;" "

Loop

Procedure HSLIDE[X]

   Hslider 0,180 To 319,190,319,X,5

End Proc

Procedure VSLIDE[Y]

   Vslider 0,0 To 10,170,170,Y,5

End Proc
```

Well okay, I've never seen any sliders like that before, but then neither have you. The configuration of the sliders is all done with the SET SLIDER command at the beginning. Like our resized window, the sliders must have a Zone around them in order to function, so if you wanted to have windows and sliders resizing in the same area you're going to have to do some very clever maths or make sure that at no time your Zones collide.

In this case the Zones are around the sliders, and they sense the mouse in pretty much the same way as before, but this time instead of resizing the slider, it simply repositions the box in the slider at the mouse position. You can then feed that position back to scroll a screen or a piece of text in a buffer or anything like that. All the usual reasons you'd want to grab a handle on a slider and pull it, in fact.

No Text Please

Text in your programs is something easily taken for granted. I have in the past, and I know it's hard to think beyond the kind of things that have been possible in clunky old AmigaBASIC, which is what most people's programming experience consists of before they enter the world of AMOS. But AMOS opens up whole new vistas of programming scope, and very simply too. So let's look at how you can spice up your text, wether it be a game title, hi-score table, or just title screens of utility programs.

Text in a computer program tells you two things. The words on the screen tell you what to do, and the style with which they do it tells you a lot about the programmer's attention to detail. Normal text tricks include clever formatting and changes of colour. But more impressive are changes of font and size. It's like the difference between typing on a typewriter and making up your text in a DTP program.

To use text in windows you just have to do a print statement after you select the window, but you can also change the font using GET FONTS then use WINDOW FONT to choose the font you want to use.

Using fonts in any screen, even a window, is easy in AMOS, so let's look a bit more into the kinds of text you can use.

Two Types Text

There are two kinds of text in AMOS, normal text and what they call *graphic text*. Normal text is printed to the screen with a PRINT statement, but graphic text needs to be put to the screen using TEXT, like so:

```
Rem * Simple Font Change.AMOS *
Rem
Get Fonts
Paper 8
Set Font 8
Ink 2 : Text 5,50,"Mastering AMOS"
```

The GET FONTS command scans the ROM and FONTS: directory on disk for fonts, and SET FONT sets the font to be printed to the appropriate font in the pecking order. The colour of graphic fonts is set using the INK command rather than PEN (they're drawn rather than printed, being graphics!)

Once you have graphic text under control you can do all manner of technical tricks like putting shadows under the text:

```
Rem * Fontshade.AMOS *
Rem
Paper 8 : Curs Off : Hide : Cls
Get Fonts
```

```
For F=1 To 30
   If Font$(F)<>""
      Clw
      Print Font$(F)
      Set Font F
      For Y=20 To 150 Step 20
         SHAD[10,Y,"Mastering AMOS",1]
      Next
      Wait Key
   End If
Next
Procedure SHAD[X,Y,A$,D]
   Gr Writing 0
   Ink 0
   For DX=-D To D
      Text X+DX,Y-D,A$ : Text X+DX,Y+D,A$
   Next
   For DY=-D+1 To D-1
      Text X-D,Y+DY,A$ : Text X+D,Y+DY,A$
   Next
   Ink 2 : Text X,Y,A$
End Proc
```

This uses JAM1 mode via the GR WRITING command to ensure a good impression. Or if you're particularly clever you can even add a drop shadow using the same program, by simply changing the last two lines:

```
   Ink 2 : Text X-2,Y-2,A$
End Proc
```

This offsets the final white printing of the characters above and to the left of the black outline, creating a drop shadow. Experiment with the code and see how many effects you can do, like for example how about making the last print in the same INK as the PAPER colour for an outline font? Or to get really flashy.

1. Use a grey background.

2. Then print in white the first time offset two pixels up and left.

3. Then second offset in black or dark grey two pixels down and right.

4. Finally the last time in the same grey as the background.

Voila! what you have is a method of turning any font into bas relief. Clever isn't it?

A Word about CText

More exotic effects can be obtained using Aaron Fothergill's CText program, in which graphic text is taken to its extreme. If you get this program (either from Aaron's AMOS Club or Deja Vu Software) you can create a font in Deluxe Paint and include it in your program just like the pros do. The font is stored in an IFF picture file like the example screen on this page, and then scanned into CText a letter at a time. Then you can print it to the screen in the same way you would ordinary text, or even do a scrolly message across another screen. But I'll be going into that in more detail in Chapter 19.

Curse of the Cursors

You can also alter the look of your cursor, not only turning it off/on using CURS OFF. If the cursor gets in the way maybe altering its appearance will be more appropriate.

SET CURS allows you to input a simple graphic to replace the cursor line, like so:

```
Rem * Arrow Cursor.AMOS *
Rem
C1=%10000000
C2=%1000000
C3=%100000
C4=%10000
C5=%100000
C6=%1000000
C7=%10000000
C8=%0
Set Curs C1,C2,C3,C4,C5,C6,C7,C8
Wait Key
```

This might not do what you think it does. The binary digits are clipped to remove any leading 0s. When I put them in it looked like this:

```
C1=%10000000
C2=%01000000
C3=%00100000
C4=%00010000
C5=%00100000
C6=%01000000
C7=%10000000
C8=%00000000
```

Where the 1s are in the binary image of the cursor there is a colour 3 pixel, so the little arrow points to the right, just like a *greater than* symbol or the AmigaDOS cursor.

So you've got windows coming out of your ears, sexy text, different shaped cursors, what else do you need to make your application complete? Right, menus.

Simple Menus

If you are coding something other than a game then you'll have to get used to generating menus. This is much easier in AMOS than it is in say AmigaBASIC, where you have to specify everything so precisely you might as well draw it on the screen with a biro.

Getting a screen together is easy enough with the Screen Open command, but what do you have to do to make the menus act like a normal Amiga program? Let's take it step by step:

```
Screen Open 0,640,256,16,Hires
```

Nice and simple to start with. Just a med-res screen to give you that utility look. Now we define our menus:

```
Menu$(1)=" Project     "
Menu$(1,1)="Load        "
Menu$(1,2)="Load As... "
Menu$(1,3)="Save        "
Menu$(1,4)="Save As... "
```

That's menu 1 sorted, and as you can see it's a very simple procedure to name the menus, with 1 being the menu title, and 1,1 being a sub menu. We do the same for the next menu, but with a little twist:

```
Menu$(2)=" About This Game "

Menu$(2,1)="Start New Game"

Menu$(2,1,1)="Are you sure? "

Menu$(2,1,1,1)="Yes - GO!!"

Menu$(2,1,1,2)="No - Abort"

Menu$(2,2)="New player..."

Menu$(2,3)="New Opponent..."

Menu$(2,4)="Edit playing field"
```

You can go on and on adding sub menus like 2,1,1,1,1,1 to infinity, but bear in mind anything other than one or two sub menus really gets on the operator's nerves after a very short while. Finally we turn the menus on:

```
Menu On
```

and at this point the menus are active. You can of course turn them off later if you don't want anyone using the menus at a certain point in the program. Finally, for the benefit of our listing, a few cosmetic and diagnostic details:

```
Curs Off : Cls 0
Do
  Print "Menu= ";Choice(1);" Selection= ";Choice(2)
Loop
```

You can now run the program. Notice how the menu and selection numbers change when you select a different menu item. This is how you know what the user has selected, and it's simply that. Find out what choice 1 and 2 are and you know what menu item was under the pointer when the user let go of the right mouse button.

More Advanced Menus

To really get to grips with the menus, especially if you have a number of them, you have to use the AMOS auto menuing system with ON MENU ON. This takes a little bit of practice, but it's really quite simple. The revised program starts the same, pretty much:

```
Screen Open 0,640,256,16,Hires
Cls 0 : Curs Off
Menu$(1)=" Project      "
Menu$(1,1)="Load         "
Menu$(1,2)="Load As... "
Menu$(1,3)="Save         "
Menu$(1,4)="Save As... "
Menu$(2)=" About Game "
Menu$(2,1)="Start new game"
Menu$(2,1,1)="Are you sure? "
Menu$(2,1,1,1)="Yes - GO!!"
Menu$(2,1,1,2)="No - Abort"
Menu$(2,2)="New Player"
Menu$(2,3)="New Opponent"
Menu$(2,4)="Edit playing field"
```

But at this point it diverts into new territory:

```
On Menu Proc PROJECT,ABOUT
On Menu On
Menu On
Wait Key
```

This turns on the AMOS auto menuing system and waits for you to either make a selection from the menus or press a key on the keyboard. The PROCs you mentioned in the ON MENU ON statement are then defined somewhere else in the program, like right now for example:

```
Procedure PROJECT
  Cls
  Y=Choice(2)
  Locate 0,22 : Print "Menu: Project"
  Locate 0,23
  If Y=1 Then Print "Load what?"
  If Y=2 Then Print "Load as what?"
  If Y=3 Then Print "Save what?"
```

```
            If Y=4 Then Print "Save as what?"
            OM
         End Proc
         Procedure ABOUT
            Cls
            Y=Choice(2)
            Locate 0,22 : Print "Menu: About Game"
            Locate 0,23
            If Y=1 Then Print "Yes Or No? Which is it?"
            If Y=2 Then Print "No I won't!"
            If Y=3 Then Print "He'll do it himself"
            If Y=4 Then Print "Feature not implemented"
            OM
         End Proc
         End
         Procedure OM
            On Menu On
         End Proc
```

And there you have it, the responses are put into PROCs and this makes the whole thing a lot simpler. You only have to scan for one variable CHOICE(2) because the first one, the menu itself is chosen for you automatically, and you're sent right to the PROC that deals with that menu. Once you've got subroutines accepting input from menus, you've got yourself the basis for a menu driven utility program. (There will be more about menus in Chapter 15 on Advanced AMOS.)

Hyper Hypertext

To what use can we put this windowing menu and text system? Well the obvious choice is a Hypertext system, just like the kind of thing you can do with INOVAtronics' CanDo system or one of those other systems. All you need to do is set up buttons on screen with Zones on them and you can load pictures from a CD drive, or text files in scrolling windows with slider bars to control the flow, and Zones over certain items of text to take you onto other areas. The possibilities are endless.

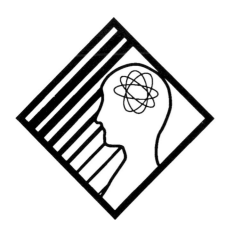

6:
Maths
Functions

Computing is all about maths when all's said and done. The fact however is that, although computing at the high end may use maths which makes your brain squirt out of your ears at high pressure, for the most part O Level maths will get you through without any personal injury. If you intend including a lot of maths in your programs, I feel bound to persuade you to get a book on basic maths. From this you can glean all the essential materials for you to include mathematical formulae in your programs if you, like me, never paid attention in school. It's handy to know things like, for example, how to calculate the area of a circle although, having said that, AMOS can take a lot of the weight off your shoulders by supplying much of the hard number crunching power in the form of its mathematical functions. I'll delve into the built in functions a little later on in this chapter. But for now.

Let's Talk about Maths

When you mention maths in polite conversation in most circles, and people turn off. People react as if you've said something really offensive, and this becomes even more offensive it seems in print. Stephen Hawkins says in his book *A Brief History Of Time* that there's a saying that every formula you include in your book halves the readership of said book. This needn't be the case, especially if the point of your book is programming, in which case a certain amount of maths talk is unavoidable. The main stumbling block for people is to realise that maths is actually good fun as long as you don't get out of your depth, a bit like swimming. Take easy steps and soon you'll treat every outing as a pleasure rather than something to be feared or dreaded.

The secret with mathematics is to get the right reference books and read them very carefully. I like two which spring to mind as inspiring maths books, which make it fun. The first is *Mathematics For Everyman* by Laurie Buxton (Dent 1984), which is a very readable and friendly book about the joy of maths. It takes you through a lot of the very easy stuff and, more than that, explains reasons why maths can be fun. The second book is the more wordy and slightly more learned *Mathematician's Delight* by WW Sawyer (Penguin 1943) which has appeared in paperback a number of times. (You may have to buy it from an out of print book service like that offered by Waterstones, or order it from the library!) Buy both these books and read them to bits, then you'll be ready to take on almost any thick book of formulae without so much as breaking a sweat.

Basic Functions

AMOS contains a lot of maths functions, and although a small amount of mathematical knowledge is good for a programmer, it's more a case of knowing what you need to know and leave it at that. You don't need to know the equation for calculating the amount of black holes in the Universe off the top of your head, you just need to be able to look it up somewhere and understand enough to know an equation when you see one. Although it might not ever occur to you to actually use any maths functions in your programs, they can in fact be incredibly useful, and this is the reason why. You can bang bang nails into wood by hand, especially if you're a karate expert. But a more elegant and less painful solution is to use a hammer, a purpose built tool for the job. This is why maths functions are useful, and this is precisely why you should use them. The right tool for the right job.

AMOS Maths

The maths functions in AMOS use the standard Amiga maths library found on most Amiga disks, at least the ones with most of the Workbench files on anyway. So in order to use maths functions from an AMOS program you need to ensure you have the MATHTRANS.LIBRARY in the libs: folder of the disk from which the program is booting. This includes any compiled programs and obviously any programs running from RAMOS (see the Chapters 15 and 16 for more details about this). For the most part this is dealt with by booting from your AMOS disk anyway, but if you run into problems this is sometimes a good thing to check.

Obviously you need to use the correct AMOS number types to perform any operations, so trying to use integer numbers with a function that expects a floating point number will cause problems in your output. Check the various variable types I mentioned in Chapter 3.

Now what sort of maths are we talking about? Well, in most cases the way you'll be using maths is if you want to draw complex shapes like 3D, unless you stump up the cash for AMOS 3D that is. Vectors they are called, and basically they are points in space. You'll have to read up on angles and moving vectors (transformation that's called) before you embark on a project. But basically what you have to know about angles in AMOS is that they will be expressed in radians.

A Few Degrees

For the treatment of angles (for the creation and movement of points in space for example) AMOS will use radians as a default, as opposed to degrees. Why this is I don't know, because I never studied radians and don't know them from Adam. Francois Lionet obviously knows radians better or they are easier to code, I don't know. But what I do know is that if you want to have AMOS recognise degrees all you have to do is type:

Degrees

and all will be well. This affects all the trigonometric functions and all their input and output will be translated accordingly. Obviously to switch back from degrees to radians you will type:

Radians

which apart from sounding like some new washing powder is in fact the way you switch back to the default method.

A Slice of PI

Another branch of maths which will be of interest to the budding top end programmer is geometry and trigonometry. This is all about angles too, but geometry is more familiar territory for those of us who thought we'd never need to know how many men it takes to half fill a bath of water. Diameters of circles, areas of triangles, space and volume. That's trigonometry country.

As you will doubtless recall from your maths lessons, PI is a constant much used in trigonometry to calculate angles, eg the circumference of a circle is calculated by 2 times PI times the radius, or 2PIr. The AMOS version of PI is PI#, with a special version of the # symbol to help distinguish it from any other variables. So to calculate the circumference of a circle we could do this:

```
Rem * Circumference.AMOS *

Rem

Screen Open 0,640,256,16,Hires

Paper 0 : Pen 2

Cls 0

Input "The radius of the circle is ?";R#

Print "The circumference is";2*Pi#*R#

Wait Key
```

The word trigonometry comes from the greek meaning *the measure of triangles*, and so knowing a bit about angles is a good thing. All this maths isn't just good for its own sake, you see. It's handy to have a little maths if you want to create a really original game, for example, as you can speed your way by knowing how to divide up things like memory and screen space, using formulas rather than the old fashioned *brute force and ignorance.*

Triangles and a certain Pythagoras are linked by the theorem which we all learn in school "the square of the hypotenuse of the right angle triangle is equal to the sum of the square of the other two sides", and the joke about *squaws on hippopotamus hides*, etc. The angles of the corners of a triangle add up to 180 degrees, so there are a number of ways to calculate the area of a triangle. One of my favourites, by a strange coincidence, employs another of the AMOS trigonometry functions, SIN or sine. The area of a triangle is equal to half the sum of the length of two of the sides (let's say sides b and c for argument) and the sine of the angle between them. Obviously if you know the length of the sides and one of the angles, it's easy to figure the remaining angles.

But sines are better known perhaps for generating sine waves like this one:

```
Rem * Sine Wave.AMOS *

Screen Open 1,640,256,16,Hires

Degree

For X=0 To 640
```

```
Y#=Sin(X)

Plot X,Y#*50+100
```

Next X

As a sound wave the sine has a pure sweet tone, like a flute or pipes but we'll go into that a bit more when we cover sound (see Chapter 13).

Trigonometry Fountain

To fully appreciate the sort of effects you can get using maths rather than plain graphics, check out the effect from this program using a range of the various trigonometry functions available to you in AMOS:

```
Rem * Triginomitry Fountain.AMOS *

Rem

Screen Open 1,320,256,32,Lowres

Curs Off : Cls 0 : Flash Off

NM#=81

P1#=4*Atan(1)

DE#=0.05

SX#=160/Sqr(3) : SY#=230

For N=1 To NM#

    A#=P1#*(-1+2*N/NM#)

    Gr Locate 160,100

    For T#=0 To 3 Step DE#

        X#=T#*Cos(A#) : Y#=T#*(Sin(A#)-T#/2)

        If Y#>-0.4

            Z=Rnd(15)

            Ink Z

            Draw To SX#*X#+160,100-SY#*Y#

        Else

            T#=3

        End If

    Next T#

Next N
```

It's a recursive program, meaning it takes the basic premise of running a curved line down the screen and runs through the procedure a number of times via the FOR NEXT loop. The word recursive brings us to another kind of geometry much used in computers over the last ten years, and that is fractal geometry.

Fractal Maths

The word *fractal* was first coined in the late '70s by an IBM scientist called Benoit B Mandelbrot, and has since passed into popular usage. People now know what one looks like (which is more than they did when I was banging on about them years ago) and they can usually mumble a few words about where they come from and what they're for. But few people really know much about them.

Fractals are a part of a bigger field called *chaos theory*, which is based on a little understood series of experiments and theories which produce unpredictable results for no reason. You send random data to an object or program and the result is a strangely ordered pattern, which is odd considering the random input. The theory was invented years ago before computers, but it's only since computers have been around that people have been able to see what these curves look like. Computers use fractals to produce imitations of natural phenomena, and AMOS can do this too.

We've touched on fractals and mandlebrots, but how do you actually go about generating them? It's complicated, but like our previous example the answer is a recursive approach, where a formula is fed repetitively with random information, and the distribution of the output is displayed on the screen. You can do this in one of two ways. Either plot each dot to the screen, which takes ages and doesn't give you a very good screen display. Or you can draw the whole thing line by line, which is the way almost all mandelbrot programs work. Here's a simple example of that process:

```
Rem * Simple Mandelbrot.AMOS *

Rem

Screen Open 0,320,220,32,Lowres

Flash Off : Hide On : Curs Off : Cls 0

Pen 2 : Paper 0

'

Do

    X=320

    Y=200
```

```
      Z=32
      Cls 0
      FRAC[X,Y,Z]
      Wait Key
Loop
   '

Procedure FRAC[X,Y,Z]
   CY=Y : CX=X : K=Z
   XN#=-2.25 : XX=0.75 : YN#=-1.5 : YX#=1.5
   H#=(XX#-XN#)/CX : V#=(YX#-YN#)/CY
   For A=0 To CY-1
      For B=0 To CX-1
         M#=XN#+B*H# : N#=YN#+A*V# : D=0 : X#=0 : Y#=0
         '
         L:
         W#=X#*X# : Z#=Y#*Y# : R#=W#+Z# : Y#=2*X#*Y#+N# :
         X#=W#-Z#+M# : Inc
         If R#<4 and D<K Then Goto L
         '
         If D=Z Then D=0
         Plot B,A,D
      Next B
   Next A
   '

End Proc
```

All the work is done in the procedure FRAC, and first it sets up the basic integer variables CY, CX and K and some other variables of a more floating point nature. These are minimum and maximum values of X and Y. The loop takes the initial values and pumps them through the function repeatedly and a line is plotted to the screen of a certain distance of a certain colour. An entire basic mandlebrot curve is printed line by line to the screen. Obviously you can add zoom routines which redraw a certain part of the formula and the screen in more detail. If you decide to take a pop at this I'll advise that you make sure the level of magnification is compensated for by levels of precision in your maths.

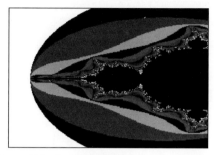

Figure 6.1. A mandelbrot from the program.

More AMOS Maths Functions

The beauty of having built in maths functions is that, like a scientific calculator, the AMOS program can accept data directly from a formula in a book. So from any of those maths books I mentioned earlier you can lift a formula and build a program around it. The formula forms the basic *routine* of your program.

$$Xf = Xb + \frac{Xr}{3} + \frac{SINX}{TANXr}$$

Figure 6.2. A nice maths formula.

Like for example the formula in Figure 6.2 translates as the following:

```
XF=XB+(XR/3)+(SIN(X)/TAN(XR))
```

This formula isn't to do anything in particluar, so running it won't answer any big questions in the cosmos, but it does demonstrate how to translate a mathematical formula into AMOS code.

Gimme a Vector, Victor

Finally, another area where maths can help you is in the field of vectors, like the ones I mentioned earlier.

Vectors are basically a change in direction of an object or point in space. Hence their use in transport especially aeroplanes and space vehicles like the space shuttle. As an AMOS idea vectors are interesting for the construction of games and graphics, as exemplified in Aaron Fothergill's *Brickout* and *Ping* games.

The thought is this: you have to use two variables to hold the x and y coordinates of the sprite position. You use these two variables to hold the x and y movements of the Sprite in each frame of the animation. Like so:

```
Rem * Vectors1.AMOS *

Rem

Curs Off : Hide : Flash Off : Cls 0 : Ink 4,4 :
Paper 0

Input "X Vector ";DX#

Input "Y Vector ";DY#

Cls 0 : Bar 0,0 To 3,3

Get Bob 1,0,0 To 4,4

Cls 0

X#=160 : Y#=100

While X#>0 and X#<320 and Y#>0 and Y#<200

    Bob 1,X#,Y#,1

    Wait Vbl

    X#=X#+DX#

    Y#=Y#+DY#

Wend

End
```

This shows you the principle. You start by inputting the x and y direction vectors and this has a result on the direction that the Sprite will go. It's best to try a range of numbers between -8 and 8 for each of the vectors. First the vectors you require are accepted through the unput command and stored in two variables called DX and DY. The Bob used in the program is grabbed from the screen using Get Bob, having first been placed there using a Bar command. Then the start position of the Bob is set to x=160 and y=100, or the middle of the screen. A While Wend loop is then activated to move the Sprite in the the direction given by the vectors. (Once you've learned a bit about vectors you'll be able to predict the precise direction!) The Bob is moved until it reaches the edge of the screen, either less than screen position 0 at the top or left of the screen, or screen position 320 or 200 to the right or bottom.

Each time the While Wend goes around, the DX and DY vectors are added to the current coordinates, thus affecting the direction of the Sprite. This is a very cool and efficient way of shifting objects around, and this becomes even more slick when the objects move in not just one direction but two. Obviously you have facilities at your disposal in AMOS 3D to translate objects in three dimensions, but a little vectoring wouldn't hurt sometimes for those really special effects.

Here's another example for you to chew on. In this next case the vector is flip flopped, that is to say it goes all the way in one direction until it reaches the screen edge and then bounces back to go in the opposite direction. Here's the listing:

```
Rem * Flip Flop.AMOS *
Rem
X=1 : DX=1
Curs Off : Flash Off : Cls 0
Ink 4,4
Bar 0,0 To 15,15
Get Bob 1,0,0 To 16,16
Cls 0
Double Buffer
Do
    Bob 1,X,100,1
    Wait Vbl
    X=X+DX
    If X<=0 or X>=319
        DX=-DX
    End If
Loop
```

The Bob is created as before, but this time a little bit bigger. The Bob is only moved for simplicity's sake in the X dimension, from left to right. Once it gets to the other side of the screen, it flip flops around and reverses direction to go back the other way. The DX vector is changed to a minus number, which of course reverses the movement and translates a left to right motion into a right to left motion. Simple and very effective. A subtle and much more spirited variation would be to make the X and the Y vectors flip flop on impact, so you can bounce the Bob around the screen. A further twist would be to make the vector of the bounce different when it hits the wall so it bounces around a little bit more randomly. Many thanks to Aaron Fothergill for his vector programs.

Bone Up Your Maths

One of the best sources for AMOS mathematical hints and tips, algorithms and the like is the AMOS Club (see Chapter 23 for details). Creating or computing graphics is one way of getting a flash of colour on your screens, but what about ready made screens? How can we load and manipulate them? Turn the page and find out.

7:
Screens

The screen is your canvas in AMOS, and it's up to you to fill it with every type of colour shape and animation possible, which in AMOS is quite a large palette and very easy to get to. The screen operations in AMOS allow you to create, move, shape, distort and generally doodle about with Amiga screens in any way you like. Anything you can write, print, load or draw to the screen can be manipulated as easily as you can fold a piece of paper. All it takes is a grasp of the required commands, which as usual is down to you, but also as usual with AMOS it's very easy to achieve.

Screen Open

This is the screen command that you'll use most often, and this is the way you'll start almost any program, unless the default brown LOWRES screen is adequate for your purposes.

You can access all the Amiga's screen modes with this command. Obviously if you want 80 columns of text on the screen then a 640x256 screen will be needed:

Screen Open 0,640,256,16,Hires

which would be a good start for any text driven utility programs. HAM (Hold and Modify) mode screens can be opened with:

```
Screen Open 0,320,256,4096,Lowres
```

or some such. This enables you to load pictures digitised with HAM devices or to create computed graphics on a HAM mode screen.

Of course any screens for the Digital Creations DCTV or Black Belt Systems HAM-E will be just as easy to load, as these are basically tricky versions of normal Amiga screens with the extra colour data coded into the bitmap somewhere along the line. Read the technical documentation for these devices for details about the screen types to open. As a guideline however, I would say 16 colour Hires is good for both types of screen, and a size of 736x566 for DCTV would be an idea as it's usually *overscan* without a screen border.

Probably by the time you read this, you will be able to use the new Super-hires, Super-hires-interlaced and *productivity mode* formats available to the new Release 2 Denise chip (like the ones fitted to the A3000, A500 and A600 models) in perhaps a new version of AMOS? We'll have to wait and see about that.

Interlaced Screens

The main types of screen used on an Amiga are Lowres, Hires, HAM and overscan variations on those. Also you have the option of Interlace mode, which doubles the vertical resolution with the slight disadvantage of a little bit of screen flicker. Interlace was designed to be a TV friendly mode for hires TV graphics, but it finds a use in any program which needs to have a bit more fine detail.

To open an interlaced screen just use the following syntax:

```
Screen Open 0,640,400,16,Laced+Hires
```

```
Screen Open 0,320,400,16,Laced+Lowres
```

or just:

```
Screen Open 0,320,200,16,Laced
```

Laced is a newish function for AMOS which was only added after about version 1.23 or so. Before that it was impossible to use Interlace without some tricky screen doubling and switching. It's still not perfect though, and the function is not without its limitations.

As soon as one screen is opened with interlace, any other screens become interlaced. The interlacing will only be any good for the screen actually opened with LACED. All the other ones will just have their lines doubled on the screen, so remember to reset the function before you move on to a non-interlaced display.

Interlaced mode is perfect for displaying pictures, but anything more complicated than that, like for example any kind of animation, runs at half speed, so of course games should not be written in interlaced, really. As soon as the last interlaced screen is closed the whole display returns back to normal mode. Your TV monitor might not like lots of fast switching from normal to interlace, so you shouldn't do it over much. Remember a *little* interlace is a good thing.

All normal operations are available in interlaced screens. Screen Offset, Screen Display etc. The only little problem arises because the interlacing in AMOS is software driven. The bitplanes are changed during the vertical blank and this particular interlace process is forbidden during Copper list calculation. So if you have a large Copper list, ie 4 screens, 1 of which is interlaced, and a multicoloured rainbow, and then have a Copper calculation to do, the interlaced screen will display only half of the picture during the calculation. Nothing can be done to solve this, it is simply a limitation of the AMOS system. Until the process gets an overhaul in a future version, this will have to do.

Hide and Seek

AMOS has some very powerful commands for the manipulation of screens and their contents. What about moving screens around once you have them defined and loaded? Screen Hide will take a screen you've loaded and send it away somewhere until it is needed. To show it again you just need to use the Screen Show command. As always in AMOS Show/Hide are the exact opposite. The best place to hide an AMOS screen of course is in a SPACKed memory bank and as a Packed Picture, as it takes up less memory.

Okay, so what else? Screen Copy is used as a part of the process of scrolling all or part of screens, in combination with Def Scroll, Scroll and Screen Swap, as we see in this example:

```
Rem * Screen Copy.AMOS *

Rem

Load Iff "name your path and picture here",1

Screen Open 0,320,256,32,Lowres

Get Palette 1 : Curs Off : Flash Off

Screen Copy 1 To 0 : Screen 0 : Double Buffer : Bob
Update Off

S=2
```

```
Def Scroll 1,80,80 To 240,240,0,-S : Rem scroll screen
Repeat
   For Y=0 To 199 Step S
      Scroll 1
      Screen Copy 1,80,Y,240,Y+S To 0,80,240-S
      Screen Swap
      Screen Copy 1,80,Y,240,Y+S To 0,80,240-S
      Wait Vbl
   Next Y
   Screen Swap : Wait Vbl : Scroll 1
Until Mouse Key
```

The screen you choose is loaded, and an area defined by the Def
Scroll statement is scrolled upwards using the repeat until loop.
This is done smoothly and continuously until the mouse button is
pressed, when the program breaks.

Screen swap uses an *invisible* screen called the *logical screen* on
which it renders things like scrolls, like in our example. When the
object or screen has been modified, the results are copied to the
real screen. Logical screens are very useful for smoothing otherwise
slow or clunky rendering routines (see also Double Buffering). Try
the last example and alter the settings to see how it changes when
you adapt certain parts of the program, particularly the Def Scroll
and Screen Copy lines.

Dual Playfield

Now then, this is when it starts to get really interesting. In the
Amiga's display system, a dual playfield is where two Amiga
screens are visible at the same time, overlaid one on the other,
where one is visible *through* the other. This is a handy effect for
what they call in the game reviewing business *parallax scrolling*,
like in the game *Shadow of the Beast*. (There is a good AMOS demo
which parodies this effect, called *Madness Week* by a bunch of
clever French AMOS hackers calling themselves Syntex. Get it from
the AMOS PD Library, and you'll see what I mean.)

As well as parallax scrolling, you can also do a number of other
effects which require some form of transparency and two effects
moving in sync, like this example based on an idea by Peter
Hickman.

```
Rem * Dual Playfield1.AMOS *
Rem
Screen Open 0,320,48,8,Lowres
Paper 0 : Pen 4 : Flash Off : Curs Off : Cls 0
Centre At(,0)+"Mastering AMOS"
Centre At(,5)+"It's a breeze!"
Wait Vbl : Screen Clone 2
Wait Vbl : Screen Clone 4
Screen Open 1,320,48,8,Lowres
Flash Off : Curs Off : Cls 0
Wait Vbl : Screen Clone 3
Wait Vbl : Screen Clone 5
Dual Playfield 0,1
Dual Playfield 2,3
Dual Playfield 4,5
Screen Display 2,,200,,
Screen Display 3,,200,,
Screen Display 4,,130,,
Screen Display 5,,130,,
Def Scroll 1,0,0 To 320,56,0,-1
Def Scroll 2,0,0 To 320,56,0,1
Def Scroll 3,0,20 To 320,34,0,-1
Def Scroll 4,0,20 To 320,34,0,1
Repeat
   Screen Copy 0,0,0,320,1 To 1,0,1
   Screen Copy 1,0,47,320,48 To 0,0,47
   Screen 0
   Wait Vbl
   Scroll 1
   Scroll 3
   Screen 1
   Scroll 2
   Scroll 4
Until False
```

Dual playfield mode is good for any time when you want to have two screens in motion on the screen at the same time, and obviously the best applications are going to be games and demos. But I can see an application in video titling with a little bit of thought and imagination.

Display that Screen!

Another feature, which we've seen in action in the last program to very good effect, is the Screen Display command. Once a screen has been defined with Screen Open, you can position it on the monitor screen with Screen Display. Once a screen has been displayed, it can be moved with Screen Offset. This means that you can move the screen by even a single pixel at a time for very smooth scrolling screens. Try this example for a start:

```
Rem * Display and Offset.AMOS *
Rem
Screen Open 0,640,512,16,Hires
Screen Display 0,128,45,320,200
Flash Off : Hide On : Curs Off : Cls 0
Load Iff "any hires screen.iff"
Screen Copy 0,0,0,640,200 To 0,640,0
Screen Copy 0,0,0,640,200 To 0,0,200
   X=0
   Y=0
30 Screen Offset 0,X,Y
   X=X+1 : If X=640 Then 60
   Goto 30
60 Y=200 : Screen Offset 0,X,Y
   X=X-1 : If X=0 Then 30
   Goto 60
```

The beauty of the Display and Offset types of command is that you can even have different types of screen, even different resolutions of screen, nestled up next to each other on the screen! The Amiga is one of the few computers that can do this kind of display switching.

Screen Clone

Obviously most of the programs which manipulate screens use two
or more of the available screen commands to load, create, place and
shift screens about. One of the least used is SCREEN CLONE and the
reason is that it's only in a very few applications that you'll want to
copy a screen more than once, unless it's a repeating scroll you're
after, like in the *Display and Offset.AMOS* screen scroll program. But
for now let's see what happens if we go mad multiplying screens:

```
Rem * Screen Clone.AMOS *
Rem
Screen Open 1,1000,20,16,Lowres
Rem Clones=7
C=7
For I=2 To C
    Screen Clone I
Next I
O$="Loop: For RO=1 To 125; Let X=X+4; Next RO;"
O$=O$+"For RO=1 To 125; Let X=X-4; Next RO; Jump
Loop"
For I=1 To C
    Screen Display I,120,I*40,400,10
    Channel I To Screen Offset I
    Amal I,O$
Next I
A$=" Mastering AMOS gives you the power to clone
yourself"
A$=A$+" eight times using SCREEN CLONE... wow! "
Print A$;
Amal On
Do
Loop
```

Here we've printed up a small thin screen, cloned it another seven
times and positioned it on the screen. Then we use AMAL to scroll
them back and forth. You could use the same AMAL technique to
scroll screens up and over eachother using dual playfield, and rig it
so the screen looks as though it's flipping over on itself.

Special FX

I'd like you to consider some of the options for presenting your graphics in an AMOS program. Okay so your program isn't a game, but there's no reason why this should mean it looks bad or boring. As well as the more complex screen movement commands like the ones we've gone into just now, there are other kinds of effect which are more like the kinds of transitions you see on TV. Two of the presentation tools at your disposal are FADE and APPEAR, but there are many more.

Fade does just what it says, if you want to fade to black or even another colour, then this will do it. The effect is the same as a fade in a movie, if you've got something on the screen you can fade it out to black (or even another colour!) using the Fade command.

Fade works very simply:

    Fade [speed]

where SPEED is the speed of the fade. If you don't mention any colours the fade will be to black. Why would you want to fade to anything but black? Well how about if you put a logo on the screen, very large, then fade it to red for example and then print the instructions to your program in white over the top of it? Very classy.

You can also fade to the palette of another current screen, like so:

    Fade [speed] To [x]

where speed is the speed of the fade, and x is the screen number containing the new palette. Try this for size:

```
Rem * Fade demo.AMOS *

Rem

Do

    S$=Fsel$("*.*","","Load yourself a screen") : If S$=""
Then Edit

    FADIFF[S$]

    Wait Key : Fade 2 : Wait 16*2

Loop

Procedure FADIFF[A$]

    Fade 1 : Wait 16

    Auto View Off

    Load Iff A$,0 : Screen Clone 1 : Screen To Front 0

    For X=0 To 31 : Colour X,0 : Next
```

```
    View : Auto View On

    Fade 3 To 1 : Screen Close 1
End Proc
```

Appear is another kettle of fish entirely, although in some ways similar. With this command you can *crossfade* between two screens, like so:

```
    Appear 0 To 1,20
```

This transforms from one picture to another using the last number to determine the effect of the fade, that is to say how the transformation occurs. The best numbers to choose are odd numbers which are not divisible by 5, strange but very true. Try out a few numbers with this program:

```
Rem * Appear.AMOS *

Rem

F$=Fsel$("*.*","","Select a picture")

If F$="" Then Edit

Load Iff F$,1

If Screen Width>600 Then REZ=Hires Else REZ=Lowres

Screen Open 0,Screen Width,Screen Height,Screen
Colour,REZ

Screen Open 2,320,50,2,Lowres

Screen Display 2,,250,,50

Screen Open 3,320,10,2,Lowres

Screen Display 3,,40,,10

Screen 0 : Screen To Front 0 : Get Palette(1) : Screen To
Front 2

Screen To Front 3

Flash Off

Do

    Screen 2 : Input "Enter effect ";E

    If E>0

        Cls : Screen 0

        Appear 1 To 0,E

    End If

Loop
```

Each time you enter an effect the blank screen is acted upon revealing the screen below. Okay, so it's not a very smooth crossfade of the type you see on television, but what do you want for your money, eh? A TV studio in a box? I bet you do.

A good rule of thumb for using Appear and Fade is to put them into PROCs and this ensures their proper use, like this one for APPEAR:

```
Rem * Appear Proc.AMOS *
Rem
Procedure _APPEAR[S,D,X]
   Appear S To D,X
End Proc
```

and this one for FADE:

```
Rem * Fade Proc.AMOS *
Rem
Procedure _FADE[S]
   Fade S
   Wait S*15
End Proc
```

That keeps things nice and simple, and if you just incorporate these PROCs as you go along (using Merge) you can't go wrong.

More Special FX

The amount of special effects you can achieve with AMOS are limited only by your skill at using the program, as it allows any degree of coding skill from BASIC to machine code, and if you know a lot you can do a lot. But the really beautiful routines are the simplest, like this selection of great routines originally by James Lanng:

```
Rem * Linesleft.AMOS *
Rem
Procedure _LINESLEFT[CL,LINES]
   Ink CL
   For B=Screen Width/LINES To 0 Step -1
      For A=LINES To 0 Step -1
         Draw Screen Width/LINES*A+B,0 To Screen
         Width/LINES*A+B,Screen Height
```

```
    Next A

   Next B

End Proc
```

This PROC does a simple wipe from right to left of the colour you specify in CL and for the amount of the screen from 0-320 you specify in LINES. Of course the reverse can also be true:

```
Rem * Linesright.AMOS *

Rem

Procedure _LINESRIGHT[CL,LINES]

   Ink CL

   For B=0 To Screen Width/LINES

      For A=0 To LINES

         Draw Screen Width/LINES*A+B,0 To Screen
Width/LINES*A+B,Screen Height

      Next A

   Next B

End Proc
```

Or perhaps you can do two wipes from bottom left and top right at once:

```
Rem * Bottomright.AMOS *

Rem

Procedure _BOTTOMRIGHTTOPLEFT[CL]

   Ink CL

   For A=0 To Screen Width

      Draw A,0 To A,Screen Height/2

      Draw Screen Width-A,Screen Height/2+1 To Screen
      Width-A,Screen Height

   Next A

End Proc
```

Or by extension, you can also do wipes up and down simultaneously:

```
   Rem * Leftup.AMOS *

   Rem

   Procedure _LEFTUPRIGHTDOWN[CL]
```

```
        Ink CL
        For A=0 To 320
            Draw 0,A To 160,A
            Draw 160,250-A To 320,250-A
        Next A
    End Proc
```

Although these effects are very clever (nice one, James!) they aren't really manipulating screens so much as covering them up in very pleasant ways. For some real screen hacking we need to look a little further.

Let's Splerge!

No talk of AMOS special effects for screens is complete without a mention of Splerge. Splerge is a brilliant routine written by my mate Peter Hickman, which first appeared a while back and has been broadcast on CIX, printed in magazines, and used by all and sundry since time began. I can't remember the last demo I saw which didn't obviously use Splerge or a variation on it. It's a classy effect, and one which takes a devious mind like Pete's and the programming power of AMOS to create:

```
Rem * Splerge procedure by Peter Hickman 1991 *
Rem
Procedure _SPLERGE[SPEED,SOURCE,DEST]
    Screen SOURCE
    SOURCE_SIZE=Screen Height
    Screen DEST
    DEST_SIZE=Screen Height
    V=Min(SOURCE_SIZE,DEST_SIZE)
    Screen SOURCE
    SOURCE_SIZE=Screen Width
    Screen DEST
    DEST_SIZE=Screen Width
    H=Min(SOURCE_SIZE,DEST_SIZE)
    For LOP=V-SPEED To 0 Step -SPEED
        For LOP1=0 To LOP Step SPEED
```

```
        Screen Copy SOURCE,0,LOP,H,LOP+SPEED To
        DEST,0,LOP1

    Next LOP1

  Next LOP

End Proc
```

Tap this in and check it out. What you're basically doing is taking a source screen (preferably a loaded IFF or a SPACKed screen) and copying it line by line (or at least linear chunk) to another empty screen. First you have to set up a couple of screens and turn off all the usual stuff, and also load a screen to operate on:

```
Screen Open 1,320,200,32,Lowres

Load Iff "amospic.iff"

Screen Open 2,320,200,32,Lowres

Curs Off : Flash Off : Hide : Cls 0

Get Palette 1

_SPLERGE[2,1,2]

Do : Loop
```

You could also load another screen to be splerged over, but it's not essential. Then you grab the palette of the screen you're about to load so it doesn't take on the odd palette from the blank screen. Then you activate the effect, passing it some numbers to get going on, like the speed and the numbers of the source and destination screens. Then you can either add a do loop at the end like I have or you can just do a wait key to take you on to another bit of your program. Make sure there is a prompt to press a key on the screen or the user will just sit there waiting for something to happen.

It's a great effect for a title screen to a game, especially if you add perhaps a sample of water pouring into a glass, or even something a little more rude! I love it.

What Now?

So you've got your screens sorted out, loading them and SPACKing them and special FXing them. What now? You'll be needing to run some sprites around the place, that's what. Which is what we're looking at right now.

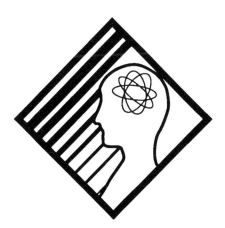

8:
Sprites
and
Bobs

In all computer games you see on the Amiga, you will see lots of Sprites and Bobs, the characters on the screen which glide around over the backgrounds, shooting each other or running around mazes in pursuit of a wild few hours away from it all. These characters on the screen are called *sprites* for a reason long lost in the history of computer programming.

At the back of my mind I vaguely recall something about insects called water sprites, and the way they skim around on the surface of the water. I imagine an Atari programmer looking at these things skimming about and wondering if they were trying to tell him something about how aliens should move over the surface of a background without touching it. Until then any characters on the screen had obliterated and redrawn the background behind them as they went, because they inhabited the same plane of graphics.

Anyway even if this story about water sprites is bogus, (I kind of like the sound of it) Sprites are now built in to the hardware of any computer capable of games, and are usually called *hardware sprites*. They are discreet chunks of graphics that are separate from the main display, on a separate plane you might say, so that they skim over the surface of the background without disturbing it. The Amiga has eight hardware Sprites, and these are pretty much the state of the art for 1985.

But when the Amiga was designed they also incorporated a facility for what they called Blitter Objects or Bobs. These are better than Sprites for a couple of important reasons.

1. Sprites are limited to eight per horizontal line on screen

2. Sprites can only have 15 colours.

Bobs on the other hand make use of the Blitter Chip in the Amiga, capable of copying images to the screen at rates of a million pixels per second. Bobs are just like Sprites, but instead of being limited in any way they are unlimited. They can have as many colours and resolutions as Amiga screens, and they can be as numerous as you like as there are no limitations on number. Obviously the more Bobs you have on screen the more stress you put the processor under, but don't worry about that. Chances are you'll rarely push AMOS that far with your programs. But bear in mind that Bobs are slower than Sprites and use up more memory. This may be a consideration no matter how small your program.

Sprites are limited in size, and their palette can only be the last 16 colours of a 32 colour display. So if the Sprite's palette takes some of its colours from the first 16, those colours will change with different backgrounds. Great care is needed in the creation of Sprites.

As a rule of thumb use Bobs for slow moving, and big shapes and use Sprites for fast moving small shapes, that's a fair division of labour.

Don't Get Confused

It's easy with all this talk of Sprites and Bobs to get a little tied up in knots. When you see a character on the screen in a game, it's always called a *sprite*, but this is a generic term, and not intended to imply that the object is a Sprite or a Bob. Like hoovers and biros, the word has a lower case first letter and means *any moving object on the screen*. When I talk about specific routines etc, pay attention to what we are actually talking about. I'll try to make it plain, but you'll have to concentrate, that's your end of the deal.

One other thing, Sprites can be made to be bigger than the limit of 16 pixels, and that is by using what they call in AMOS *computed sprites*. The computer automatically sticks Sprites together to make bigger Sprites. You can only have up to 128 pixels in width, as there are only eight hardware Sprites. (Tsk! Nothing but limitations!)

Creation of Sprites and Bobs

Making your own Sprites is very easy. You can grab a Sprite from an IFF picture using the GET SPRITE command, (and some very good special effects can be had this way) but by far the best method is to use a Sprite designer like Sprite Editor.AMOS from your AMOS disks, or better yet SpriteX. (See Chapter 21 for more details)

The Sprites can actually be designed and drawn in SpriteX or simply grabbed from an IFF file. This is good because you might feel more comfortable drawing in DPaint or something like that than you will diving straight into a strange *sprite engine.*

Once the Sprite or Bob has been drawn and grabbed, it can be saved into an ABK file on disk, and then loaded into AMOS programs for use. Great care must be taken when you create the Sprites that you use the right colours for the palette you will be using. To keep the same palette in DPaint between two pictures, simply load in the picture whose palette you want, clear the picture, and then draw your sprites and save them. The palette will then be identical to your picture. (Bear in mind also what I said about Sprites using the second 16 colours in a 32 colour palette!)

Animation

It is possible to use animation without using AMAL, and with the advances in AMOS, like for example the AMOS Compiler, such routines needn't be slow. When compiled, the movements can be as fast and smooth as AMAL, and in some cases depending on how well you write and structure (optimise in other words) your code, they can even be as fast *without* compilation.

Simple animation can be performed by changing the image in a Bob or Sprite command quickly, like this:

```
Rem * Bob Animation.AMOS *

Rem

Load "Sprites.abk" : Rem Load your favourite sprite
file here

'

Main:
Bob 1,100,100,1
Wait Key
Bob 1,100,100,2
Wait Key
Bob 1,100,100,3
```

```
Wait Key
Bob 1,100,100,4
Wait Key
Goto Main
```

This case shows you that you can look at each frame in a Sprite and create an animation from it. Each time you press a key the animation advances a single frame, and although this is very nice, animating is usually a bit faster than this. To animate the images properly, you simply have to add a loop to the proceedings:

```
For A=1 To 10
   Bob 1,100,100,A
   Wait Vbl
Next A
```

The Wait Vbl smooths the animation by waiting for the next vertical blank of the screen before flipping to the next image. You can change the Wait Vbl to a Wait n with n=5 or something like that. This slows down the animation to a sensible speed. The images are flipped through from 1 to 10 (most animations are a little less complex than that) and rapidly enough that the illusion of movement is given. If you want to know how to do animation itself... well, that's a more weighty subject and enough for a book in itself. Get a book on animated film-making and employ the techniques given there, or how about getting a copy of Disney Software's *The Animation Studio*, which has a lot of very good tutorial stuff on how to draw animation.

The key thing in animation is animating only when needed. Very few Sprites will require animating all the time, and most only animate when they move. If you require constant animation then I suppose AMAL is the best idea, because it all works independently from the AMOS code. This can be a drawback though in some cases, especially when you need to pass information to and fro from AMOS to AMAL, and if you're going to compile the program I'd say avoid AMAL.

So try to animate on the move, meaning that for example if your little man or whatever has to move to the left, then a Sprite showing him walking to the left is useful. You don't *have* to draw all the Sprite moves (especially if the Sprite looks the same from both sides) as you can flip the Sprite from side to side by adding a hexadecimal number $800 to the Sprite definition. So that's creation and animation. What about moving about and bumping into things?

Moving

Moving Sprites and Bobs about without AMAL is very simple. Sprites can be whizzed around the screen anywhere you like, simply by adjusting the x,y coords on the screen. These numbers can be INCed and DECed and FOR NEXTed to any value you like, and controlled by any external controller like the mouse or joystick, and many other types of control as we'll see in Chapter Nine on controls and movement. So try this:

```
Rem * Movit.AMOS *

Rem

Load "sprites.abk" : Rem don;t forget to load your
favourites

For Z=1 to 80

   Bob 1,X,80,1

Next Z
```

So you just have to alter the coords on the screen, and this doesn't have to be just a simple loop. You can adjust the point that a Bob is traced onto the screen smoothly or jerkily, and these positions can be drawn from anything, even the sound of the music playing in the background, as with the VUBARS commands.

Collision Detection

Unless what you are doing with AMOS is not a game of any kind, you'll want to detect collision. There's no point in having Sprites whizzing around the screen unless you can tell when two or more of them bang together, or when one shoots, that the others are going to explode.

There are two facets to the detection of Sprite or Bob collisions, first the BOBCOL, SPRITEBOBCOL, BOBSPRITECOL, or SPRITECOL commands, which detect if any Sprites have collided. In other words "has anyone hit anything?" Second you have to employ the function COL() which tests to see which individual sprite sustained the damage, or "who hit what?".

For example if your hero is Sprite 8 and the bad guys are Bobs 1, 2, 3 and 4, you would do something like this:

```
C=Spritebobcol(8,1 To 4)
```

returning a value of -1 if you've hit any of the mentioned Bobs, and a 0 if you haven't. So obviously you have to have a test after the command to test IF THEN -1 or 0 GOTO somewhere else.

The first *somewhere else* you go to is to the COL() function, like so:

```
If Col(3) Then Print "Crash"
```

or more appropriately GOTO the animation images for an explosion and replace them inplace of the current Sprite. This is a program which explains all that very simply:

```
Rem * Collision Detect.AMOS *
Rem
Screen Open 0,320,200,16,Lowres
Curs Off : Flash Off : Hide : Cls 0
Load "df0:sprite_600/aliens/alien1.abk"
Load "df0:sprite_600/space/ship3.abk",1
Get Sprite Palette
Double Buffer
Bob 1,0,80,
Bob 2,320,80,
Shared M
M=320
'
Do
   _ANIMSHIP
   _MOVEALIEN
   If Bob Col(1) Then _BOOM
Loop
'
Procedure _MOVEALIEN
   M=M-5
   Bob 2,M,80,1
End Proc
'
Procedure _ANIMSHIP
   For Y=18 To 21
      Bob 1,,,Y
```

```
        Wait Vbl
     Next Y
  End Proc
     '

  Procedure _BOOM
     Boom
     For X=35 To 43
        Bob 1,0,80,X
        Wait 4
     Next X
     Pen 6 : Paper 0 : Centre "Bang! You're dead!"
     Wait Key
     End
  End Proc
```

This program has a number of features worth looking into. Obviously the Sprites are from the Sprite 600 set, available from your AMOS disks or via one of the various AMOS PD outlets. These are the same Sprites in the simple AMAL game I've described in the AMAL chapters, in fact this is a sort of prototype of that idea. In this example the spaceship meekly waits at the end of the screen, and you can't move it at all. The alien ship comes from the right of the screen, and when the ship is touched by the alien it explodes beautifully.

All the image information for the explosions etc are in the Sprite files, and like other examples which use the example Sprite files, the Sprites are loaded one after the other into the same Sprite bank. If you wanted to make this program a little bit easier to handle (and cut out the wait for the Sprites to load from disk) you should load them in direct mode and save them off with the program. Or to be really kind you could load the Sprite files into the bank, merging them by adding the positive number to the end of the filename, and then save off the bank to disk as a new ABK file.

Once we have loaded the Sprites we've set up DOUBLE BUFFER to prevent any flickering of the Sprites, and GET SPRITE PALETTE will make sure our Sprites are the same colours as they should be. In this case the Sprites are from the same set so they are all the same colours. If your Sprites are of different palettes, you may have to re-edit them and alter the palettes to fit.

Next we set up the initial positions of the Bobs, and then define a variable as shared for the position of the Bob in the proc called _MOVEALIEN. The reason this is shared is that the proc is called each time the Bob is moved, and so the variable has to be defined outside the Proc. If the variable isn't shared, then it is always 0, as it never gets defined, according to the Proc. In this case this means that the Sprite would suddenly turn up in the same position as the ship and explode the ship right away, rather than travelling gently across the screen.

So we're all set. The main loop of the program is the DO LOOP, which will go on forever until the <Ctrl-C> combo is pressed. The loop runs through the main parts of the program, calling procs and then looping back to the start again. Each time it calls the _MOVALIEN proc the alien moves to the left. (I've put an underscore character at the beginning of the proc names so I can then use any words I like, rather than sticking to proc names which aren't commands or reserved words!) Each time the _ANIMSHIP proc is called the ship's tailflame animates. And at the bottom of the proc we have the collision detect routine which will trigger the Proc called _BOOM when the alien makes contact with the ship.

The _BOOM proc makes a BOOM noise and then animates the explosion sequence from the sprite bank. This won't work if the Sprites are any others than the ones specified, as they have specific images in the bank which do certain jobs.

The sprite movement is a little jerky, even with double buffering. But you can spruce this up a little with careful organisation. For example, only animating things that need animating is a good one. The old Paul Daniels' ploy is a good one too, that is to say *distraction.* If your Sprite moves fast and all over the place, nobody is going to notice how jerky it is are they? This works well with scrolling screens too, if something is going on over the screen then it won't be quite so obvious. Planning is everything, but obviously all these problems vanish to a certain extent when you compile a program.

Another method is to make sure that if something which has a constant animation is moving, try shutting down any loops which could slow it down. Set a variable to toggle on and off when certain processes are going along, and then you can simply check what's operating and if you have more than a certain number you can close a few down. It's a complex way of doing it but it works.

The way you toggle a variable between two values is like so:

```
S=2

Do

    Print S
```

```
    S=12-S
Loop
```

This toggles a variable called S between 2 and 10, by making it equal to 12 minus whatever it is at the time. As it is equal to 2 one time and 10 the next, it flip-flops back and forth between 10 and 2. Clever, eh?

Sprite Viewing

One of the hardest things to do when working with Sprites, especially other people's, is to know what image in the bank does what. If you think about it though, it's remarkably easy to fix up a simple program to look into a bank for you and show you interactively what is there. To check the vital statistics of your Sprite banks, let this program do all the work:

```
Rem * Sprite Bank Viewer.AMOS *
Rem
F$=Fsel$("*.abk","","Load sprite bank","to show on
screen")
If F$="" Then End
Load F$
Flash Off : Curs Off : Get Sprite Palette
N_SP=Length(1)
For N=1 To N_SP-1
   A=Sprite Base(N)
   If A
      Clw
      Bob 1,160,100,N
      Print "Sprite number";N
      Print "Size in X:";Deek(A)*16
      Print "Size in Y:";Deek(A+2)
      Print "Number of bitplanes:";Deek(A+4)
      Print "Position of hot spot in X:";Deek(A+6)
      Print ' " " Y:';Deek(A+8)
   End If
   Wait Key
Next
```

Each time you press a key, after loading the Sprite file in question, the file will flip to the next image and give you a read-out of the Sprite image and its important statistics like length, width, image number and so forth. As a project for you, try creating a variation on this program which has a two way flipping effect, so you can go back and forth through the Sprites.

Bullets

A sort of sub-skill in producing games is that of releasing, tracking and colliding with bullets and even multiple bullets. This is a mega problem but with a little bit of clever maths, it can be solved with the minimum of fuss.

This routine was originally created by Aaron Fothergill of the AMOS club, and I'm printing it here as it's one of the best and most concise routines of this type that I've seen:

```
Rem * Multi-bullet.AMOS *

Rem

Dim BX(10),BY(10),BDY(10),BS(10)

Curs Off : Flash Off : Cls 0 : Paper 0 : Pen 1 : Ink 2,2

Bar 0,0 To 7,15 : Hide On

Get Bob 1,0,0 To 16,16 : Hot Spot 1,4,0

For A=0 To 9 : Cls 0 : Locate 0,0 : Pen A+2 : Print "*"

Get Bob 2+A,0,0 To 16,8 : Hot Spot 2+A,4,4 : Next A

X=160 : Y=180

Cls 0 : Double Buffer : Colour 2,$FFF : Colour 1,$FF0

Fade
1,$0,$FFF,$F00,$F0,$F,$FF0,$FF,$F0F,$F80,$8F0,$F8,$8F,$80
F,$F08

While Mouse Key<2

    Bob 1,X,Y,1

    If NB>0 Then Gosub BULLETS

    GTG=1-GTG : X=X Screen(X Mouse)

    If Mouse Key=1 Then Gosub FREBULLET

Wend : End

'

BULLETS:
```

```
For A=0 To NB-1

   Bob 2+A,BX(A),BY(A),2+BS(A)

   BX(A)=BX(A)+1 : BY(A)=BY(A)+BDY(A)

   If GTG=0 Then BDY(A)=Min(A,BDY(A)+1)

Next A

NB2=NB

For A=NB-1 To 0 Step -1

   If BY(A)>199 or BX(A)<0 or BX(A)>319

      Bob Off 1+NB2

      Swap BX(A),BX(NB2-1) : Swap BY(A),BY(NB2-1)

      Swap BDY(A),BDY(NB2-1) : Swap BS(A),BS(NB2-1)

      Dec NB2

   End If

Next A

Return

'

FREBULLET:

If NB<10

   BX(NB)=X : BY(NB)=Y

   BS(NB)=Rnd(9)

   BDY(NB)=Rnd(2)-12

   Inc NB

End If

Return
```

The beauty of this routine is that it doesn't waste time on bullets which are no longer moving, and sorts the remaining bullets so that they are more efficient. Fiendish.

As well as anything else, the program first creates the Bobs we'll be using, and in this case it's a sort of firework which moves left and right in tune with your mouse movements. If you press the mouse button, the *sparks* shoot out of the end of the firework. The bullets and their motions are stored in arrays, and when the mouse button is pressed, the fire routine is actioned and a number of bullets come flying out of the top and curve upwards under the influence of gravity. Study the BULLET and FREBULLET procs and how they work. Use the SWAP command to sift the bullets into the right order depending on their status.

For Your Information

The mouse pointer in AMOS is a Sprite, and so is the AMOS logo at the top of the screen in the editor. These are all stored in a special bank called Mouse.abk on your AMOS disks. In this special bank Sprite 1 is the normal mouse pointer, Sprite 2 is the crosshairs, Sprite 3 the clock and Sprite 4 the AMOS logo. You can load and edit these Sprites but you must keep the same resolution and amount of colours or AMOS will crash. The cursors are all 2 bitplanes (4 colours) Hires, and the AMOS logo is 4 bitplanes (16 colours). Keep to these boundaries and you can create your very own pointer set.

Let's Get Moving

So now we can animate and move about, what sort of processes can we use to get the Sprites and bobs to do what we want? Onward to Object Movement.

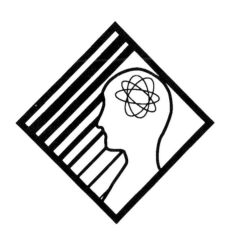

9:
Object
Movement

Once you've got the hang of Sprite moves, you'll doubtless want to start interacting with these Sprites. How do you move them, and with what? If you've had your Amiga for longer than about 10 minutes you'll be used to having a joystick in one port and a mouse in the other, so these are obviously the first choices of input devices. Then there's the keyboard, perfect for Tetris type games, or an option for those people who hate joysticks. (They do exist, I assure you. Ex-PC owners mostly!)

Moving Experience

You interact with AMOS programs using the keyboard, mouse and joystick, and although the keyboard is easy (if you know BASIC), getting the computer to understand what you want using the mouse and keyboard are harder to master. Until now that is.

HIDE is the first command that springs to mind, and this is a fairly simple mouse control command which has nothing to do with object movement but as we'll see in a sec has something to offer the programmer of mouse moves. This command hides the mouse pointer, and the reasons you would want to do this are manifold. Mostly it's to free the screen for a really good picture and not allow the user the distraction of wanting to click on something.

If the mouse pointer is not being used, but instead you're using a character which is in fact a Sprite (like a digitised picture of a human hand, for example) then obviously you won't want the old pointer still on screen, will you?

So HIDE sends the pointer away. To get it back just do a SHOW command, so a typical structure would go like this:

```
Screen Open 0,640,256,4,Hires

Load Iff "load a hires picture here"

Hide

Centre "<It's gone!>"

Wait Key

Show

Centre "<It's back!>"

Wait Key
```

It's handy to be able to hide the mouse pointer on main title pictures, and draw in a *Press Any Key* prompt on the picture to make people trigger the Wait Key command to carry on. And clearly if the method of control is something other than the mouse, like the joystick, you don't want to have the mouse pointer hanging about clogging up the screen.

Another useful mouse command is CHANGE MOUSE. This allows you to alter the shape of the mouse pointer to another preset design or even one of your own. You can do this in your *system-configuration* and load this onto your RAMOS disk, but there is an elegant way to do this from within AMOS. The way you use CHANGE MOUSE is like so:

```
Change Mouse 1
```

where the 1 could be any number from 1-3. The preset pointer shapes are.

1. for a normal pointer
2. for a crosshair
3. for a mouse clock

And if you choose a 4, then the mouse pointer will be taken from your Sprite bank. It's not that simple though, as the Sprite number is derived by subtracting 3 from the number given. So for example:

```
Change Mouse 4
```

gives you Sprite 1 of the current bank, and:

Change Mouse 5

gives you Sprite 2, and so on and so forth. This means you can have your Sprite attached to the mouse, without having to hide the pointer, because in this case the pointer *is* a Sprite.

AMOS is really good at simplifying the reading of hardware, and this is because it's been thought up long after all the old world BASIC commands have been tried and tested and been found wanting.

For example for reading if a mouse button has been pressed, you just use either the MOUSE KEY or MOUSE CLICK commands. To set or read the position of the mouse pointer on screen you use the much more simple X MOUSE or Y MOUSE instructions. (Much more simple than *BASIC Ordinaire*, that is.) And finally you can limit the mouse to certain areas of the screen with the LIMIT MOUSE command. This program shows you roughly what I'm talking about:

```
Rem * Mousing around.AMOS *
Rem
Print "Mouse pointer on"
Wait Key
Hide
Cls
Print "Mouse pointer off"
Wait Key
Show
Cls
Change Mouse 3
Print "Mouse back again, but altered"
Print "Move mouse and press button"
Cls
Proc _CHECKMOUSE
End
'
Procedure _CHECKMOUSE
Do
```

```
            Home
            X1=X Mouse : Y1=Y Mouse
            Print "Mouse location = ";X1,Y1
            K=Mouse Key
            If K=0 Then K$="None"
            If K=1 Then K$="Left"
            If K=2 Then K$="Right"
            Print "Mouse key pressed = ";K$
        Loop
        End Proc
```

Obviously once you have the mouse being read from the AMOS program, you can just as easily pass the information from the mouse to a Sprite and relate its moves to those of the mouse:

```
        Rem * Mouse follow.AMOS *
        Rem
        Screen Open 0,320,256,32,Lowres
        Flash Off : Hide : Cls 0
        Load "df3:sprite_600/space/ship3.abk"
        Get Sprite Palette
        Double Buffer
        Do
            X1=X Mouse : Y1=Y Mouse
            Bob 1,X1-150,Y1-50,1
        Loop
```

This example shows you how this is done. (Obviously you could simply change the mouse pointer, but this is how to control a Bob with the mouse!) The X MOUSE and Y MOUSE values are stray by about 150 in the x dimension and about 50 in the y direction due to a little difference of opinion between hardware and screen coordinates, but I'll look at that in a moment. LIMIT MOUSE suffers from a similar problem, but here's what it looks like:

```
        Rem * Mouse Limit.AMOS *
        Rem
        Curs Off : Cls 0
```

```
Ink 7

Bar 0,0 To 319,150

Ink 2

Box 0,0 To 319,150

Box 100,100 To 200,50

Pen 0 : Paper 7

Locate 0,1

Centre "* LEFT button mouse limit *"

Locate 0,3

Centre "* RIGHT button no limits *"

Do

    If Mouse Key=1

        Limit Mouse X Hard(0,100),Y Hard(0,100) To X
        Hard(0,200),Y Hard(0,50)

        X Mouse=X Hard(0,150) : Y Mouse=Y Hard(0,70)

    End If

    If Mouse Key=2 Then Limit Mouse

Loop
```

Notice the use of X HARD and Y HARD to get the head of the mouse pointer limited to the right spot on screen. I'll explain why this is in a moment.

The mouse can't move outside the confines of an invisible box on the screen, which is good for the kind of game where an attack wave is coming onto the screen from the righthand side and you might smack into a few Bobs as they appear. If you can't reach that side of the screen your player will be safe, until they start shooting at least.

One thing to bear in mind with mouse control is the difference between hardware coordinates and screen coordinates. The X MOUSE and Y MOUSE commands return a hardware coord so you have to convert that to a screen coord for the position to be right. Same with LIMIT MOUSE. In order for the coords from X and Y MOUSE to be correct you have to convert them using X and Y SCREEN.

Mouse moves are easy to follow and even control, as in this final mouse example, which takes the form of a famous toy. (How I miss it!)

```
Rem * Retch-As-Ketch.AMOS *
Rem
Curs Off : Cls 0
Paper 0
Pen 3 : Centre "R e t c h - A s - K e t c h"
Locate ,4 : Pen 4 : Centre "Press 's' key to save a pic-
ture"
Locate ,6 : Pen 2 : Centre "Right mouse to clear screen"
Locate ,24 : Pen 1 : Centre "Press a key to start"
Wait Key : Cls 0
Y Mouse=X Screen(160) : X Mouse=Y Screen(100)
Do
    X=X Mouse : Y=Y Mouse
    M=Mouse Key
    I$=Inkey$
    If M=1 Then Plot X Screen(0,X),Y Screen(0,Y),2
    If M=2 Then Cls 0
    If I$="s" Then SAVIT
Loop
'
Procedure SAVIT
    F$=Fsel$("*.IFF","","Save your picture")
    Save Iff F$
End Proc
```

Press the s key on its own to save your doodles to disk, and press the right mouse button to erase your etches from the screen. Okay so it isn't DPaint, but it's fun, and it only takes about 10 minutes to type in. Notice carefully the use of X SCREEN and Y SCREEN here to convert the X and Y MOUSE functions from hardware coords to screen coords. This is the best way to do it.

Deep Joy

And so we move on to the joystick, which is read in a similar no nonsense way. Obviously the main difference between the joystick and the mouse is that the mouse has a coordinate on the screen, whereas the joystick only has eight directions and a fire button. There are ways of reading the stick in AMAL, and even Autotest, but we'll get into that in Chapters 10 and 11. For now let's concentrate on the ways of reading joysticks through AMOS itself.

The Joy command returns a figure telling you what state the joystick is in. Take a look at this segment of code:

```
Do
    Bob 1,X1,Y1,I
    J=Joy(1) and 15 : Add X1,X(J),10 To 30 : Add
    Y1,Y(J),10 To 20
    Exit If Joy(1)>15
Loop
```

Just look at this, but don't type it in because it won't work. Although this example requires that you set up DIM statements etc, you can read joystick port 1 and pass the information to a Sprite (or in this case a Bob) move command to shift the thing around the screen.

As well as using the comprehensive Joy command, you can look specifically at each direction one at a time with the Jup, Jdown, Jleft and Jright commands, along with Fire to check the mouse button. Try this example which will give you the idea:

```
Rem * Joystick Tester *
Rem
Do
    If Jleft(1) Then Print "Left"
    If Jright(1) Then Print "Right"
    If Jup(1) Then Print "Up"
    If Jdown(1) Then Print "Down"
    If Fire(1) Then Print "==FIRE!=="
Loop
```

Obviously the action taken on trapping the joystick can range from simply passing information to a program (like change a page of information) or it can action some animation for a certain Sprite on the screen. Direction is important to animation as we've heard from the Sprite creation chapter, but here's how it's done in AMOS:

```
Rem * Directional Joystick.AMOS *
Rem
Flash Off : Hide : Curs Off : Cls 0
Load "df0:sprite_600/vehicle/superbik.abk"
Ink 2
Polygon 100,75 To 200,75 To 319,200 To 0,200 To 100,75
Ink 1
Polygon 150,75 To 155,75 To 159,100 To 155,100
Polygon 156,110 To 164,150 To 170,150 To 159,110
Polygon 174,159 To 185,200 To 176,200 To 170,159
Locate ,3
Paper 0
Centre "Use the joystick to lean the bike!"
Double Buffer
Get Sprite Palette
X1=100 : Y1=100 : I=11
Bob 1,X1,Y1,I
Do
    If Jleft(1) Then Dec I
    If I<1 Then I=1
    If Jright(1) Then Inc I
    If I>20 Then I=20
    If I>11 Then A=25
    If I<=11 Then A=0
    Bob 1,X1+A,Y1,I
    Wait Vbl
Loop
```

The Sprite we're using is the SuperBike from the Sprite 600 set. It has a series of images of a bike leaning over from the left to the right, with the central image of the bike upright being image 11. The main loop of the program checks the joystick's left and right sensors to see if the stick is pressing in those directions. If it's pushing left it decrements (subtracts) 1 from the image number, giving you the next image down, which makes the bike appear to lean to the left. The reverse happens if the joystick is being pushed to the right. The image number I is incremented (added to) by I, and the next images show the bike leaning to the right.

The short tests to see if I is equal to 11 are to shift the image on screen by 25 pixels in the X dimension between images 11 and 12. The wheels of the Sprite flick from one side of the screen to the other if you don't make sure they stay put. Testing to see which image you are using enables you to add the amount of pixels difference (stored in A) to the X coord of the Sprite, meaning that it will always seem to be on the right spot and not jump.

The Sprite image changes whichever way the joystick is moving, and this improves the reality of the Sprite's movement. Obviously you can incorporate various other routines to improve the animation, like making a little puff of grit when the bike leans a lot, making it lean further the faster you go, and even let the bike slide a little across the road when you go around corners. It's all done with Bob image changes and a bit of intelligent programming. It's all a matter of what happens when, as with all programs.

Obviously joystick control needn't be passed simply to a Sprite. You could pass the joystick movements to the mouse pointer, and ask someone to move the mouse. When they think they've got the hang of it, you can divert them with the joystick. (A silly joke, but I got a kick out of it). Or perhaps this is more your line:

```
Rem * Joystick Screen Move.AMOS *
Rem
Screen Open 1,320,256,32,Lowres
Flash Off : Curs Off : Hide : Cls
Load Iff "df0:iff/amospic.iff",1
Screen Display 1,X Hard(0,0),Y Hard(0,0),320,256
X=0 : Y=0
Screen Copy 0,0,0,319,100 To 0,639,0
Do
    If Joy(1)=%100 Then X=X-6
    If Joy(1)=%1000 Then X=X+6
    Screen Offset 1,X,0 : Wait Vbl
Loop
```

The picture in the program is of course our old friend AMOSPIC.IFF, but it could really be any lowres picture. Once the program is run you can move the joystick to the right, and hold it there. A number of copies of the screen roll by, and when you push the joystick the other way the screen scrolls back. If you scroll back to beyond the first screen you'll discover that we haven't made provision for a leftwards scroll, although it would be a simple matter of copying the screen to the left of the current screen as well as the right, in the SCREEN COPY routine.

Keyboard Controls

There comes a time in every programmer's life when he wants to write something which has more controls than the simple up, down, left, right and fire that a joystick can offer. Flight simulators are a good example of this, and although that is a slightly complex example, it serves the purpose. Flight simulators usually have a number of controls, obviously a joystick is a good start, but for things like setting your flaps, throttling the engine, launching rockets etc, this is a task that requires a few more control keys. This is where the keyboard comes in.

The simplest method for controlling things using the keyboard is to examine individual keys and check if they are equivalent to certain ASCII characters. ASCII is a standard code for computers where every key on the keyboard has a number, and although these numbers are usually only used internally for the computer to identify certain characters, the codes do have uses in computer programs.

Commonly the computer language you use has a sort of translation of the codes built in, so you can do a:

```
If A="Y" Then _GOFORIT
```

kind of thing. This means that if a key you have pressed is in fact the capital Y key, the Proc called _GOFORIT is actioned. To grab the key in the first place you have a few options, the simplest of which is the INKEY$ statement:

```
Do
    X$=Inkey$ : If X$<>"" Then Print X$
Loop
```

INKEY$ waits in the background until a key is pressed, and then when it is, the value of that key is stored in the variable you assign it to. Testing that variable allows you to check which key it was that was pressed. To check the ASCII codes of keys you can test them with the ASC and CHR$() functions. ASC generates the ASCII code of a character and CHR$() converts that code into a character on the screen.

A more sophisticated function is the SCANCODE keyword, which allows you to check for keys which don't actually print on the screen, like Help, Del or the function keys. This means that all the keys on the keyboard can be trapped and used as control keys for your program. This short program gives you the basic idea:

```
Rem * Scancode.AMOS *
Rem
Screen Open 0,640,256,16,Hires
Hide : Paper 0 : Cls 0
Do
    While KEE$=""
        KEE$=Inkey$
    Wend
    If Asc(KEE$)=0 Then Print "**Special Key!**"
    Print "Scancode for key is";Scancode
    KEE$=""
Loop
```

The function keys can also be accessed with this command, and this can be handy for utility programs, and even creating keyboard short-cuts from menus.

New Control Extensions

New extensions to the language are coming out from time to time, and the primary source of these is the AMOS Club. Only recently they've been running a series on writing your own extensions to AMOS, and including a new interface for controlling analogue joysticks as part of the AMOS Club/Shuffle extension! Interesting stuff. Obviously it's easy to include support for anything which plugs into the joystick port, like Koala pads, graphics tablets etc, but some things need a little more control. Writing extensions is not for the faint hearted.

Moving Faster?

You need some animation fast, and you don't have a compiler? In that case the next stop on this ride has to be the AMOS Animation Language. Yes, it's time for a spot of AMAL.

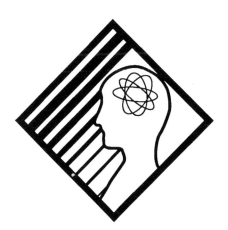

10:
Introducing
AMAL

I've been saying I was going to get around to AMAL for a few chapters now, and now is the time. Although you might think you know about AMAL, I bet you rarely use it and think that it's rather complicated, don't you? Well relax, because as well as the tutorial element, I'll also be explaining a bit more about the theory of AMAL. So just skim forward to the program to type it in if you like, and ignore the technical stuff till later if you already know heaps about AMAL. (But then if you know heaps about AMAL and AMOS in general, what are you doing reading this book?)

AMAL is the AMOS Animation Language and it's one of the most important parts of AMOS. It's a powerful way of animating Sprites and Bobs (or anything you move around the screen in fact) without taxing the processor. You see AMAL commands are specially optimised BASIC program commands which are compiled before running, making them super fast. You can easily incorporate AMAL programs within your regular AMOS code, and this is how you do it.

The first thing to know is that AMAL code can be written in one of two ways:

1. as string statements in a normal AMOS program.

2. using the AMAL Editor program.

It is possible to write a whole program using just AMAL and letting AMOS run the boring stuff. The trade off is that AMAL is harder to learn and implement well if you're a beginner. But being harder to learn it's more minimalist and does the job very efficiently with the minimum of programming. Anyway look at it like this, a skill acquired is never a waste of time, eh?

Using AMAL

The easiest and most accessible way of using AMAL code in your programs is to embed the commands in strings in AMOS statements like so:

```
Amal 1,"S: M 300,200,100 ; M -300,-200,100 J S"
```

then run the AMAL program (or more properly *channel*) number 1 by typing:

```
Amal On 1
```

which runs AMAL program number (or *channel*) 1. Each of the AMAL commands is a single letter, like M for Move, A for Animate, and L for Let. If you type the letters for the rest of the word, they will be ignored by AMAL, but will be easier to read and understand, especially by people who didn't write your program. For clarity it's best to type the initial letter in upper case and the rest of the command in lower case. Why? Well, the commands are embedded in strings, so the computer won't alter them in the same way it does ordinary commands.

AMAL contains very clever commands like the Play (or PL) command, which is for recording a set of mouse moves, for an attack wave for example, and playing them back to a Sprite. There are also commands for reading the joystick and mouse positions. These are much faster than the normal AMOS commands, and are very useful for the kind of fast, hard action type games, or even for something like a graphics program where fast mouse reading and movement is desirable if not essential.

If the AMAL program is a single line then putting:

```
Amal 8,"program"
```

is okay. But if your program uses more lines you have to add each line to a variable, and then call the variable an AMAL program at the end. This is the way it is done in most AMAL programs, in this case with C$, but it could be any string variable like B$, or Z$:

```
C$="For R=0 To 10 ;"

C$=C$ + "For RO=1 To 320 ; Let X=X+1 ; Next RO ;"

C$=C$ + "Let Y=Y+8 ;"
```

and so on, with each line adding the current line to the last, by physically adding it to C$. At the end of the addition statements, you make the C$ string equal to the AMAL program by adding the *Amal n* command, and running the program with Amal On as the last line, like so:

```
Amal 8,C$ : Amal On 8
```

Saying Amal 8,C$ is like saying Amal 8, "insert your program here", and the Amal On 8 line immediately after runs the program you've just created in your string statements.

Command Set

The commands in AMAL are much fewer than the commands in AMOS itself, and although the instruction set is very restricted, it can do a great deal, especially in the creation of games. The command set falls into two categories, the commands and the functions. There are basically just 13 commands, see Table 10.1 for details.

Option	Hot key
Move	(or M)
Anim	(or A)
Let	(or L)
Jump	(or J)
If	(or I)
For To Next	(or F T N)
Play	(or PL)
Pause	(or P)
Autotest	(or AU)
Exit	(or X)
Wait	(or W)
On	(or O)
Direct	(or D)

Table 10.1. AMAL command set.

And there are 15 *functions*, and these are just simple ways of getting information to and from the screen, joystick and mouse. These are detailed in Table 10.2.

Command	Action
=XM	returns x coord of mouse
=YM	returns y coord of mouse
=K1	status of left mouse button
=K2	status of right mouse button
=J0	tests right joystick
=J1	test left joystick
=XH	convert x coord into hardware coord
=YH	convert y xo-ord into hardware coord
=XS	ditto only)
=YS	in reverse)
=BC	checks for bob collisions
=SC	checks for sprite collisions
=C(n)	returns status of object n after BC or SC
=Z(n)	see below
=V(v)	see below

Table 10.2. AMAL Functions.

A couple of the functions don't fall in to any category, and these are the Vu meter and the random number function, and I must say that AMOS must be the *only* language in the world which features a VU meter function of *any* kind! The Vu meter function is handy for creating Vu meters (those nice bouncing sound level gauges you get on stereos) in your latest demo, where you can make sprites and graphics bob up and down or left to right in time to the music. Check the function of both this and the VuMeter AMOS command in your manual.

Not everyone needs VU meters, but everyone needs random numbers from time to time, and although you can get them from AMOS and pass the data to AMAL, you can get much better (and faster) results by using the =Z(x) function, where x equals the number range. For example using 255 for n will return a value between 0-255.

Using AMAL Editor

If you intend to print out your program in a magazine or to distribute to friends, then putting your AMAL code into the AMOS listings is a better way to go. But if you are the only person going to see the code, if you're going to compile your program or lock it for example, then the AMAL Editor is better. The AMAL Editor takes your AMAL programs and puts them into a memory bank. Then you can call the AMAL programs from a bank, saving space in your AMOS program and stopping anyone inspecting your code. I'll be looking at the AMAL Editor in depth in Chapter 11.

Sprite Movement

The main strength of AMAL commands over the regular AMOS commands is that they are compiled, and so run much faster than the equivalent regular strength commands. So they are the perfect way to animate your sprites. To move a sprite you use the format:

    M w,h,n

where w is equal to the amount of pixels horizontally, h to the amount of pixels vertically and n equals the speed of the move. So for example:

    M 75,75,100

is a very slow move 75 pixels to the right and down, so if the Sprite started at 100,100 it would end up at 175,175. If you then did a move like this:

    M 0,-75,20

it would be a very fast move straight up. Negative values of w and h will give you moves to the left and up, so the sprite would now be at 175,100. The speed of the move is governed by the n number, ie the amount of steps in the move. Obviously if you have a lot of steps, then the move will be slow and precise. If you have a very few steps the move will be fast.

Sprite Animation

Animating sprites is simple in AMAL, but then again this is the AMAL speciality, and the reason why the commands are compiled before runtime. Animation is usually very slow because of the amount of work the computer has to do, but in AMAL the animations run independently of the rest of the AMOS program.

The Anim command is a single letter A, and the format is like this:

    A n,(x,y)(x,y)

where n equals the number of times the animation cycles around, and x,y equal image number and duration. A zero in the number of animation cycles means the animation runs in a loop continuously. So this:

    A 0,(1,4)(2,4)(3,4)(4,4)(5,4)

is a continuous animation with five frames, and each frame duration is 4. The number of the animation frame is the number of the sprite in the sprite bank.

AMAL On!

To start your AMAL programs, even if they have been loaded as an .abk file, is to use the Amal On command. You can specify an AMAL program number like so:

```
Amal On 8
```

or just leave it blank to run all AMAL programs currently resident:

```
Amal On
```

As a default situation, the AMAL programs you run affect a hardware Sprite with the same number, although this situation can be changed with the Channel command. But in the default situation, this is the way it works:

```
Amal On 2
```

activates an animation involving hardware Sprite 2.

When I Say Jump

Just like normal AMOS, the AMAL programs can use labels to mark certain points in the program, which can be jumped to using the Jump (or J) command. To set up a label, simply type it in with a : on the end, like this:

```
Start:
A 0,(1,4)(2,4)(3,4)(4,4)(5,4)
M 0,-75,20
etc
```

Now at any point in the program you could Jump to that point again using:

```
Jump Start
```

Labels can be anything, but it's the first letter that counts, as in all AMAL operations. So to label the program you might just as well have put:

```
S:
A 0,(1,4)(2,4)(3,4)(4,4)(5,4)
M 0,-75,20
etc
```

and to jump to that point in the program to have typed:

J S

AMAL is a little bit confusing like that. It might look very complicated and high technical to only use the AMAL keywords as single letters, but I find it helps if you pad them with extra lower case letters to make them more readable, even much used things like Move and Anim. Obviously it's a free country and I can't come round and beat you with a fistful of kippers if you don't do this. But that's my advice.

Put it all Together

And what have you got? A little AMAL program, that's what. You can either do the program like this in the AMAL Editor on channel 8:

```
Anim 0,(1,3)(2,3)(3,3)(4,3)

Move 0,75,50

Move 75,0,50

Move 0,-75,50

Move -75,0,50
```

being sure to load and position Sprite 8 first of course. Or you can do it in AMOS itself, like so:

```
Rem * Simple AMAL Anim.AMOS *

Rem * It's octopus time again *

Rem

Load "AMOS_DATA:Sprites/Octopus.abk"

Get Sprite Palette

Sprite 8,100,100,1

M$="Anim 0,(1,3)(2,3)(3,3)(4,3)"

M$=M$+"Move 0,75,50"

M$=M$+"Move 75,0,50"

M$=M$+"Move 0,-75,50"

M$=M$+"Move -75,0,50"

Amal 8,M$ : Amal On 8
```

Of course you can use your own Sprites (produced with SpriteX, perhaps?) instead of the ones on the disk. I know if I see that stupid octopus any more I'll scream.

BOING!

You can not only move Sprites but also whole screens. This program bounces a screen around. The repeat of the effect is handled with a bunch of loops, all following through to a bunch of labels. See if you can follow where the program is going at any point, and how the program flow changes as things happen:

```
Rem * Screen Bounce.AMOS *
Rem
Channel 0 To Screen Display 0
Channel 1 To Screen Offset 0
F$=Fsel$("","","Pick a picture")
Load Iff F$,0
A$="Boing:Let Y=-256"
A$=A$+"Let R0=256"
A$=A$+"Let R1=8"
A$=A$+"Let R2=45"
A$=A$+"Move 0,R2-Y,R1"
A$=A$+"Loop:Move 0,R2-Y-R0,R1"
A$=A$+"Move 0,R2-Y,R1"
A$=A$+"Let R0=R0/2"
A$=A$+"Let R1=R1-1"
A$=A$+"If R0 Jump Loop"
A$=A$+"For R0=0 To 25"
A$=A$+"Pause"
A$=A$+"Next R0"
A$=A$+"Move 0,320,50"
A$=A$+"Let RA=RA+1"
A$=A$+"Jump Boing"
B$="Boing:Let X=0"
B$=B$+"Let R3=RA"
B$=B$+"Let R0=320"
B$=B$+"Let R1=10"
B$=B$+"Move 0-X,0,R1"
```

```
B$=B$+"Loop: Move O-X+RO,O,R1"
B$=B$+"Move O-X,O,R1"
B$=B$+"Let RO=RO/2"
B$=B$+"Let R1=R1-1"
B$=B$+"If RO Jump Loop"
B$=B$+"Sync:"
B$=B$+"If RA=R3 Jump Sync"
B$=B$+"Jump Boing"
Amal O,A$
Amal 1,B$
Amal On
Direct
```

The last command means that the Direct mode window is activated, so you can type:

```
Amal Off
```

if you want to, to stop the movement. Fast isn't it? You could also make the routine stop by adding a Mouse Key command and then throwing in the Amal Off.

The words Loop, Boing, and Sync are all labels not commands. The Jump command is putting you through each small routine a great number of times, and because Amal is compiled the movement is very fast, almost a vibration rather than a wobble. See if you can alter the program to make the screen bounce off to the left or right randomly as if it's made of rubber.

A more manual version of the same gag, which may come in useful for something (but God knows what) is this screen grab trick. Basically what you do is click on the screen and then you can move it around as if it was attached to the mouse Pointer. I suppose if the screen was a super-bitmap (that is to say bigger than the screen) you could hide the mouse Pointer and use it to allow a user to scroll around a big map with the mouse. The mouse is limited so it only ever inhabits a certain space on the screen, so you don't have to see where the Pointer is. (The screen I'm loading here is AMOSPIC.IFF from your AMOS data disk, but any screen will do.)

```
Rem * Screen Grabber.AMOS *
Rem
Load Iff "df0:iff/AMOSPIC.iff",1
```

```
Screen Display 0,,,320,200

Channel 0 To Screen Display 1

Limit Mouse 130,50 To 320+130,50+255

Amal 0,"Loop: Pause; If K1=0 Jump Loop; Let Y=YM-
128; If XM-160<64 Jump Loop; Let X=XM-160; Jump
Loop"

Amal On

Screen 0

Repeat

Until Inkey$<>""
```

To stop the effect you have to press the space bar or any other key:

```
REPEAT UNTIL INKEY$<>""
```

is a good way to scan for a key while letting another process go on, especially AMAL progs which will rattle on until they are stopped with AMAL OFF.

Extreme AMAL

To see the kind of extreme things you can do with AMAL, how about filling the screen with Bobs? Imagine the worst attack wave of your dreams, with hundreds of wriggling aliens all over the screen. You can make things pretty hot for your players, if you follow this program. It takes a Bob from an ABK file, and animates it and moves it about in the confines of the screen, then it turns on a load of other Sprites too, using the loop, and fills the screen with wriggling beasties. (Jeff Minter would be proud! Just a little in joke there for all old C64 game fans.)

There is normally a restriction on how many AMAL programs (and therefore events) you can have running, but there is a simple way around this if you really want to go crazy. Again this program uses the octopus that Francois included in his original program disks, but the only reason I'm using that one is because it looks better:

```
Rem * Amal Madness.AMOS *

Rem

Screen Open 0,320,200,8,Lowres

Load "df0:sprites/octopus.abk"

Cls 0

Double Buffer : Flash Off : Fade 4 To -1

Synchro Off
```

```
A$="Anim 0,(1,1)(2,1)(3,1)(4,1);"
A$=A$+"Update: Let R0=Z(255)+Z(63)-X; Let
R1=Z(127)+Z(63)-Y; Let RZ=Z(15)+4;"
A$=A$+"Move R0,R1,RZ; Jump Update"
For I=0 To 63
   Set Bob I,1,%111,
   Bob I,Rnd(320)+1,Rnd(200)+1,Rnd(3)+1
   Channel I To Bob I
   Amal I,A$
Next I
Amal On
Repeat
   Synchro : Wait Vbl
Until Mouse Key
```

The trick is done using Synchro, which is used here to exceed the normal restriction of 16 programs running at once. You do it by saying SYNCHRO OFF before you define your AMAL programs, as in this example. Then you can use AMAL channel numbers higher than 15 without getting an error.

One interesting point is that the movements of the Sprites are randomised using the =Z(x) function to provide random values for the Move command, so all of the X, Y and step values are randomly generated in real time. There's really no predicting where those little monsters will go.

Joystick Juggling

Control for AMAL animations must come from either the joystick or the mouse. Let's face it if you're animating a Sprite of some kind, you will probably want to move it around, and these are the only two ways to do it.

Using the joystick is good for games, and reading it from AMAL is very easy, in fact a lot easier than with AMOS itself. This example program uses the machine gun toting monkey from the demo disks:

```
Rem * AMAL Joystick.AMOS *
Rem
Rem * Don't forget to load a sprite.abk file *
Rem * the one called MONKEY_RIGHT.ABK is best *
```

```
Rem
Curs Off : Flash Off : Hide : Cls 0
Double Buffer
Get Sprite Palette
A$="Begin:"
A$=A$+"If J1&4 then Jump G ;" : Rem joy left
A$=A$+"If J1&8 then Jump H ;" : Rem joy right
A$=A$+"If J1&2 then Jump P ;" : Rem joy up
A$=A$+"If J1&1 then Jump Q ;" : Rem joy down
A$=A$+"Jump Begin;"
A$=A$+"H: Anim 1,(1,4)(2,4)(3,4)(2,4)(1,4) ; Move
16,0,16 ; Jump Begin ;"
A$=A$+"G: Anim 1,($8001,4)($8002,4)($8003,4)
($8002,4)($8001,4) ; Move -16,0,16 ; Jump Begin ;"
A$=A$+"P: Anim 1,(1,4)(2,4)(3,4)(2,4)(1,4) ; Move
5,16,16 ; Jump Begin ;"
A$=A$+"Q: Anim
1,($8001,4)($8002,4)($8003,4)($8002,4)($8001,4) ;
Move -5,-16,16 ; Jump Begin ;"
Bob 1,160,100,1
Channel 1 To Bob 1
Amal 1,A$
Amal On
Direct
```

The direction the Sprite faces is entirely dependent on the way the sprite was drawn, but the directions are read from the stick using the J1 function. Using the AND operator in concert with the input from J1 you get the direction the stick is going. One interesting feature of this program to note is that if you add a $800 to the front of the image number of a Bob, you flip it horizontally. This works for all kinds of Sprites and Bobs, and comes in handy as you only have to draw the Sprite for one direction. You have to bear in mind with the design that it looks good both ways, although for most types of Sprite this really doesn't notice.

That's all for the basics, what about some more advanced techniques? Let's move on to Advanced AMAL.

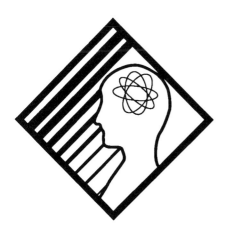

11: Advanced AMAL

Now is the time to be covering AMAL routines for AMOS in more detail, showing you ways to make your AMOS programs faster and more productive. AMAL is a very important part of what makes AMOS a special programming environment, so the more time we spend on this the better.

AMAL is a sort of subset of AMOS which primarily allows you to carry out very fast animations, and run a number of them in parallel with very little slowing up of the finished effect, like some of the programs we featured in the last chapter. So you can have a number of animations going on, a number of AMAL programs working together, in effect at the same time. AMAL is simple to use and the command set is restricted to a handful of commands which I detailed in the last chapter.

The speed of the commands is achieved by the fact that the system is automatically compiling them before they are run, allowing for faster execution than normally possible through BASIC, even AMOS BASIC. Using AMAL you can animate everything from a single Sprite to an entire screen. Up to 64 of your AMAL programs can be run simultaneously, although you can only run up to 16 without interfering with the flow of the regular AMOS commands using Synchro. (If you're getting a deja vu sensation here, don't worry! I did actually say this before, but it needs to be clear.) I talked about how you use the AMAL commands, in very simple terms.

Now by way of an introduction to advanced AMAL techniques, I want to draw your attention to the AMAL Editor you got free with your AMOS Extras disk. AMAL Editor is an AMOS program so you either need to run it from AMOS, RAMOS or compile it and run it from the Workbench. Or even better you can install it as an AMOS Accessory to be available from AMOS at any time, although this will chop down your available memory quite a bit, so don't do that unless you have *bags* of memory. In any event *do* use the AMAL editor next time you have the chance, because this will improve your AMOS programming no end.

Another AMOS Editor

Although for simple AMAL programs, the usual approach of making your AMAL programs in string variables and adding them together to make one big program is the best approach, for larger effects the AMAL Editor is the best way. This allows you to construct a perfect AMAL program and compact it into a regular AMOS memory bank, and load and save it as an .abk file. As well as allowing you to enter and edit the AMAL programs just like a normal AMOS program, the Editor allows you to save the memory bank files so you can use the same sequences in many programs, handy for animated logos and the like.

Figure 11.1. AMAL Editor.

From the main Editor screen you can write your AMAL programs or test them. A menu selection takes you to the AMAL Monitor, where you can examine the progress of any of the AMAL channels you have running. Another menu selection allows you to set up movements like the PLAY command in regular AMAL, only this is all automatic and you can save your mouse moves to a memory bank.

Once an AMAL program has been written using the editor it can be saved to a memory bank and loaded into an AMOS program. Then the AMOS channels can be called as if you'd done them the conventional way.

Through Channel Tunnels

Each channel is viewed and used by clicking on its channel number at the top of the screen. The main screen shows the text editor, information line and the channel selector. You type your programs into the editor, changing channels using the selector, and typing a new programs into each channel.

Editing using the AMAL Editor is a fairly simple affair, and the controls are as listed in Table 11.1.

Keys	Function
Return key	Inserts a line
Ctrl-Y	Deletes a line
Tab	Jumps to next tab position
Cursor keys	Moves cursor one step in any direction
Shift+cursor keys	Start/end of line or Top/bottom of screen

Table 11.1. Editor commands

Once you've written your AMAL programs to the Editor you can run one or all of them with commands from the Menu Bar. The *Run All* and *Run Current* options run every AMAL channel or just the one you have up on screen respectively. The DEBUG menu option takes you into the AMAL Monitor, allowing you to run and debug your AMAL programs very precisely.

Environment Editor

As most AMAL programs aren't able to run in isolation from AMOS, there is an Environment Editor (EE on your channel selector) which is a special channel for you to type the special environment commands. Before you can use a lot of AMAL commands, some kind of initialisation is required from AMOS itself. To do this in the Editor, you need to use the environment commands (See Table 11.2). These are basically a range of important AMOS commands, which are executed at the start of you running the AMAL programs.

The environment commands are exactly like their AMOS equivalents, and are used to make the AMAL programs in your editor run as if AMOS was running too.

The Set Reg command sets one of the AMAL registers A to Z to a value between 0-25. As well as these basic AMOS commands, there are a number of useful test commands

If Screen <number>

This command returns a true result if the numbered screen is open.

If Not Screen <number>

This command returns a true result if the numbered screen is closed.

If Bank <number>

This command returns a true result if the numbered bank is reserved.

If Not Bank <number>

This command returns a true result if the numbered bank is not reserved.

If Reg <letter>,<value>

This command returns a true result if the AMAL register mentioned equals the stated value.

If Not Reg <letter>,<value>

This command returns a true result if the AMAL register mentioned is not equal to the stated value.

Once you've entered the environment commands into the EE channel, they will be a part of the .abk file, for the next time you load the AMAL programs into the Editor. The EE channel isn't executed as part of your AMAL programs when it's all loaded into an AMOS bank, so any commands you used in your EE channel must be typed in by hand at the head of the AMOS program. You can, like me, use a universal *cut and paste* type program like PowerSnap to do this, to save you having to write it all down.

As an important footnote to using the AMAL Editor, you must remember to open an AMOS screen if you intend using Bobs, or the Bobs will appear over the AMAL Editor (screen number 7 always).

Bugs R Us

The AMAL Monitor is another similar screen which enables you to run and debug your AMAL programs easily and quickly. If your AMAL isn't running quite as sweetly as you intended, just slip into

Variables
Sprite Off
Bob Off
Rainbow Del
Screen Open
Screen Display
Screen Offset
Screen
Screen Close
Screen Clone
Double Buffer
Dual Playfield
Dual Priority
Load IFF <name>, <screen>
Colour
Get Sprite Palette <mask>
Flash
Flash Off
Set Rainbow
Rainbow
Load <name>,<number>
Erase <number>
Bob
Set Bob
Sprite
Set Sprite Buffer
Hide On
Update Every
Channel To Sprite <channel>,<sprite>
Channel To Bob <channel>,<bob>
Channel To Screen Display <channel>,<screen>
Channel To Screen Offset <channel>,<screen>
Channel To Screen Size <channel>,<screen>
Channel To Rainbow <channel>,<rainbow>
Set Reg <number>,<value>

Table 11.2. The Environment variables

the AMAL Monitor and you have a range of debugging commands at your disposal. You must first initialise everything by selecting Init from the menus or pressing I on the keyboard. Then you can use one of the following commands:

R	Run	Runs selected AMAL programs until a keypress
G	Go Until	Runs until a certain Reg = a certain value
S	Single Step	Runs the programs one step at a time

Go Until is a neat way to test parts of your programs, as you can insert a sort of breakpoint into your AMAL program. All you have to do is set an AMAL Register to a certain value at a certain point in the program, and as soon as the program in that channel reaches the breakpoint, the program breaks and returns to the AMAL Monitor. To quit out to the main Editor again you just press the Esc key.

As I said before, do use the AMAL Editor if you can, as it's one of the best ways of adding AMAL to your programs as painlessly as possible.

Holy Scrolly Screens

Now we've looked at the Editor, how about some interesting bits about what else you can do with AMAL rather than the obvious Sprites whizzing about all over the shop? How about screens?

Some games have really sexy super-bitmapped scrolling screens, but as we all know this takes up a monstrous amount of memory unless you know how to compress screens into the size of a matchbook. But using AMAL and a tricky little PROC, we can do a similar effect for very little typing or using any bitmaps at all:

```
Rem * ScrollyScreen.AMOS *
Rem
Screen Open 0,960,100,8,Lowres
Screen Display 0,130,150,320,100
Palette 0,$80,$90,$A0,$B0,$C0,$D0,$E0
Flash Off
Set Rainbow 0,1,64,"","","(8,2,8)"
Rainbow 0,1,149,150
HILLS[640,0,50]
Screen Copy 0,0,0,319,100 To 0,639,0
Channel 1 To Screen Offset 0
S$="Loop: For R0=0 To 80; Let X=R0*8; Next R0; Jump Loop"
Amal 1,S$
Amal On
Do
```

```
Loop
Procedure HILLS[Y,X,Z]
    Ink 1 : Bar X,0 To Y+X,99
    For T=0 To Z
        Ink Rnd(5)+2
        TX=Rnd(Y)+X : TW=Rnd(Y/8)+4 : TH=Rnd(50)
        Polygon TX,99 To TX+TW/2,99-TH To TX+TW,99
    Next T
End Proc
```

The key commands in this program, the ones which are doing all the work, are the SCREEN DISPLAY, SCREEN COPY and SCREEN OFFSET commands. They set up the screen, position it, and copy it to the right so as the screen scrolls it keeps coming, or so it seems, giving the effect of a much larger screen. The next important bit is the AMAL program running in Channel 1. The SCREEN OFFSET is fed to Channel 1 in the line immediately before the AMAL program is entered, and when the AMAL program is turned on with AMAL ON. The AMAL CHANNEL command normally takes a SCREEN DISPLAY command to move the screen named (in this case 0), but this time we're feeding it a SCREEN OFFSET to slide the screen to the left. The AMAL loop is set in motion and keeps going until you press Ctrl-C or AMAL OFF.

We could for example run some Sprites over the top of it, simply by opening up some Bobs and running them around over the screen.

```
Rem * ScrollyScreen 2.AMOS *
Rem * insert the spritefile of your choice *
Rem * anything but that octopus, in fact!! *
Cls 0
Screen Open 1,1000,160,8,Lowres
Load "spritefile.abk"
Set Sprite Buffer 150
Flash Off : Curs Off : Hide
Get Sprite Palette
Sprite 4,-100,100,1
Screen Display 1,112,100,400,160
Cls 0
For I=1 To 100
```

```
        Ink Rnd(15)
        HILLS[Rnd(1000),160,Rnd(160),Rnd(100)]
    Next I
    For I=0 To 3
        Sprite 8+I,82*I,125+I*32,I+1
        Channel I To Sprite 8+I
        Amal I,"L: M 500,0,250 M -500,0,250 J L"
    Next I
    Channel 10 To Screen Offset 1
    C$="L: For RO=1 To 250 Let X=X+2 Pause Next RO For RO=1
    To 250 Let X=X-2 Pause Next RO Jump L "
    Amal 10,C$
    Amal On
    Wait Key
    Direct
    Procedure HILLS[X,Y,W,H]
        Polygon X,Y To X+W/2,Y-H/2 To X+W,Y To X,Y
    End Proc
```

The hills are drawn in a similar way, but this time I've made them random, rather than all green and pleasant! Next we've added Sprites from the Sprite file you chose, and this can be any one on your demo disks or from SpriteX. The Sprite is copied onto the screen, just single unmoving images for the sake of simplicity, and the images are staggered down the screen using the SPRITE command. The little AMAL program after that scrolls the Sprites back and forth 500 pixels across the screen. Next we do the old CHANNEL to SCREEN OFFSET number again, only this time just because I feel like it we're going to channel 10. Why not? The AMAL program after that takes the screen and scrolls it back and forth too, like the Sprites. Try a combination of the two programs, and add the Rainbow from the first program to the second, for the full effect.

Autotest

Some of the programs in this book use an AMAL process called AUTOTEST. This is almost the subject of a small book in itself, but here's a quick rundown on what it can do for you.

Basically what AUTOTEST does for you is speed up programs which require a test of some sort, like looking for the coords of a point on the screen, or checking a mouse position etc. Instead of waiting every time a loop in the program goes around to test for something happening in an AMAL program, you use AUTOTEST and everything you specify is tested after every vertical blank (or Vbl) of the screen display, which means your tests happen every 50th of a second. This means if your tests are slowing down a mouse movement, the tests will be pretty much invisible and the movement will be smooth and in real time.

This is a quite advanced AMAL technique, and deserves a bit more explanation. Look at this simple example:

```
Rem * Followmouse.AMOS *

Rem

Load "load a sprite here.abk"

Get Sprite Palette

Sprite 8,130,50,1

Amal 8,"Loop: L RO=XM-X; L R1=YM-Y; M RO,R1,50; J Loop"

Amal On

Direct
```

In this example the mouse is followed everywhere on the screen by the Sprite. It's a simple program but a neat one. In the AMAL program the mouse position is put into registers 0 and 1, via the XM and YM functions. Then a move is transmitted to the Sprite you have activated, based on the information about where the mouse is.

But the movement of the mouse is so fast and fluid that even with AMAL you can't get the tests for the position of the mouse as fast as the movements of the mouse. This means that the Sprite lags behind and looks clunky and slow. Now see what happens when we use Autotest to do the tests rather than AMAL itself:

```
Rem * Followmouse 2.AMOS *

Rem

Load "yes, the same sprite again.abk"

Get Sprite Palette

Sprite 8,150,60,1

A$="AU (I RO<>XM J Update"

A$=A$+"I R1<>YM J Update else X"

A$=A$+"Update: L RO=XM; L R1=YM; D M)"

A$=A$+"M: M RO-X,R1-Y,20 W;"
```

```
    Amal 8,A$

    Amal On

    Direct
```

The same effect but look how smooth the Sprite is! It follows the mouse smoothly and carefully, and that's the wonder of Autotest. Each time the screen is refreshed the information about the mouse is fed to the registers holding the coords for the movement of the Sprite. So the moral of the story is: the greater the resolution, the finer the movements. The faster the tests the more sensitive your programs are to rapidly changing human input.

Although this lends itself to arcade games where reflexes are more in use than brains, you could just as easily use these fast tests for keyboard input, or the rapidly changing input from a sound sampler plugged into the parallel port perhaps.

AMAL Games

Okay it's time to come clean. One of the reasons you'd use AMAL, in fact a lot of the time AMAL comes into the picture, what you are doing is programming a game. Let's face it, we all do it from time to time, and there's no shame in that. (Grin.) Here is the way you use AMAL to make killing games.

I've devised this simple game using AMAL, you can't shoot anything, you can only avoid, and to keep it easy to understand I've made the alien moves static, although you can get as fancy as you like. Here's the listing:

```
Rem * AMAL Game.AMOS *

Rem

Load "Extras:Sprite_600/aliens/alien1.abk"

Load "Extras:Sprite_600/space/ship3.abk",1

Screen Open 0,320,200,16,Lowres

Hide : Curs Off : Flash Off : Cls 0

Get Sprite Palette

Double Buffer

Autoback 0

Bob 1,0,80,18

Bob 2,320,80,1

'

A$="Anim 0,(18,4)(19,4)(20,4)(21,4) ;"
```

```
A$=A$+"Main:"
A$=A$+"If J1&1 Jump Down ; "
A$=A$+"If J1&2 Jump Up ; "
A$=A$+"Jump Main"
A$=A$+"Down: Move 0,-2,1 ; Jump Main"
A$=A$+"Up: Move 0,2,1 ; Jump Main"
'
B$="Anim 0,(1,4)(2,4)(3,4)(4,4) ;"
B$=B$+"Movealien:"
B$=B$+"Move -10,0,10 ; Move 0,-50,10 ; "
B$=B$+"Move -10,0,10 ; Move 0,50,10 ; "
B$=B$+"Jump Movealien"
'
Channel 1 To Bob 1
Amal 1,A$
Channel 2 To Bob 2
Amal 2,B$
Amal On
Wait Vbl
'
Repeat
   Inc SCORE
Until Bob Col(1)
Boom
Paper 0
Pen 2
Centre "Game Over, Man!"
Locate 0,20 : Print "You lasted : ";SCORE;" clicks,
bozo!"
Update
```

Notice I've used a pair of Sprites from the Sprite_600 collection, which you should be able to find on your Extras disk. If it's not on your disk you should be able to obtain it from the AMOS PD Library.

The Sprites are in different Sprite files so the second ABK file is loaded using a *,1* after the load command, which appends the second Sprite file to the first. If you forget to do this you'll overwrite the first Sprite file with the second and you'll only have one Sprite in the bank.

After the Sprites are loaded I get their palette, which fortunately coming from the same collection of Sprites is the same for both Sprites.

Then we've got the usual CLS, CURS OFF and HIDE type things that you will get used to putting at the top of all your programs. Then we're DOUBLE BUFFERing the screen, which makes a second invisible copy of the screen, and all graphic operations are performed to this screen to make the animation and movement a little smoother. It follows that we'll next use AUTOBACK to sync the drawing of the Sprites with the movements.

Next the Bobs we are using are turned on using BOB. In this case Bob 1 is the space ship, Bob 2 is the alien. The start images for each Sprite and the position on the screen are set here, the left side of the screen for the ship and off the right side of the screen for the alien. (The alien is started off the screen so it can enter the screen when it starts to move.)

The next bit is the interesting part. We've created the AMAL programs, destined later on to be two channels 1 and 2. The first channel is defined using the variable A$ and the second B$.

In A$ we set off the animation of the ship Bob so the little flame coming out of the back of it moves. Then we check the joystick port to see which way the stick is pointing, and depending on which way it's pointing we jump to the label containing the up or down moves, which move the ship up or down 2 pixels, at a rate of 1, each time an up or down movement is detected. If you hold the stick in any one of these directions of course, the ship will move smoothly up or down.

In B$ we specify the movement of the alien and his animation. First we set off the animation loop using Anim, then we go into a loop which moves him 10 pixels left, and 50 down, 10 pixels left and finally 50 up, over and over. This advances the alien towards your ship until it either hits it or passes it. As this is a simple example, I've only made the alien make one pass, but you could very simply keep it all going by looping the alien movement to continue back at the righthand side of the screen and even at a different position.

Next we assign a channel to each Bob, so its movements are controlled by one or other of the programs we've created. And when we turn the AMAL programs on and off it all goes. The WAIT VBL waits for the next vertical blank between each move.

Finally we set a REPEAT UNTIL in motion until the two Bobs collide, again no explosions (so violent, don't you think?) because this is a simple example. When the two Bobs collide we hear a BOOM sound effect, although this could easily be our own sample, and a message is printed to the screen to tell you how long you lasted. And there you have it, in essence, the guts of a simple game using AMAL. You can make a lot of this faster and more heart pumping by using Autotest of course, but for something this simple it's not necessary. Which brings us to what you can do with this shell of a game.

I'm a Game, Build Me!

Now you have the makings of a game. Some of the refinements you could try include having a number of attack waves with aliens at different heights and speeds, allowing shooting from both the ship and the aliens, allowing the ship to move forward or back within a limited area, and from there on all the refinements you can add get a little out of hand: sound effects, samples, hi-score tables with rainbow text, and Uncle Tom Cobbly and all. All of the other routines you need for each part of your program are somewhere in this book, and it's up to you to piece them all together into the best game ever made!

12:
Icons and
Screen
Blocks

Icons mean something different in AMOS from what they do in the real world, for example in AmigaDOS. Mostly in the wide world of computing they are a pictorial representation of something, for example a picture of a disk on the Workbench which lets you manipulate files *graphically* with the mouse rather than textually by typing things into the computer. The Icon concept stems from research done at Xerox Palo Alto Research Center in the US, and later used by Apple Computer Inc in its Apple Macintosh range, as part of the Windows, Icons, Mouse and Pointer system. Of course the WIMP system is also used by Amiga in the form of the Workbench, but this isn't what AMOS Icons are all about.

Icons in AMOS are pieces of background graphic, which can be stored in a memory bank like any other kind of Sprite, Bob, sound, music or graphic screen. Once stored they can be pasted to the screen in any order to make up custom backgrounds which, because they are made from small repeated pieces of graphic, take up less time and memory than storing and unstoring whole screens each time you want a new background. It's like tiling a bathroom with patterned tiles, each tile is the same and only very small in size, but put a lot of them together and you cover a large area with an interesting pattern.

Tiling for Beginners

Most games consist of loads of different screens, and like I said just now, if these were full size IFF screens, your average arcade game would be about 3Mb in size. So the easy way out is to make small square graphics, called tiles in the trade, and paste these to the screen. Say you have a graphic of a wall. Most of the tiles are the same, except for the one which has a lamp-fitting, a bit of moss or a door in it. This means that you can build the whole wall from just five tiles, repeating them over and over as you go along.

The Icons are printed to the screen in replace mode, so anything on the screen will be erased by the new graphic. This is different from the modes for Sprites and Bobs which don't appear to touch the background at all. Sprites and Bobs will however float over Icon built backgrounds with the same ease that they would over a complete IFF screen graphic.

Icon Do That!

Does anyone do *Giz A Job* jokes anymore? I doubt it. Anyway, Icons is what we're talking about, so let's get into it. Icons, as I've already said, are the more permanent way of storing backgrounds as memory banks full of small portions or tiles of graphics, and this is the most memory effective way of creating backgrounds.

You can get an Icon tile from an IFF file like you can with Bobs or blocks (see Blocks Away below), but the best way is to create your Icon tiles in an editor of some sort and save them as a bank. You can create them in SpriteX or a similar Bob program, and if the editor doesn't save as Icons you can always run the resultant Bob bank through a program like ICON_CONV.AMOS by Shadow Software.

To save you the trouble if you can't find a program to do the job, here is how to write your own simple Icon grabber:

```
Rem * Icon Grabber.AMOS *
Rem
Flash Off : Cls 0
Shared N,X,Y,X1,X2,Y1,Y2
N=1
Dir$="df0:"
F$=Fsel$("*.iff","","Pick an IFF file")
Load Iff F$,0
Do
    X=X Mouse : Y=Y Mouse
```

```
      If Mouse Click=%1 Then BEGIN
      If Mouse Click=%10 Then FINISH
      X$=Inkey$
      If X$="a" Then SAVIT
Loop
   '
Procedure BEGIN
      X1=X Screen(0,X) : Y1=Y Screen(0,Y)
      Shoot
End Proc
   '
Procedure FINISH
      X2=X Screen(0,X) : Y2=Y Screen(0,Y)
      GRAB
End Proc
   '
Procedure GRAB
      Get Icon N,X1,Y1 To X2,Y2
      Bell
      Inc N
End Proc
   '
Procedure SAVIT
      F$=Fsel$("*.abk","","Save your icon bank")
      Save F$,2
End Proc
```

A little crude, but it gives you the idea of what you are aiming at. I've stripped it down to its bare nothings so you can understand what's being done.

First the usual setup guff, plus a little file requester call to load a picture. This picture should be some background patterns you wish to grab, and in IFF format from a program like DPaint 4 (Electronic Arts). To grab an Icon using the program you press the left button at the top left corner of the Icon, and press the right button at the bottom right corner. The left button press is confirmed by a Shoot sound, and the right by a Bell sound. The indicated rectangle is then grabbed into an Icon in bank 2. The number of the Icon is given by the variable N, and this is incremented as you go to place the Icon in the next slot along in the bank.

Finally, when you are ready to save off the Icon bank, press the a key, and the save requester will pop up, allowing you to save the bank to disk as any filename you like.

As I say this isn't the best and most efficient program, but this is how it's done. Take this basic framework and add to it, testing for bugs as you go, and you'll be well on your way to producing your own Icon grabber.

If you're a bit unhappy about bashing in all that code, or just want something a bit more powerful, try SpriteX 2 (see details in Chapter 21) for effortless production of Sprites, Bobs and Icons.

Blocks Away!

As well as Icons, the AMOS system provides you with a system of what it calls Screen Blocks, and these are just like Icons (pretty much) except that they are really only temporary measures. The blocks you create are not stored with your program and cannot be saved to a memory bank. There's no real need to save them either, as they are grabbed from the screen anyway, and chances are you have the screen from which the block was grabbed anyway, right?

This program demonstrates the grabbing of a screen block and moving it around:

```
Rem * Screen Blocks.AMOS          *

Rem * load some picture or other *

Rem

Load Iff "load your picture choice here.iff",0

For X=0 To 7

    For Y=0 To 9

        Get Block X*10+Y+1,X*32,Y*20,32,20

    Next Y

Next X

Do

    Put Block Rnd(48)+1,Rnd(Screen Width)+1,Rnd(Screen Height)+1

Loop
```

Of course once you know that the command is grabbing the correct area of the screen for the block, you could grab it under the main screen in screen 1 or something like that, so the user doesn't see the grab happen. It looks sloppy if the user of a program can see stuff like that, as it should all happen under the surface and the user only gets to see what he *should* see.

A Block Alert

Blocks are not just good for game backgrounds. You can use them to good effect to create more technical effects. Take this alert box for example. The block covering the words won't destroy them, just look:

```
Rem * CBlock Alert.AMOS *

Rem

Paper 7 : Flash Off : Curs Off : Cls

Locate 0,10 : Centre "Notice this text will still be
here..."

BOCKSALERT

Wait Key

Procedure BOCKSALERT

    W=160 : H=100 : X=80 : Y=50

    Get Cblock 1,X,Y,W+16,H+16

    Paper 0 : Pen 2

    Ink 0 : Bar X+5,Y+5 To X+W+5,Y+H+5

    Ink 0 : Bar X,Y To X+W,Y+H

    Ink 2 : Box X+1,Y+1 To X+W-1,Y+H-1

    Locate X Text(X),Y Text(Y)+2 : Centre "Under the box"

    Locate X Text(X+W/2)-3,Y Text(Y+H)-4

    XB=X Graphic(X Curs)-7 : YB=Y Graphic(Y Curs)-7

    Print Border$("Yeah!",2);

    Reserve Zone 1

    Set Zone 1,XB,YB To X Graphic(X Curs)+7,Y Graphic(Y
Curs)+15

    While Q=0

        While Mouse Key=0 : Wend

        Z=Mouse Zone
```

```
        If Z=1
            Paper 2 : Pen 0
            Locate X Text(X+W/2)-3,Y Text(Y+H)-4
            Print Border$("Right",2)
            Pen 0 : Paper 2
            Play 30,40 : Q=1
        End If
    Wend
    Put Cblock 1,X,Y
  End Proc
```

When you click on the clickbox, which is a complete AMOS construct rather than any kind of automatic alert box, it will go away leaving the words underneath intact. Note the clever use of CBlock to ensure that the words stay unharmed, or are at least replaced. A lot more subtle effects can be made like this with a little bit of thought. Just think of any area of screen that you might want stored and replaced, and you'll get the idea.

Get Block Put Block

This program does a neat trick with an area of screen. The effect is not unlike a TV digital effect, where a picture is moved around the screen. You can do this better in fact, if you load another screen under the current one, mess up the top screen with a block from that screen, then float in segments of the hidden screen onto the top screen and place them.

```
    Rem * Get Block Put Block.AMOS *
    Rem
    Load Iff "any iff picture",0
    Get Block 1,10,10,110,100
    Double Buffer
    Wait Key
    For X=0 To 320 Step 16
        Put Block 1,X,Y
        Put Block 1,Y,X
        Screen Swap : Wait Vbl
    Next
```

The block is first grabbed from the screen you loaded, and then it's stamped using the For Next loop across the page, inverting the X and Y variables to swap over the X and Y coords for the places the blocks are placed on the screen. Messy but fun.

Play On

If music be the food of love, give me a plate of it and a Coke to go. Joking aside, how can you make music in AMOS, and how can you make sounds and use the complex music production system in your Amiga to best effect? Turn the page with a small rustling sound to find out.

13:
Music and
Sound

One of the major things which sets AMOS aside from other forms of BASIC is its grasp of the Amiga's astonishing sound playing ability. But then the whole point of AMOS is that you are able to access all the features of the Amiga quickly and simply by using one command where before only a few hundred would do.

The Amiga can capture and play sampled sounds very easily, and this means that a lot of high quality stereo music can be made just using the Amiga's internal sound generation. Although there are built in sounds like:

```
Rem * Basic Sounds.AMOS *

Rem

Shoot

Wait Key

Boom

Wait Key

Bell

Wait Key
```

The sound chip can be used, and also samples can be put into a bank for you to use in your own programs. Plus AMOS can play music, like the ABK files on your demo disks.

AMOS can play a music track as easily as most other BASIC's can print *Hello World*. All you have to say is:

```
Music 1
```

and the first piece of music you've stored in the music memory bank is played until you type:

Music Stop

to halt the current piece of music, or the more drastic:

Music Off

It's easy, once you get the music into the Amiga in the first place, that is. In most cases this means that a series of samples are stored in the memory of the computer and a little piece of code tells the sounds at what pitch to play and when. The normal way of doing this using an Amiga is using a *tracker* program, like Soundtracker, Noisetracker, Protracker or the totally brilliant MED. Any of these programs can be used with AMOS, as once the track has been created you can convert the track to an ABK file and from there on it's plain sailing.

Using Trackers

The various tracker programs you need are all public domain, with the exception of certain versions of MED which are what they call *licenseware*, that is to say the program costs a bit more than a £2.50 PD disk, but the author of the program gets a royalty every time the program is sold. If you know a little bit about music then you won't be too surprised as to how the trackers work, but for the uninitiated here's what they're all about.

They almost always feature what we call in the trade a *pattern editor* like you find on most modern drum machines, only the keyboard of your Amiga turns into a musical keyboard and the *beats* you put into the program can have a pitch. The sounds in trackers are almost always samples, like the kind you can make with your own sound sampler, with the exception again of MED which also uses the sound chip in the Amiga to create synthesised sounds. Most trackers come with disks of sounds for you to get started from, most of which include samples from some of the most expensive synthesizers you can buy!

The way they work is that you assemble patterns, short sequences of music lasting for 64 beats, and then when you've made a pattern for your verse, chorus and other little fill-ins etc, you finally chain them all together to make a complete piece of music. You say which pattern you'd like to play when, and the program will play each pattern in turn to make meaningful music.

So for example you could have an intro on pattern 1, a verse on pattern 2, a chorus on pattern 3 and a fill-in on pattern 4. (Tunes are usually more complex than this but you get the gist.) So the patterns could be played in this order:

Step 1	Pattern 1
Step 2	Pattern 2
Step 3	Pattern 2
Step 4	Pattern 2
Step 5	Pattern 3
Step 6	Pattern 4
Step 7	Pattern 2
Step 8	Pattern 2

...and so on. The beauty of a pattern based system is that you only have to input your patterns once and then they can be played and arranged as many times as you like, rather than a more linear system which would mean you'd have to type the tune in every time you wanted it to play.

Creating music with a tracker is easy, as you can have four tracks (in some cases even 8 with programs like OctaMED Professional) and you can either put the notes in one at a time in what we call *step time*, or play along with the other tracks live on the keyboard in what is termed *real time*. Step time is easier for learners as you can fiddle about with each track of the pattern until it sounds right, like typing words into a word processor and editing them until the spelling and syntax is perfect.

There are of course a number of disks of tunes available for you to use in the public domain, and these are free for you to use (with a credit obviously) in your own programs. There is another way to get tracker tunes and that is from demos. Those exotic demo disks you get from PD houses usually have a few tracker tunes hidden away on them, but they are buried deep within the code as 9 times out of 10 they are coded in assembler. But if you have a Datel Action Replay cartridge you can strip out the tracker music and save it to disk. Then you have access to all the gorgeous samples and arrangements that these guys use. Worth £50 for the cartridge I'd say.

Converting

Once a piece of tracker music has been made, or produced, you can convert it to AMOS ABK format and load it into a bank. The AMOS disks contain many different converters to serve most of the different kinds of editor, like Noisetracker, Soundtracker, StarTrekker, Protracker, Games Music Creator, Sonix etc. All you do is run these very clever little AMOS programs and they read in a tracker file and spit out an ABK file onto disk ready to be loaded.

Some of these programs work fine, but the problem is that so many of the tracker programs (being in the PD for some time now) have all been revamped and rewritten so that they are marginally different in format from the original programs. Some tracker tunes will not play properly once they've been converted for some reason and that is probably it. Either the tracker has a pattern length which is variable and not fixed at 64, or it stores its samples in a different way. Now if only there was a way to access one of those CLI based player programs. Ah, but there is.

Music Engine

A recent and very popular edition to the Deja Vu licenseware library is *Music Engine* by Paul Townsend and all at Technical Fred Software. This allows you to use tracker music *without* first having to convert it. You see although AMOS hides the Amiga's Workbench, it's still there somewhere (accessible still through the AMOS TO BACK command) and if you have the right routines you can access any program on the Workbench, including the CLI. So what this program really provides is the interface between AMOS and the CLI. The ability to play many different music file formats is achieved by running *player programs* which means you can hear the music without having to convert them first to an AMOS music bank. This program makes it all possible.

Once you've bought the Music Engine program from Deja Vu, you are free to use the source code, if it's for Public Domain, Shareware or Licenseware use, providing of course you acknowledge the source of your source (chuckle). If you want to use the routines in a piece of commercial software however, then you have to contact the programmers to arrange a suitable fee.

The program you are given is filled with useful routines to steal, and although as a program it only allows you to play files and samples that you have on disk (very useful if your tunes have all got stupid names like mine), it is the routines that have made this disk famous. Even the 3D requester used in the program, written by Len Tucker by the way, reminiscent of the one used in Oxxi/Aegis Spectracolor, has been borrowed by a number of recent releases on the AMOS scene and is excellent so I'm not surprised.

The Music Engine gives you a handful of buttons on screen to choose from. File selection can be set to Auto or Manual. In Auto mode when you load in a tune the program senses what type of music the file is. It seems to know Med, OctaMED, Soundtracker, Sonix and AMOS. If the file type is recognised then a player will be selected and an attempt (usually successful) will be made at playing the tune. The success of the tune playing depends on a few factors, like you having enough memory to process the tune, and the correct file type being recognised and/or selected. If Manual file selection is active another screen will appear which gives you the option of deciding what type of music you want to play. If the type is not recognised, or recognised incorrectly, then the music will probably just not play, but it may just crash the computer! The Help button toggles the Help Mode and a message will be displayed to show you if Help is currently active. When you're in Help Mode, further selection of any of the buttons on the screen will display a short message giving you a reminder of what that button does. Full manuals are supplied, so although the help feature is nice, it doesn't replace the docs on the disk.

Music Engine is a very powerful tool, and not just for driving music programs. The trick is a very good one, and although it's handy for music, it's powerful enough to run any program from the Workbench, effectively making your AMOS system multitask with other programs. For more details of Music Engine (disk number LPD79) get in touch with Deja Vu Software at the usual address or write to:

> Technical Fred Software, 117 Hilton Lane, Walkden, Worsley, Manchester, M28 5TB. Phone or Fax: 061-703 7842.

Sampling Your Own

Obviously if you're going to be using samples in your AMOS programs you'll be needing to glean some samples from somewhere. You can pick up disks full of samples from PD libraries, but it's much more fun and far more creative to make them yourself, which is much easier than it sounds. In fact it takes longer to explain it than it takes to do!

Sampling is just a means of recording sound using the digital memory of the computer rather than a tape machine. The sound is stored digitally in the computer, and after recording, the sound can be edited and replayed. To sample sounds with your Amiga, all you need is a sampler, a microphone and a piece of sampling software.

Samplers

There are three samplers I use, and each one has its own merits. The first two are Stereo Master and AMAS 2, both by Microdeal. Stereo Master is the cheaper of the two, and although they use practically the same sampling software, AMAS is also a MIDI interface and comes with its own microphone. The other one I use is the Perfect Sound 3 program and hardware, which is simple to use and very good quality. It also has the benefit of full size audio jacks on the back, which saves you having to shell out for the usual adaptors and stuff like that.

To sample the sound all you have to do is provide an input, either your voice over a microphone or a tape from a video or record, and sample it. (Do of course bear in mind that taping/sampling records or videos is an infringement of copyright.) The sample turns up on the screen as a wavy line, representing the highs and lows of the sound. You can then edit that sound, as if you were cutting out pieces of the tape and rearranging them. When the sound is just the way you want it, you can then save it to disk.

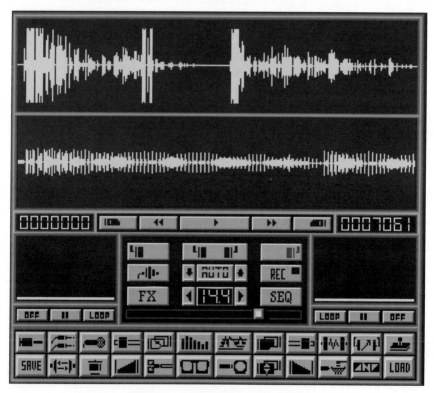

Figure 13.1. AMAS Sound Sampler.

Using Samples in AMOS

Using sampled sounds in AMOS is easy, and similar to the use of IFF picture files, in the way you can load them in form disk as they are or use them from a bank. You need an AMOS program called Sam Maker, and this allows you to load samples and put them together into a bank in memory.

The drawback with loading samples from disk is that you have to BLOAD them and specify locations in memory and all that, which is a little bit technical, not to say a touch heavy on memory and resources. It's far better to store them in a bank as they are ready to access at any time during your program, and they are loaded instantly.

Once you have your samples in a bank you can play them back at any speed, which changes the time the sample takes to play and thus the pitch of the sample. So you can either have samples of speech, snatches of music, or even single notes of an instrument which you can play in a tracker at different pitches.

As I said, playing samples in AMOS is easy. You use the SAM PLAY command:

```
Sam Play V,S,F
```

The voices your sample will use are chosen by setting a bit in V, like so:

```
%1000      voice 3

%1010      voice 3 and 2

%1111      voices 3, 2, 1 and 0
```

This is all very well documented, but here's an idea for you. The Amiga has four voices, and these are paired to play in either the left or right stereo channel. Voices 0 and 3 play through the left speaker and 1 and 2 play through the right. If you want to pan a sound around in the stereo spectrum you have to alter the volume across the two stereo channels of the same sound. (This is called mixing.) To clarify that, a sound appears in a certain position in the stereo picture, depending on how quiet or loud it is in each ear. A noise which is soft in the left ear and loud in the right will appear to come from right of centre in front of the listener.

So in order to simulate stereo panning in an Amiga sound, all you have to do is put the same sound in both speakers and alter the volume of one or the other to move the sound in space! Let's try this out:

```
Rem * Stereo Panning.AMOS *

Rem

Screen Open 0,640,320,16,Hires

Hide : Curs Off : Paper 0 : Cls 0

Load "AMOS_Data:samples/samples.abk"
```

```
        Sam Loop On

        Volume %10,0 : Volume %1,50

        X=1

        Locate ,5 : Pen 4 : Centre "This is a sample of
        Stereo Panning..."

        Locate ,7 : Centre "Notice how the sound moves from
        left to right."

        Do

            Sam Play %11,3

            PANIT

        Loop

            '

        Procedure PANIT

            P1=0 : P2=50

            Repeat

                Volume %10,P1 : Volume %1,P2

                Wait 25

                Inc P1 : Dec P2

            Until P1=50

        End Proc
```

After all the usual setup jazz, we load in some samples from the AMOS Data disk. If you don't have this in the drive it'll prompt you, because I've specified the exact disk name in the LOAD statement. Then we turn SAM LOOP ON to make the sound continuous, and so make it easier to hear the stereo panning. Next we set up the initial volumes of the two voices we'll be using, in this case voices 1 and 2, indicated by the Binary codes %0001 and %0010. This sets the volume so that the right channel is silent and the left is set at 50. Then the PANIT procedure increments the right and decrements the left at half second intervals until the sound has travelled fully from left to right. Crude but effective.

If you were very clever you could even have another sound panning the other way too, but I'll leave that one for you to play with.

Using the Sound Chip

Samples tend to be how most people use the Amiga's sound making ability, but there's a brilliant synthesiser chip in there too. You can use it with SET WAVE, or WAVE and then play the notes in the instrument or sound you've created using PLAY:

```
Rem * Power Sound.AMOS *

Rem

Screen Open 1,640,200,16,Hires

Paper 0 : Pen 4 : Cls 0 : Curs Off : Hide

Wave 0 To 15

Locate ,0

NOISE

Wait 50

Locate ,2 : Centre " Welcome to AMOS Power
Programming" : Bell

Wait 50

Locate 0,4

NOISE

'

Procedure NOISE

   For L=79 To 0 Step -1

      Play 96-(20+(L/2)),0

      Print "*";

   Next L

End Proc

Wait Key
```

SET WAVE is the command you use to create your own sounds, and the sound numbers start from 2, as 0 and 1 are already defined. Wave 0 is defined as *noise* for explosion effects. Wave 1 is a pure sine wave for flute and other whistling effects. After that it's up to you to create your own. Like this one created using the SIN function to combine sine waves.

```
Rem * Setwave.AMOS *

Rem

Hide : Curs Off : Cls 0

Pen 4 : Paper 0

Locate 0,0 : Print "This is the wave you are hear-
ing..."

S$="" : Degree

  For S=0 To 255

    V=Int((Sin(S)/2+Sin(S*2+45)/4)*128)+127

    S$=S$+Chr$(V)

    Plot S,V

  Next S

Set Wave 2,S$ : Wave 2 To 15

For N=0 To 10 : Play N,10 : Next N

Print "...and now a bit higher!"

For N=20 To 30 : Play N,10 : Next N

Print "Ahh sweet music!"

Wait Key
```

If you can draw a wave on the screen using plot, you can create that same wave as the basis for an Amiga sound. Try and create a square wave and even a triangular wave like a sawtooth.

Noisy Drums

The noise wave can be used to create an explosion effect, but like most percussive sounds it's tuneless but has a certain rhythm. Try this noise based drum set for size.

```
Rem * Drumset.AMOS *

Rem

Flash Off : Curs Off : Cls 0

Pen 4 : Paper 0

Centre "Play the drums by pressing keys..."
```

```
Locate ,2 : Centre "I particularly like the function
keys"

Noise To 15

Volume 15,63 : Mvolume 32

Set Envel 0,0 To 1,63

Set Envel 0,1 To 10,0

Do

    Repeat : A$=Inkey$ : Until A$<>""

    Exit If A$=Chr$(13)

    S=Scancode

    If S>0 and S<96 Then Play %100,S,0

Loop
```

The Scancode function returns the value of the key being pressed and passes this value to the PLAY function. Obviously if you were clever you could contrive to not only store a different sample for each key instead of an internal sound, but also make it so that every time you pressed a key it stored the rhythm in a file that you could play back. It's a do it yourself drumbox!

Sound Advice

The possibilities for sound production on the Amiga are greater than for just any other machine. Using samples you can create music that sounds professional even if you aren't. Go out and get yourself a tracker program and a sampler, and see what the dimension of sound can do for your programs.

Contact

MED and OctaMED are available from:

Amiganuts United, 169 Dale Valley Road, Hollybrook, Southampton, SQ1 6QX – Fax: (0703) 785680

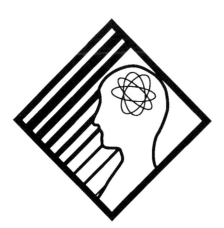

14:
I/O and
Disk Ops

Although AMOS programs will spend most of their time being loaded and run, some programs are bigger than that. Sometimes you need to load and save, do disk directories, and all manner of other disk based input/output (or more commonly I/O) commands. It may be that even though you've had your Amiga around for a while, you might not know what all this talk about files and directories is all about.

Disks are organised to provide space for files, pictures or text from programs that you use. They store them in an organised way so that they can be retrieved by the computer when they are needed. The structure is often described as being like a tree: a main or root directory, with a number of subdirectories branching out from the main stem like the branches. So the main directory has a list of all the subdirectories, and each step along the directory tree is described by using the / symbol. This description as to where files reside on the disk is called the *path*. Imagine you have a disk called DOCS, and on that disk is a directory called LETTERS, and another one called ARTICLES. Inside *letters* you have a file called MUM.TXT which is a letter to your mother, and inside *articles* you have a file called REVIEW1.TXT. To describe to the computer where the files are you would type the following paths:

```
docs:letters/mum.txt

docs:articles/review1.txt
```

Any standard guide on AmigaDOS, (like *Mastering AmigaDOS 2* by Bruce Smith and Mark Smiddy for an obvious example) will tell you everything you need to know about this kind of operation, from an AmigaDOS point of view that is. From an AMOS standpoint, we can do our own disk operations and manipulate files on disk for use in our programs.

Disk Ops

In AMOS programs we can direct the computer's attention to a particular disk or drive so that files needed by the current AMOS program can be found and used, like IFF files, ABK files and so on.

The Amiga uses a system of what are called *devices,* as you probably know, and these are denoted by the use of the : symbol. You can specify a drive number like df0 or df1 by the system:

```
df0:

df1:

fh1:
```

etc. This looks at the drive mentioned no matter what the name of the disk is. If you want to get files from a specific disk, then you can use the colon symbol to ask for it using the *volume name*, like this:

```
MyDisk:

AMOS_DATA:

Workbench:
```

If the disk you need for the program isn't in the drive, a prompt will pop up asking for that disk by name. Or you can specify a logical device, not a real drive but an assigned directory, hardware port or system folder. These are all examples of this kind of device:

```
RAM:

PRT:

CON:

SYS:

LIBS:

FONTS:
```

Using the DIR command, you can get a directory of the currently selected path, or even specify a path to look at like so:

```
Dir

Dir "df0:"

Dir "AMOS_DATA:"

Dir "AMOS:IFF/"
```

You can also add the /w switch to the command to list the files in two columns down the screen to save space.

This command is primarily for use in Direct mode. when the directory will be displayed on the current screen, usually the default brown screen.But most often you'll be wanting to direct the attention within AMOS program to a specific drive or disk using the Dir$ command. In most cases, if your program is to be used by someone else, you'll direct the attention of the computer to the boot drive:

```
Dir$="df0:"
```

Which means that the program will always look at that drive to load any programs, files or data that it needs.

Running AMOS Programs

To make programs that are more excellent and bigger than single one-off programs, or to incorporate programs which you've written before, you can do one of two things. Firstly you can merge the code with the new program. Or more simply you can load and run the program from disk using the RUN command. This is the slower of the two options as you have to wait for the disk to access and stop before the program runs. If you incorporate the program with the current program, then it will obviously be runable without any wait for loading. But for things which are not time based, the RUN option is useful.

To use it you simply have to put in a line like this:

```
Run "df0:next_level.AMOS"
```

and the program specified, in this case a fictitious program called *next_level.AMOS*. Although there are time penalties, this feature does mean that even if you have used up all the available memory for a program, you can load another program (a level in a game for example) which will replace the one currently running. So any programs you write can be as large as the disk they come on. And if you distribute the program on many disks and write an installation program to install all the files on a hard disk, well the sky's the limit.

Disk Files

Something which I personally don't like, although some people from the business programming and archaic BASIC communities will disagree, is sequential files. This is something which enables you to open files directly on the disk, add to them and close them. It's a hazardous business and not something to be taken on lightly if you're a complete beginner, but I'm including a little bit of detail about them here for completeness. The full details about sequential files are to be found in your manual, but as ever I'll take it as read you've digested that but can't really think of any applications for it.

Although sequential files themselves are fairly outside the mainstream of your interest in AMOS, I would say they do offer some interesting facilities in the form of ports and channels (what we used to call *streams* in the old days) and should be studied for those. Working with channels and ports is something I thought I'd left behind years ago on the C64, but here they are again large as life. The primary use for these types of file is in the manipulation of data, especially ongoing data to be added to or edited in some way, like a database program or something like that. They are an amazingly slow method of storing things on disk however, as they are sequential as the name suggests, serial, or one after the other, meaning the data is stored in a specific order, like the music on a cassette tape. To get to a certain point in the data, say in the middle, you have to plough your way through the rest of the data to get to it. There are more interesting ways to store data, but like so many AMOS features this was added to make it all things to all men. Anyone who's been used to using sequential files on another computer in another BASIC will be right at home with this set of commands, and this will enable you to convert your regular AmigaBASIC or other inferior BASIC into AMOS in no time.

A similar concept to sequential files is random access files, and this too is more than adequately serviced in the AMOS manual so I won't talk about them any more. A more useful twist on opening channels for output can be found later in this chapter under Outside AMOS. Okay, next I/O hint, please.

Yes We Have No LLIST

Or bananas either, but that's an old joke and I won't dwell on it. That's right, no LLIST. This command was put into early versions of the manual but later some commands weren't included for various reasons, most of which had nothing to do with the usefulness or otherwise of the commands. It would have been handy to have it, but that's the way it goes. Software development is a job for real men. If something isn't right or doesn't fit, cut it out, that's what I say.

Of course to do a LLIST or even a LPRINT you can Select All using <Ctrl-A>, and print the block (containing as it happens everything) if that's what you want to do. I suppose if the worst comes to the worst you can always save the program as ASCII, send AMOS TO BACK and use the AmigaDOS command:

```
COPY <file> TO PRT:
```

or similar.

Scancode

We've covered a lot of output in this input/output chat, but not much input. You probably know about CHR$() and all the ASCII type codes for keyboard entry. (If you don't, you'd better find out about them really soon, as they are a great bonus.) For one slightly more out of the way method of grabbing keyboard input, especially hard to grab keys like the function keys, you'll need to use the Scancode command.

Instead of reading the keys pressed from their ASCII number, you may need to read a key which doesn't produce a character when pressed. So you have to resort to pulling the internal scancode from the keyboard hardware itself. In combination with the Key Shift command, you can test for any key on the Amiga keyboard, shifted or unshifted, producing a character on the screen or producing nothing.

Outside AMOS

We've seen the AMOS program sending data to a CON: device. The same thing can be done to other Amiga devices using logical ports. Ports is a concept familiar to any of us who used a Commodore 64 before we used an Amiga. Opening ports, sending data down them and closing the ports again was the only reliable way to print stuff out most of the time! Now ports have made it possible for the Amiga to talk to the outside world too.

You can access parts of the Amiga usually outside of the control of AMOS, too, using ports. Using the Open Port command you can send data or control strings down the serial port, parallel port and printer device, or to any other Amiga device. This example shows us that you can make the AMOS program drive a Prefs printer:

```
Rem * Open Port.AMOS *

Rem

Open Port 1,"prt:"

Set Tab 5

T$=Tab$

For X=0 To 10

    Print #1,T$;"Mastering AMOS is a breeze!";T$;
"with Mastering AMOS"

Next X

Close 1
```

First a port is opened, and it's assigned to open the PRT: device or the printer. We set up the tab spaces, and then do a For Next loop which goes from 1 to 10. After that we print the words, but instead of printing to the screen, the words are printed to port 1. The words fly down the pipe and come out on the piece of paper you threaded into the printer. (You did put a bit of paper in the printer, didn't you?)

Ports are a two way thing, and you can read data in as well as feed it out. Using this method you could write a program to drive your serial port, like a terminal program for example. A terminal program is just a simple method of reading and writing to the serial port, once the port is connected to a modem of course. The information is read down the port and put on the screen, and information from the keyboard is taken and sent up the port. If you want to connect to anything a little non-standard using AMOS, then ports are the way to do it.

Beyond Simple AMOS

So now you know all the essential information you need to make the best of your AMOS program. But what lies beyond the basics? Advanced AMOS, of course!

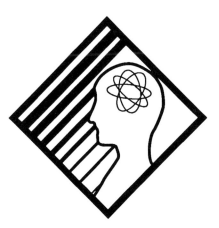

15: Advanced AMOS

Once you've been working with AMOS a little bit you'll want to move on from just banging out games try to touch on a few things which are a little more advanced. This is what this chapter is about, how to *push the envelope*, as they say in California, which is a laid back way of saying let's see what we can do if we change the rules a little bit.

Some of the things I'll be talking about in this chapter may be a little bit over your head, and that's fine. I don't expect you to be an AMOS expert, you wouldn't have bought this book otherwise, would you? What this book is really about is showing you a lot of what's possible and giving you the ammo to take things a little bit further yourself, if you want to.

A lot of things have been added to AMOS since the first revision, like for example the interlace mode we spoke about in an earlier chapter. One of the biggest additions to the system is the ability to multitask, which not only lets us create Workbench based applications but it also allows us to have a more flexible working environment. This means we can basically have AMOS up and running in the background and be working on some AmigaDOS task at the same time, like formatting disks, looking around directories and generally improving our productivity by having two programs available at once at the toggle of a button.

Multitasking with AMOS

The Amiga is a multitasking computer, of that there is no doubt, but AMOS has always taken over the system so you couldn't get at anything else while coding. Now AMOS has multitasking you can flip back and forth between the editor and AmigaDOS at the touch of a button. Pressing <Amiga-A> (okay, that's two buttons) switches you in and out of AMOS and the Workbench without the annoying blank screen. As a consequence the following commands have been made possible.

Amos To Back

Hides AMOS from view and shows the Workbench. This will bring forward the Workbench display, allowing you to access other programs, format disks and even run AMOS again. (Although you'd have to be mad to try that.)

Amos To Front

This switches back the AMOS Editor to the front of the display. AMOS is forced back onto the display with this command, leaving the Workbench hidden.

Amos Here

This is a sort of trap, which tests if AMOS is around. It returns TRUE if AMOS is currently displayed and FALSE if the WORKBENCH is on view.

You also have access to the AmigaDOS file requester too. Although the price of this flexibility is a small problem.

Request/Request On

will make AMOS generate its own requester routine and is the default. This happens if you don't type anything at all.

Request Off

This changes the situation and AMOS will always select the CANCEL button of the requester if this command is used. The actual requester will not be displayed, so this is ideal for error trapping within a program, especially if you want to add your own requester of some kind, even a nice 3D one like Len Tucker's.

Request WB

This tells AMOS to switch back to Workbench's system requester. You'll come back to AMOS as soon as you have chosen one of the options.

If you don't load the requester up (by deleting it from the extension list in the config file), the normal workbench requester will be used for displaying messages. This does have a slightly confusing side-effect though, AMOS will seem to have crashed when a requester appears. If this happens you must simply press <Amiga-A> to return to Workbench, answer the question and press <Amiga-A> once again to return to AMOS. It's only best to avoid loading the requester when memory is very low!

Machine Code

There are many ways that the more experienced programmer can access the important little places on the Amiga, and the machine code programmer has been more than catered for. The commands which you'll need to look at first are PEEK, POKE, DEEK, DOKE, LEEK and LOKE, which will give you access to bytes, words and longwords in all the memory locations on the Amiga. (Don't bother thinking about making your own assembler, because Gary Symons already did that. See below.) Hex to Dec conversion is simple with the HEX$ and BIN$ functions:

```
Rem * Hex/Bin converter.AMOS *

Rem

Screen Open 0,640,200,16,Hires

Paper 0 : Cls 0

Do

    Input "Number to convert: ";A

    X$=Hex$(A)

    Print "The hex version of this number is: ";X$

    Y$=Bin$(A)

    Print "The binary version of this number is: ";Y$

    Cdown

Loop
```

A handy little programmer's tool that, especially for the creation of graphics and bitmaps from scratch. (Find that pad of graph paper you used to have. It may save your life!)

From there on it gets kind of hair-raising, so we won't dwell on it. But if you are a machine coder, you *will* want to know about AMOS Assembler.

AMOS Assembler?

Yes, I'm afraid it's true, on AMOS PD disk LPD9 and free with AMOS Compiler, the AMOS Assembler, for those of you out there who are not just any old AMOS beginner. Some people (and who can hold it against them) have a little knowledge of machine code. It happens. If this is the case, you don't need to discard all that knowledge simply because you've taken up the obvious charms of the AMOS language. Now you can combine AMOS and machine code for fast and effective programming. Make some routines containing things that AMOS can't do and incorporate them with your AMOS programs. Add nice fast rendering routines, and pep up any area of AMOS which doesn't quite have the speed you were looking for. Or perhaps you don't know machine code (like me for example) but you think that sooner or later you might learn it. This is a fine way to use your new knowledge, and with very little hassle. Adding small bits of code as you learn makes using AMOS a tutorial process as well as a creative one.

The AMOS assembler was written by Gary Symons, and it's a very clever little suite of programs. The tricky thing about AMOS Assembler is that you just embed the machine code you want to run in your program, like AMAL:

```
C$=C$+"Example:"
C$=C$+"move.l a3,a5;"
C$=C$+"add.l #4*4,a3;"
C$=C$+"move.l (a3)+,d0;move.l (a3)+,a6;"
C$=C$+"move.l #4,d6;"
C$=C$+"lea plane_0,a0;"
C$=C$+"lea plane_1,a1;"
C$=C$+"lea plane_2,a2;"
C$=C$+"lea plane_3,a3;"
C$=C$+"lea plane_4,a4;"
C$=C$+"move.l #319,d1;move.l #255,d2;"
C$=C$+"loop:"
C$=C$+"movem.l d1/d2,-(sp);"
```

```
C$=C$+"btst #6,$bfe001;bne.b no_quit;movem.l
(sp)+,d1/d2;rts;"

C$=C$+"no_quit:"

C$=C$+"add.l 4(a5),d1;add.l (a5),d2;"

C$=C$+"move.l d1,d3;muls d3,d3;lsr.l d0,d3;"

C$=C$+"move.l d2,d4;muls d4,d4;lsr.l d0,d4;"

C$=C$+"move.l #0,d7;"
```

and so on and so forth. (Don't try running this program by the way, because it needs more code to function. It's just an example to give you an idea what you're looking at when I talk about machine code programs.) All the lines are read in as C$ and then the assembler is activated, and the code you typed in is assembled and run. The demo programs are short, and to be honest I can't tell how it works, not being an ace assembly programmer myself, but you can take it from me that it's totally brilliant and the effect is mind boggling.

The basic program to get you going is included, and a bunch of example programs to demo the speed of the thing. The results are nothing less than gobsmacking, especially the fast mandelbrot program. (Okay, so fractals are usually boring, but not this fast they're not!) If you like assembler, then this is the PD disk for you. One thing I would like to see is a C compiler written in AMOS, or an AMOS to C converter! Now they really *would* open a tin of worms. But I guess we'll have to wait for that.

Advanced Menus

When we talked about menus we didn't really go into a great amount of depth, and this is one area which has a few layers of subtlety which are rarely touched on. Keyboard shortcuts are one thing, graphic menus are another (and that's something you can't do easily in Intuition, eh?) plus the other tricky menu type, movable menus.

There's so much to the menu systems on AMOS that you'd be surprised. The system is so much more flexible than AmigaDOS it makes you wonder why people still program in C and machine code at all.

This next program is an example of using menus in a very unusual way, and one which is very hard to do using normal AmigaDOS menus.

```
Rem * Bobs on a menu.AMOS *

Rem

Load "df0:sprite_600/aliens/alien1.abk"

Load "df0:sprite_600/space/ship1.abk",1

Flash Off : Cls 0

Get Sprite Palette

Menu$(1)="(Bob 1)Bugs" : Menu$(1,1)="(Bob 2)This
Bug" : Menu$(1,2)="(Bob 3)That Bug"

Menu$(2)="(Bob 21)Ships" : Menu$(2,1)="(Bob 22)This
Ship" : Menu$(2,2)="(Bob 23)That Ship"

Menu On

Do

Loop
```

This program uses the Bobs from the Sprite_600 set so have those
ready in drive df0:. The Bobs appear on the menus, and they act
like normal menus except that they have these great pictures on
them too. The pictures can be instructive, or they could even be
graphics of text! Imagine all the menu text showing up as street
graffiti or cobwebs or clouds, depending on the tone of your
program. You can do the same with Sprites and Icons too.

Cursor the Crimson Altar II

Cursor designing? Okay, pretty low on the old priorities for the
moment, but when you get into programming things which use text
rather than pictures, you'll be glad to get rid of the standard AMOS
cursor. For everyone who wants to get busy tapping out their own
cursors, I'd recommend a program from AMOS PD Library disk 394
called *swiz* and its' a cursor editor, containing a number of example
cursors. Here's some of mine which I created with the program:

```
Rem SWIZ V1.0 data file

Rem

     '

Rem * Alien *

Set Curs
%00111100,%01111110,%10011001,%10011001,%11111111,%0
0111100,%00100100,%01100110

Wait Key

Rem * Arrow2 *
```

```
Set Curs
%00000000,%00000100,%00000110,%11111111,%11111111,%0
0000110,%00000100,%00000000

Wait Key

Rem * BigArrow *

Set Curs
%11000000,%11110000,%11111100,%11111111,%11111111,%1
1111100,%11110000,%11000000

Wait Key

Rem * Smiley *

Set Curs
%00111100,%01000010,%10100101,%10000001,%10000001,%1
0011001,%01000010,%00111100

Wait Key

Rem * SmallArrow *

Set Curs
%10000000,%11000000,%11100000,%11110000,%11110000,%1
1100000,%11000000,%10000000

Wait Key

Rem * Heart *

Set Curs
%00000000,%01101100,%11111110,%11111110,%01111100,%0
0111000,%00010000,%00000000

Wait Key
```

The joy of the Swiz program is that it allows you to concentrate on the precise design of your cursor while it stores away all the information for later transmission to disk as an ASCII file which can then be merged with your programs. Okay it's not earth-shattering, but it is a nice little go-faster stripe for your AMOS system.

You can do other types of tricks with cursors too, using the CLINE, CUP, CDOWN, CLEFT and CRIGHT commands:

```
Rem * Cline, Cup & Friends.AMOS *

Rem

Screen Open 0,640,256,16,Hires

Hide : Paper 0 : Pen 4 : Cls 0

Wait 100 : Bell : Print "Hello playmates!"
```

```
Cdown : Wait 100 : Cdown
Bell : Pen 6 : Centre "The cursor just jumped
down... to here" :
Cdown : Wait 100
Bell : Pen 2 : Print "then here..."
Cdown : Cdown
For LEFT=1 To 50
   Cleft
   Wait 1
Next LEFT
Wait 100 : Pen 12 : Bell
Print "now over here";
Wait 100 : Cdown : Cdown
Wait 100 : Cright : Cright : Cright
Bell : Pen 14 : Print "Now over here";
For UP=0 To 6
   Cup
   Wait 1
Next UP
Wait 100 : Bell : Pen 10
Print "and finally up here" : Wait 100
Cmove 5,20
Pen 3 : Wait 50 : Print "Or what about snapping 5,20
to this location with CMOVE?"
Wait 100
Pen 4 : Locate ,24 : Centre "AND NOW ERASE EVERY-
THING A LINE AT A TIME"
Wait 100
Home : Paper 6
For X=0 To 30
   Cline
   Locate ,X
   Wait 10
```

```
Next

Wait 200

Locate ,10 : Pen 2 : Centre "And that my friends is
the Cursor commands"

Wait 500 : Edit
```

This is a simple demo of the cursor command set, which throws the lines of text around the screen in various interesting ways and pings a bell to draw your attention to what's happened. The demo flips you back to the editor when it's finished.

Speech Demons

Speech is another little used area of the AMOS system, which bears a little experimentation. You may have used your Amiga's speech before, perhaps with the little SAY demo on your Amiga disks. Well AMOS is capable of using speech too. The speech capability is simple but effective, having only two commands SET TALK and SAY.

How about this little speech toy of my own. Imagine your computer has had too much to drink, but like most drunks is trying to ignore that and talk to you anyway:

```
Rem * Drunk computer.AMOS "

Rem

Screen Open 0,640,200,16,Hires

Paper 0 : Curs Off : Cls 0

Locate ,10 : Pen 4

Set Talk ,,65,50

Print "I've had a few drinks, but I'll try to talk
for you..."

Cdown

Do

    Input ">";A$

    Say A$

Loop
```

Anything you type into the computer will be spoken, but the speech will be slow and slightly slurred. Very realistic. In fact it might be a scientific breakthrough! Yes, a computer program that drunk people can understand, a sort of *text to inebriated person* filter.

NEO Converter

So you've got a complex technical problem. AMOS to the rescue. The problem here was having a number of Atari ST low resolution pictures in the NEOCHROME format, which needed to be converted to IFF. There are a few picture converters on the market, but few will do this particular job. Enter AMOS and a clever little routine.

The original program was written by a very clever chap called Terry Mancey, and the original version before I got my hands on it and adapted it to my needs was originally printed in the *All About AMOS* *magazine*. Since I edited this program I've seen a number of other file converters and all of them use a similar technique to grab the file, put it to the screen and save it off. Here's the listing:

```
Rem * NEOchrome to IFF Picture Converter *
Rem
Screen Open 0,320,200,16,Lowres
Flash Off
Curs Off
Reserve As Work 10,32128
'
PINKY:
Show
F$=Fsel$("*.NEO","","Load Your NEO pic")
Bload F$,15
Hide
GROWNEO[15]
Bell : Wait Key
Show
F$=Fsel$("*.IFF","","Save Your IFF pic")
Hide
Save Iff F$,0
Bell : Wait Key
Input "Convert another NEO picture? (y/n)";A$
If A$="y" Then Goto PINKY
End
'
```

```
Procedure GROWNEO[B]
   PALT=Start(B)+4
   For C=0 To 15
      Colour(C),Deek(PALT+(C*2))*2
   Next C
   PICT=Start(B)+128
   For Y=0 To 199
      For X=0 To 19
         Doke Phybase(0)+(X*2)+(Y*40),Deek(PICT+0)
         Doke Phybase(1)+(X*2)+(Y*40),Deek(PICT+2)
         Doke Phybase(2)+(X*2)+(Y*40),Deek(PICT+4)
         Doke Phybase(3)+(X*2)+(Y*40),Deek(PICT+6)
         Add PICT,8
      Next X
   Next Y
End Proc
```

When the program is run the Load requester will appear. Select the first NEOCHROME image you wish to convert, and either double-click on its name or type it in and click OK. The file will be read in and scanned onto the screen. A bell will sound when the conversion is finished. Press any key and the save requester will pop up. Type in the name you want the file to be saved as, preferably appended with the .IFF extension to distinguish it from the NEO version, and click on OK. A bell will sound when the file has been fully saved. Press any key and the program will prompt you to type in a y or n if you want to convert another NEO image. If you type a y then the whole process starts again with the load requester. If you type a n, the program will terminate.

The drawback of the program is that it won't as yet convert or display high res Atari pictures, or any other format other than NEO. Obviously you can do hires if you change the format of the way the files are read. The technique is here for you to see, and all you'll really need to make it a universal converter program is the right size buffer to take the input pictures and the technical specs of the bitmap files in question. That takes a lot of research and a lot of programming time, but I'm sure you can do it! (Smile.) As long as you can print the bitmap to the screen, you can save it off as an IFF. This is a big project, so good luck.

Onwards to the Future

So there is life after basic AMOS. And there are still more ways you can press the boundaries of what's possible. And this is mostly done with AMOS in concert with other things like AMOS 3D and AMOS TOME, and like our next example, the AMOS Compiler, which contributes more to the overall power of what can be done with AMOS than just about any other extension to the language. Strap yourself in, you're in for a fast ride.

16:
AMOS
Compiler

One of the most exciting developments since AMOS itself was the release of the compiler package, enabling you to compile your AMOS programs into near perfect machine code. As the early forerunner to AMOS (a program on the Atari ST called STOS) had an excellent compiler, the AMOS Compiler was waited for with much impatience by the Amiga community at large. Well it arrived, and in case you haven't read any old reviews of it, you'll be thrilled to know that it's brilliant.

The compiler itself exists in a simple CLI command called *acmp*, which you can in fact just type at a CLI or Shell prompt and pass it some parameters (I'll tell you a bit about this in a minute.) Or you can boot up an AMOS program called Compiler.AMOS which is a graphic front end for the compiler, allowing you to compile your programs with a simple click of the mouse. (See Figure 16.1.) The whole shebang is run from an extension to the basic AMOS language and, as with all extensions, it needs to be installed before it can be used.

Programs compiled with AMOS Compiler can be run from the CLI, the Workbench, or even from within AMOS. Why should you want to run a compiled program from within AMOS? Well, you can run AMOS programs from within an AMOS program, loading and running another segment

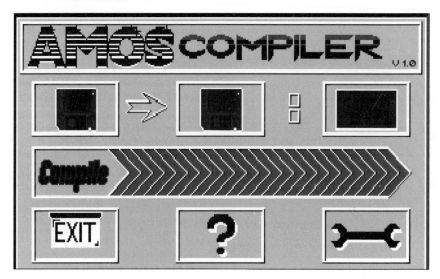

Figure 16.1. Compiler.AMOS front end of compiler.

of a game for example. Well, if this segment of your game is compiled (for reasons of speed or secrecy) then it'll be pretty rapid and safe. The other two types of compiled programs can be almost anything, and although there are certain limitations as to what you can compile with AMOS Compiler, most things will compile and run properly. Compiled programs are a lot faster than the normal AMOS counterparts, and AMAL is to a certain extent made obsolete once you have Compiler installed. Having said that, AMAL will run from compiled programs, although the AMAL sections are already compiled so they won't run any faster. You have to pay attention to certain simple timing errors, where the animations get out of sync with screen blanking, but I'll advise you on that a little bit towards the end of this chapter.

Compile Me

The beauty of the compiler is that you don't need any expert knowledge to run it, and the product of the compiler improves the performance of your programs by three or four fold. What's the catch? There has to be one, and the major catch is that in the main compiled programs are much larger than their AMOS counterparts. There is a certain amount of runtime code which is permanently welded to the program when it's compiled. This allows the program to be run on its own without any of the AMOS program or any libraries having to be present on the disk. This is a trade off, and it's unavoidable. One thing you *can* do is compact the program with a PD program called PowerPacker. This means the program is compressed by the PowerPacker program, and then later your compressed program auto-unpacks when run. PowerPacker is available from your local PD library.

The Compiler comes with two disks, one of which is an updater disk to convert your AMOS master disk (or at least a backup of it) to give you AMOS 1.34, as the only versions of AMOS that will run the compiler are 1.3 and upwards. The other disk is the compiler, and although this works very well in a normal Amiga, obviously the thing works better if it has more legroom in the memory department. To help users of unexpanded A500s, a number of memory saving routes have been worked out for you, so you can compile as large a program as a big-memoried 2000 user. For example using direct mode, you can compile programs using a new command called *compile,* strangely enough. This allows you to employ memory saving features such as the ability to compile direct to and from disk, rather than load the whole program into memory to do so.

The updating goes along automatically with a little program which you run which does all the hard work for you, installing the extension and copying the various parts of the program disks across to your AMOS disk or hard disk partition.

There are some PD programs and other types of example program on the disk. AMOS Assembler is also included on the master disks, just in case you hadn't seen this excellent program already. This is one way of expanding the capability of AMOS by using machine code stored in AMOS banks. (If you know about machine code that is!) I've included a little blurb about this program, AMOS Assembler by Gary Symons, in Chapter 15. AMOS Assembler is a separate program and doesn't need to be installed in order to run.

Using the Compiler

The compiler uses a number of methods to run. The first method which you should be aware of is the COMPILE command which can be used in direct mode. First you have to close window 0 by going to direct mode and typing:

```
Screen Close 0
```

This saves 32K of memory and forces the compiler messages to be displayed in the direct mode window rather than on the current screen. Then you are free to compile your programs.

Compilation essentially takes your AMOS code and reduces each command to its vital elements, interpreting the meaning of the code into assembly language and then into raw code. The file you're left with cannot be read into AMOS, or printed like a text file, because it is an executable file, a program in itself. It can be run from the CLI or the Workbench like any other Amiga program, and is indistinguishable from *the real thing.*

To compile your programs you type:

```
compile <filename> [parameters]
```

or for example:

```
compile "your program name.AMOS -D11 -T3"
```

The parameters at the end I'll go into in a sec. The other option is to compile the program using the AMOS front end. A front end is a graphic interface to a program, and this is the friendliest way to compile your programs. Just load Compiler.AMOS and run it. The screen will tell you what to do. Click on the buttons and compile away!

The third method is from the CLI in AmigaDOS. You run the ACMP program like so:

```
acmp <filename> [parameters]
```

perhaps like so:

```
acmp "your program again.AMOS" -OMyProg
```

Where the output file is called *MyProg*, and that is what you type to run the program in this case.

Fine Tuning

Those are the basic methods, but here's the detail. In the Compiler.AMOS front end you have a nice easy method of running the compiler and setting up the options. But a power user will like to fine tune the compilation process himself. Here are the parameters you'd use. Each option is chosen with a dash, -, followed by a single letter.

-O<filename>

This stands for OBJECT FILE, and means the output file. If you omit this command the compiler will simply strip the .AMOS part of the input filename and use that as the output file. In most cases this is enough, but sometimes you'll want the program to have a different name to the input file. It happens.

-Dnn

The D option allows you to specify the source and the destination of the AMOS compilation. The 1 signifies a disk and the 0 signifies the Ram Disk, the first number is the source and the second number the destination. The permutations are as follows:

```
-D00 RAM to RAM

-D01 RAM to Disk

-D10 Disk to RAM

-D11 Disk to Disk
```

So if you're compiling from disk to Ram Disk, your program in AMOS format is on the disk and the finished compiled program ends up on the Ram Disk.

-Tn

The T option specifies the type of program that the output file is. The types are as follows:

```
-T0  Workbench program with icon

-T1  CLI program without icon

-T2  CLI program with automatic multitasking

-T3  Compiled AMOS program
```

The last option produces a program which is compiled but can be run from AMOS.

-Sn

where n=0 or 1. AMOS will always create the default brown screen with the flashing cursor. If you don't want to see that (it's a dead giveaway that your compiled program is written in AMOS) then you must set the -S0 toggle. If you want to reset this feature use the -S1 toggle.

-Wn

where n=0 or 1. This prevents AMOS erasing the current Workbench screen when the compiled program is executed. -W1 holds off displaying the AMOS program until your program does an AMOS TO FRONT. Or you can write a routine which creates and writes text to a CLI window. -W0 is the default setting.

-L

Used for compiling large programs.

There are some other options you can set but these are available in the AMOS Compiler manual.

Using the Front End

The front end program, Compiler.AMOS, is very useful for compiling stuff on the fly, where you don't want to be doing with anything complex. The program window specifies source, destination and type of program, and has some configuration options too. The program runs all the direct mode commands, so the only difference between this approach and the more technical direct mode or CLI approach is that with the front end you don't have to really think about what you're doing too much.

Commercial Release

There is an interesting note in the manual concerning the commercial release of compiled AMOS programs. Obviously if you compile a program written in AMOS, it can't be distinguished from any normal machine code program without examining the file. The note in the manual says if you create a program for the PD or Shareware/Licenseware, you *must* say that the development program used was AMOS. If you are selling the program commercially, then you must let Europress know, but they will keep quiet about it being done in AMOS until the program comes out. The reason for this is that certain programmers are noticing a reluctance of software houses to accept programs written using *game creators*. Europress will then publicise the fact that the program was AMOS-based two months after release. Very neat.

Good Vibrations

I like the compiler very much, as you can probably tell, and it really does make programs fly along. Although the speed difference isn't quite as marked as I was expecting, it does make a difference, especially for many tasks operating at once, like animation, music and so forth. Where in certain programs you will have noticed a marked slow down in the music score when there's a lot happening on screen, you now see a definite improvement. This is the area in which the compiler is most useful, that and the ability to run your programs without having to use the RAMOS runtime program. Not only that but it prevents people listing your program and stealing your ideas. I would hate to see the end of RAMOS driven programs, as I think that a lot can be done with plain vanilla AMOS. The compiler has its place, sure, but it's not the answer to all your problems. The way to better programs is (unsurprisingly) through better programming.

Compiler Hints and Tips

There are some things which you should know for using the Compiler effectively. For a start, you may notice some graphics movement will flicker a little bit when you compile a program. This is entirely due to the speed of the AMOS compiler, and not a problem. The loop you have set up is going so fast it's flickering, and the best way to synchronise it with the screen speed is to use a

WAIT VBL at the end of each loop. If you're using UPDATE, you must ensure that at least one vertical blank occurs between any two UPDATES.

If your program won't compile you probably haven't tested it. Test the program and then save it to disk or Ram Disk (wherever you want to save it) and then recompile it. Certain extensions can cause problems, but only really if you haven't got the latest versions. (Contact AMOS Club for further details about this.) The PRUN command isn't supported from AMOS, and has to be replaced with RUN if you intend to compile your program.

More Dimensions

AMOS Compiler is one way to beef up the performance of your AMOS system, but there is a far more complex way of making AMOS into something else entirely. AMOS 3D does something that no other BASIC language can do and that is 3D graphics! If you want to know about AMOS 3D, turn the page.

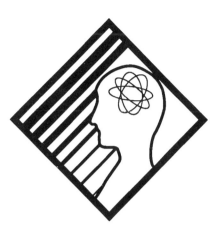

17:
AMOS 3D

I waited what seemed like a long time for AMOS 3D, and as the days stretched out into months, it began to seem that perhaps it was impossible, that you couldn't create 3D objects and move them around in real time with a BASIC interpreter. But the module was promised, and so far Europress had delivered all the support it promised for the AMOS system, so the prospects looked good.

Sure enough it appeared, and we all breathed a sigh of relief. It's out, I've tried it and it works! More to the point it's the single most simple way of creating 3D games and demos known to man. The Red Sector Demo maker (and all its copies) is too hackish and tricky to be of any use for such things as full-blown games design, so the only option, AMOS 3D, is certainly to be considered the best!

A 3D World

AMOS 3D, like the compiler and AMOS TOME, is an extension, and it runs in the same way. You have an editor program called the Object Modeller, OM for short, and an extension which must be installed on your master AMOS disk or hard disk partition.

To install AMOS 3D all you have to do is run the install program on the Install disk. This is an AMOS program, and it allows you to either install

AMOS 1.3 or over (needed to run both AMOS Compiler and AMOS 3D) on a floppy or hard disk version of AMOS. The 3D part of the program is an extension, so it isn't a physical program that you run, it's installed as an integral part of the AMOS system. After you've installed AMOS 1.3 and 3D, you can tell you are running 3D because the words *Voodoo 3D extension I 1.00* are included with the other extensions on your AMOS startup screen. The Voodoo bit means that the 3D extension was created by Voodoo Software rather than the usual Francois Lionet/JAWX. It's still a genuine AMOS product however.

AMOS OM

Although there are alot of example objects on the disk to get you going (see Table 17.1) you have to create your own objects using the object modeller. This program will enable you to create shapes and bolt them together into meaningful objects. The objects you make can be shaded in any colours you like, and you can even draw small bitmaps to map them onto the sides of the shapes to make them more lifelike. The OM isn't a proper 3D shape creator, that is to say you can't expect to turn out proper ray-traced shapes like the *Lawnmower Man* or anything like that. But it is a very powerful vector graphics engine, and this enables you to create objects which, while not being perfect 3D objects, will at least mimic the shapes of real 3D objects, enough for the purposes of a 3D game or a demo.

You run OM either by typing OM if you're a shell user, or simply clicking on the icon if you are running from Workbench. OM prefers to run alone, so free up memory by quitting any other programs you may have running.

OM is a program which runs separately from AMOS, to allow you to create objects for use within AMOS. The program features alot of tools for stretching, squashing and forming primitives, like squares, circles, cubes and pyramids. You copy the primitives to work areas on the screen called *shelves* (I don't know why, so don't ask), where you work on them with the mouse, selecting a point, line or face with a series of keypresses, and deforming it by clicking on the exotic roll and tilt control or the arrows whilst holding the button down and moving the mouse. Although this sounds very complex, it couldn't be simpler. Selected faces have a marker on them so you know which face is the active face when performing an operation on it.

Once you have reshaped the primitives into something a little bit more diverse, you can glue them together to make other more complex objects. This is done simply by selecting the faces that need to be glued together on the two objects, and once selected this is done automatically.

Then you can apply surface detail, patterns in four colours which you can map to the selected face of the object. This is done by drawing lines on a grid, which are then filled before they are attached to the face of the object. The neat thing about these surface detail grids is that they can be copied from and to objects at will, so you can copy a face back onto the grid if you forgot how to draw it, even if the object is one you did a while back.

alphabet	letterh	ship2
amidisk	lettert	ship4
amiga	lines	ship5
amos3d	lorry	ship6
car	manual	ship8
chain	missile1	ship9
chess	missile2	station1
chess1	mis_front	station2
coffin	mother	struct
copter	one_ton	summer_house
disk	phone	sun_shade
enterprise	plane	threedee
face	poise	voodoo
gallows	punt	within
hereboy	ring	
insect	ship1	

Table 17.1. Objects included with the OM.

More AMOS 3D

Recently the AMOS 3D system received a shot in the arm with the release of the AMOS 3D Object Modeller Disk 1.2. This update has some great new objects on it. The new OM disk is essentially the same as its predecessor, but with the addition of some new objects for you to use in your own programs. Okay, so there were quite a few anyway, now there's even more.

Of these new objects one of the most interesting is the idea of using *inside out* blocks. Blocks that have been turned inside out by using the group sizing tool are displayed with only *invisible* faces drawn. This is what you would see if you were inside the block. New objects *Punt* and *summer_house* on the examples disk use this effect. In *summer_house* two cubes, one regular and the other inside out, have been glued together to yield an object with an outside and an inside. Surface detail windows in the regular cube let you see inside. A further block has been placed inside. For all of this to work correctly the block numbers are important. The example object *within* demonstrates another effect called double nesting, which is a variation on this theme. As with *summer_house*, the order in which the blocks are glued together is vital.

Figure 17.1. AMOS Object Modeller.

The disk also features details of some interesting undocumented Td Commands like the one to define the order in which objects are drawn:

```
Td Priority n,p
```

where:

n = object number.

p = object drawing priority.

This allows you to specify the order in which objects are drawn by the 3D system. In other words objects that are drawn first appear in front of other objects. The command makes some interesting special effects possible:

```
Priority,p       Object drawing order
```

which translates as:

0	Draw the object in the normal way (by depth).
>0	Draw the object in front of all other objects with a lower priority.
<0	Draw the object behind all other objects with a higher priority.

By default all objects have a priority of 0. Note that if two objects have non-zero priority the one with the highest priority will be drawn first (in front).

The other undocumented feature is Td Set Colour which sets a specified object block's colour combination, like so:

Td Set Colour n,b,c

where:

n = Object number.

b = Block number.

c = Colour combination code of the block (same as in OM).

This command is the language equivalent of OM's colour combination tool described in the 3D manual. It sets the colour combination code of the specified block. Valid colour numbers range from 0 to 16; colour combinations 0 to 12 are the same as in OM, colour combinations 13-15 are new. An out of range colour code will be truncated to the nearest valid code without causing an error.

Contact Europress Software for further details about the OM disk update.

Using Objects

Once the AMOS 3D extension has been fitted to your AMOS program, you can load and move 3D objects in your normal AMOS programs, using a series of new commands.

Now you have to come to terms with the idea of space, 3D space. The world now has a trio of axes, called x, y and z. X and y are the ones we are used to on the computer screen, and translating objects around that screen merely involves adding numbers to their x,y coordinates. Like the numbers which tell a move sprite command to shift the position of a sprite. But now you have an extra dimension, that of depth, and this is the z dimension.

With AMOS 3D there are a new set of commands called *Td* commands, and these preface any 3D commands you put in your programs, like this example I knocked up in about 10 seconds using one of the simple examples on the disk as a basis:

```
Rem * Object Roll Demo.AMOS *

Rem

Td Dir "disk_containing_3D_objects"

Hide

Double Buffer

Autoback 0
```

```
Td Load "test_object"

Td Object 1,"test_object",0,0,5000,0,5000,-4000

Palette ,,,,,,,,,$FFF,$F,$777

Repeat

    Td Angle 1,A,0,A

    A=A+1000

    Cls 0

    Td Redraw

    Screen Swap

    Wait Vbl

Until False
```

Now that's what I call a simple program. And it does so much! Substitute your own object or one from the demo disk in place of the Td Dir and Td Load commands. Double buffering is definitely required as this smooths the transition between one redraw and the next, and is in fact the way it is done in professional 3D programs written in assembler.

As well as rotating the objects and moving them in and out of the screen, you can animate the surface detail, animate the shape, do collision detection with other 3D shapes, and generally do all the things you'd associate with a top flight 3D game or PD demo disk by a really talented vector graphics crew.

It all sounds like a bit of a dream really, doesn't it? But it's all true. All the demos I created on the first day of using the program worked like a dream, and although they are not as silky smooth as I would like, the effect is undeniably solid and professional looking.

Obviously you have to learn to think in three dimensions, but that goes with the turf. Vectors are hard to do in normal circumstances, but this program should make the whole thing really that much easier to cope with. You can sketch out your 3D ideas on graph paper beforehand, just to give you an idea of what you want, but in most cases the best idea is just to plough into it and make it up as you go along. Not only will you learn the program more quickly that way. Who knows, you might have fun along the way.

Summing Up

AMOS 3D completes the AMOS system with a bang. Now it's possible to not only make games, but a whole variety of new and high tech programs which now suggest themselves. Virtual reality? Well no, not really, but certainly a very good 3D program, and as a modeller I much prefer it to 3D Construction Kit. I can't really fault it, and although I could say I'd like to see it faster, I know this isn't really possible. Compiling obviously smooths things out but not all that much. I'd like a utility to transfer objects from one disk to another as an object is made of a number of obscurely named files, and you have to load them into OM and save them to another disk in order to be sure of getting all the files. How about precompiling the movement, a sort of 3D AMAL? I don't know, it's good enough for most things so why worry.

All this talk of 3D may sound a little bit advanced for you, but if you are still struggling with AMOS even after all my tutoring and all the listings to type in, relax. Help is on the way in the form of Easy AMOS.

18:
Easy AMOS

AMOS was released onto an unsuspecting public, and at once people began to realise this wasn't just any old ordinary language for game production. It was in fact a very complex and powerful thing and you could take it just about as far as you liked. But the very power of the language was its problem too. Some people found it a little hard to get into, through no fault of their's or of the designers. AMOS is simple to learn but hard to apply fully, and that is when the idea of a tutorial came up. This idea grew until Easy AMOS was born.

The idea behind this new version of the program is that new users or kids can get a grip on AMOS without a lot of the very technical stuff getting in the road. EA isn't just a cut down version, although it features about 300 commands instead of the usual 600 or so. Its main objective is not necessarily to be smaller, but easier, hence the name. The main thrust of the package and its programs is to become a tutorial for programming and using AMOS and, despite having less commands, it's actually got more accessories than before. So less really *is* more. It's easy to see that once you have this program under your belt you will have more than enough to get you going on the full-grown AMOS program.

Easy as PI

Obviously most of the changes are going to be cosmetic to appeal to a different audience. The main change you notice right away is the editor has changed quite a lot, and it now looks a lot more like Workbench 2.0. It does look nicer, although the function of the screen isn't altered much for all the 3D effects and colour changes. The reason for the cosmetic changes are apparently to be more appealing to kids. It's more like a cosmetic change to make it look different to what I call these days *Classic AMOS*. You can bet that a lot of the processes and interesting twists that make Easy AMOS so easy to use will be incorporated into any future versions of AMOS.

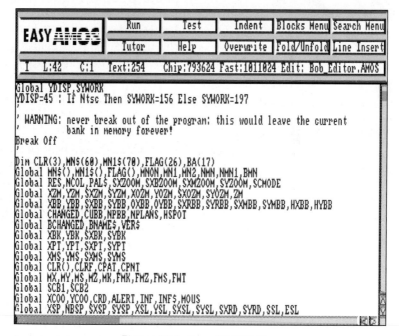

Figure 18.1. Easy AMOS Editor.

Wot? No AMAL?

The most major omission compared with AMOS is the exclusion of AMAL, one of the key animation tools in the AMOS arsenal. This is more than compensated for by the Easy AMOS Tutor, which is a most advanced programming tutor I've ever seen. The Tutor features three windows: one for your AMOS code, one for variables and expressions with their values, and finally a window with your program output. The programs execute line by line so you can see all the program's important little places whilst it is actually running, meaning not only can you trap bugs but you can also see how your program works. Teriffic. The Tutor can run at different speeds too, so you can slow it down to see it all in action, or speed it up to real time to check it all looks okay!

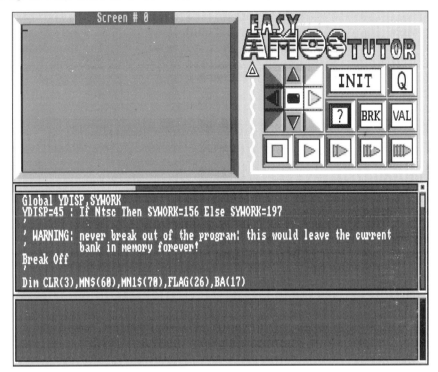

Figure 18.2. Easy AMOS Tutor.

Simple Setup

Because it is a beginner's program it won't allow you to run the master program but it makes a working copy for you before you begin. It does this automatically and, obligingly enough, it supplies you with labels for your working disks. Once it's all set up you have three disks, one master program disk, one tutorial disk, and one examples disk.

The examples are manifold, covering all manner of useful utilities to show how AMOS copes with programming *proper* programs, such as one of the example programs called AMOS Disk, for example, which is a sort of disk utility clone like SID or Directory Opus.

A lot of other utilities are bolted onto the main system, rather than being separate AMOS programs, so the bob editor (there are no sprites in Easy AMOS) is a menu option rather than a program you load. Another snappy option which Easy AMOS has over conventional AMOS is the ability to load Soundtracker and Noisetracker type tunes, using the TrackLoad command. This is good news to everyone except the people who are writing programs and procedures to make AMOS do this. Hopefully the new versions of AMOS will have this ability too.

Of more interest still is another program to be included in the package, a sort of progress tester. This is an AMOS program which plays a kind of interactive quiz to see how well you are doing in your quest to learn AMOS, by asking you questions and logging your answers. In this way, you can see how much you are taking in about AMOS. If you pass a certain stage you get a diploma on screen. This is another bit of zippy design for the younger user, and is sure to go down well.

Easy AMOS is a foretaste of what to expect with the next major revision of AMOS, AMOS Professional. Obviously the design is not by accident, and if you added AMAL and sprites to Easy AMOS it wouldn't be that different from the real thing. Both AMOS Pro and Easy AMOS will only run in 1Mb Amigas, which is one thing that will make a few people a bit cross. Mind you anyone who's still only running a half Mb machine will run into this sort of thing all the time by now, so it's not AMOS's fault but the onrush of technology. Besides, new Amigas all have 1Mb on them, so no worries for complete Amiga beginners who've only just bought their machine.

Bob's Your Uncle

The sprites have been dropped in Easy AMOS to make the program easier to grasp. Like most reasons for changes in the Easy AMOS environment, the change is for ease of understanding rather than ease of use!

The original sprite editor by Aaron Fothergill has long since passed away and been replaced by SpriteX. So the time had come for a new AMOS bob editor. When the original editor was released people complained it was a little bit buggy. Not surprising really as Aaron was writing the sprite program at the same time that Francois Lionet was writing AMOS. More than a few revisions later the program was expected to work, and all credit to Aaron it did, but not nearly as well as it should.

Europress took all the suggestions for improvement to heart and they've incorporated all the suggestions in the Easy AMOS Bob Editor. Although not as good as SpriteX (particularly the new version 2) the Bob Editor is definitely one of the easier movable object editors around. The buttons are big and have very descriptive pictures on them, and the program couldn't really be easier to use. But then that was the idea, eh?

Omissions

A lot of commands have been withdrawn from Easy AMOS, and the reason for them being taken out is to prevent the user being distracted from the task of learning. Some of the more technical commands have been shed, and as I said before the highly complex (it says here) AMAL has been axed too. Most of the changes I agree with but a few are a bit mystifying. The disk font system is still in place. All the joystick commands, like =JUP, =JDOWN, =JRIGHT, and =JLEFT in fact all except =JOY have been excised. The extremely useful reserved variables Screen Height and Screen Width have been dropped. Why? It's crazy but true.

Aaron Fothergill has come up with a routine to compensate for this, namely:

```
SCRW=Deek(Screen Base+76)

SCRH=Deek(Screen Base+78)
```

but I have to ask why did he need to? There was nothing wrong with those variables so why the change? Perhaps the code was all joined together like chewing gum, and they had to pull those variables out with a few other things that were attached. Ah well.

The lack of AMAL is really more than compensated for by the fact that you can compile Easy AMOS programs, of course, provided you have the AMOS Compiler program and extension.

Nice Weather for Docs

Despite the wealth of internal tutorial matter, and programs to test you and as examples, there is also a paper manual containing all the information you'll want to know. I'm not much of a one for on screen manuals anyway, so I was very pleased to see that Easy AMOS has a manual to follow.

The manual has a funny cartoon character to appeal to the kids, and it's written by the writer and wacky ideas man Mel Croucher, who also I seem to recall designed the funny character and wrote the manual for the ill-fated Sam Coupé.

I'm not convinced that this approach really works, and some kids and older beginners might find this sort of thing a bit patronising. But the content is okay, and in spite of my poking fun at Mr Croucher's style, he has done a nice job on the manual, making it easy to read and apply. (He did write the Pimania and Deus Ex Machina games for the Sinclair Spectrum, so he can't be all bad! Ah those were the pioneering days, blah blah...) It is a little bit oddly organised, but most of the people Europress tried it on were up and running in a few moments.

Figure 18.3. Easy AMOS Disk.

It's Good, but is it Art?

I have to say that this is one of the best beginners programming languages available, and I've seen quite a few. AMOS is in itself an easy approach to programming and so something which makes the learning curve that much shallower is only to be welcomed with open arms. The documentation is readable and nicely printed, the program itself is easy to use, and the Tutor program is the most powerful program utility for a small system ever devised.

This is the first time which a language has been used to create a program to teach people how to use itself, and it's a very well-designed piece of Computer Aided Teaching as well, something which I'm on record as saying could never exist. If you want to learn AMOS fast then get this package without delay.

Right, onto the more knotty topic of producing text in your programs. How do you make text more interesting? Why, you slap on another module of course! Let's take a look at the very best option, namely Shadow Software's CText.

19: CText

I've made a lot of references to CText and other types of extension to the AMOS language, but not as yet gone into any details about how you would use it. But now is the time. CText is another extension to the AMOS language written by Aaron Fothergill of Shadow Software, and you bolt it onto your AMOS system like any other extension. First you use the INSTALL program to copy the library CTEXT.Lib into your AMOS_SYSTEM directory, and then you make use of the Config1.x.AMOS program, whatever your system is, to ensure that AMOS knows the extension is loaded and ready to go. Once installed the extension appears on the startup screen in AMOS and the commands become part of the AMOS command set.

I, CText

CText stands for Colour Text, and it is an extension to the AMOS language which enables you to use colour fonts (and much more!) which are in fact icon bank based fonts. In other words the font is made from icons rather than text, and where you would normally use TEXT commands, you now can use CTEXT commands instead to give you glorious colour fonts.

These can be drawn in up to 64 colours using any Amiga paint program, and can be displayed on the screen using proportional spacing and even kerning. CText Fonts are loaded in as icon banks, and once loaded don't need to be loaded again. When they're needed you just call them up and if they are loaded into the correct bank they are typed up to the screen like any normal font.

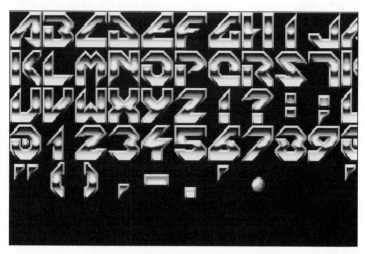

Figure 19.1. A colour font for CText.

In use in an AMOS environment, CText works exactly the same way as the TEXT command, and in fact displays faster than using TEXT with a disk based font. On the CText disk, you have two versions of the CText extension, one for AMOS 1.23 and one for V1.3 and upwards, what you'd call the *compiler versions* of AMOS.

Installing

These are installed with an AMOS program called CText_INSTALL.AMOS, which you run. In the new version of CText, called CText 2.0, there is a new version of the FONT_SETTER.AMOS program, which is used to set up your Ctext fonts for use. Also on the disk are a number of demos for you to run and examine, and a huge directory of fonts for you to try out. Table 19.1 gives you a list of these, and those who've had lots of font experience with DTP on Amiga and Mac will recognise some of these names.

All of the programs on previous versions of CText were supplied in two forms, for V1.23 and V1.3 of AMOS, and this was because the extension systems for these versions of AMOS are slightly different, and require slightly different versions of the CText extension. There's only one version of the new system as this CText 2.0 is only available as an upgrade to the original system.

Akashi22	digital16uo	PaloAlto15
Aldous12	digital32uo	Park_Ave
Andover	DPAINT	Peignot44
AvantG12	fsstencil	Pica11
Bigtext	Futurebig	Ruby
Bookman11	futuresmall	RUBYSTENCIL
bubbles16	Garnet9	SanFrancisco
Bubbles21	Ham	SAPHIREBIG
Camelot21	Helvetica12	sapphire16
Celtic15	LINEAL24	Stencil15
Courier11	Longl15	stripe
cutout32	LOSANGELES14	stripes32
DemoFont1	Manhattan	Swansong15
DemoFont2	Microsoft15	TIMES12
DemoFont3	MONACO11	TimesStencil
Diamond	Opal9	Tiny
DIAMONDBIG	outline32	

Table 19.1. Demo fonts with the CText System.

Using CText

Ctext is designed to be used as a replacement to the TEXT command in AMOS. Instead of using the usual methods of getting coloured text, that is to say IFF fonts and a lot of judicious programming, it simply uses an ICON bank (bank swapped to bank 10) to store all the characters, and a small 768 byte data table to show which icon to use for each of the 256 characters, and the Width and the Baseline of each character (for proportional spacing mode). If you're only using non-proportional text with a set width and baseline, then bytes 2 and 3 are ignored. One of CText's neat tricks, is that you can assign the same icon to several characters.

CText requires its icons in Bank 10, so normally you would load them into Bank 2 as normal, using NO ICON MASK or MAKE ICON MASK as required and then use the BANK SWAP command to swap them into bank 10, like so:

```
Bank swap 2,10
```

The only other thing you have to load for the font is the 768 byte font data table:

```
BLOAD "afont.abk.CFNT",font data
```

The Fontsetter program always saves the font data as the name of the icon bank with a .CFNT on the end.

This routine will load a Ctext font into memory:

```
F$="Bigfont"
Load F$+".abk"
Make Icon Mask
Bank Swap 2,10
Bload F$+".abk.cfnt",Font Data
```

Once you have your own copy of CText 2.0 you could try this program to run through a few of the fonts to see what they look like:

```
Rem * Show CText Fonts.AMOS *
Rem
Do
    Curs Off : Flash Off : Cls 0
    Erase 2
    Erase 10
    F$=Fsel$("CTEXT2:fonts/*.abk","","Load a CFont")
    Load F$
    No Icon Mask
    Get Icon Palette
    Bank Swap 2,10
    Bload F$+".cfnt",Font Data
    Autoback 0
    Font Size 0,0
    Ctext 10,30,"Hello World, CText here!"
    Wait Key
Loop
```

The program will pop up a file requester for you to load a font and then load it. NO ICON MASK means that the font isn't transparent on colour 0, but then on a black screen it doesn't have to be. If you wanted to overlay text on top of something else, you could set MAKE ICON MASK instead.

GET ICON PALETTE obviously grabs the palette of the icon bank, in this case the font we loaded. BANK SWAP switches the iconised font to bank 10 where CText operates from, and BLOAD etc loads in the Font Data file. The word FONT DATA is a reserved variable and this is where the 768 bytes of data will go into memory. The font is displayed, and waits until you press a key, when the whole business starts over again.

CText Commands

In CText 2.0 there are a number of new commands you can use, and they go something like this:

Font Size x,y

This sets up the width and baseline of the font. If zero is used in X or Y, then the relevant width or baseline table will be used from the data area. e.g:

```
Font Size 32,16 : All characters 32 width, 16 base-
line

Font Size 0,16 : Use Proportional width, but fixed
16 pixel baseline

Font Size 11,0 : Use Fixed 11 pixel width, with pro-
portional baseline

Font Size 0,0 : Use fully proportional
```

CText x,y,string$

The command to use the text is the CText command, which uses exactly the same parameters as the TEXT command, so you can simply change all your TEXT commands to CText, and your programs will run as normal.

Font n

Multifonts are a new feature and this command allows you to choose the font number from your program, where n is the number of the font.

Font Banks a,b

Normally CText uses bank 10 to store the icons and bank 11 to store font data for multifonts. But you might want to switch banks for some reason, like something else in your program is already inhabiting the space. Well, this command allows you to set the multifont bank (a) and the icon bank (b).

Font Shift x

This is a method of kerning the text, so that the letters tuck into each other a little more or less. This makes text take up a little less room, but it also makes it more attractive in some cases.

Font Step y

This makes it possible to angle the text up or down in steps.

Ct Double x,y

This prints the font twice with a small offset.

Set Ctab n,x

This sets up tab points across the screen. If you've ever used a word processor or a typewriter then this will make some kind of sense to you.

There are also a number of new functions for use with the system, like:

=PLEN(string)

Returns the pixel length of the string. This is so you can predict the length of the string on the screen.

=PHEIGHT(string)

The height of the string, just like PLEN.

=LAST CTX

Detects the position of the last pixel in the last string.

=CFONT$(n)

Changes fonts mid string

=KERN$(n)

Similar job as CFONT but for kerning.

=CTAB

Tabs text from within a string.

=FONT BASE

=FONT DATA

Returns the location in memory of the Ctext and Font Data areas. Useful for creating special effects in machine code.

All these new functions improve the way you can use the program about a hundredfold, and quite a number of the commands allow you to create moving text with great ease. The creation and manipulation of text couldn't be simpler. So how do you create a font for use with the CText extension?

Making a CText Font

Ctext fonts are very easy to make. You need to create a bank of AMOS icons, each icon being a character in the font. There are already a number of disks in the Public Domain which contain colour fonts as IFF files. And the beauty of it is that there are no colour, bitplane or size restrictions either, so if AMOS can display the IFF file, CText can display the font. PD disks abound but one of the best ways to do it is to take a PD font and adapt it, so you can steal the brilliant design ideas but use your own palette, or variation on their theme etc.

Okay so you want to create your own font. You'll need Deluxe Paint for this. I could cover all the bases by saying "you can use any IFF compatible paint program for this" but who am I kidding? Everyone uses DPaint so what's the use in fighting it! You create a font by placing all the characters onto the screen in rows, like this:

A B C D E F G H I J

K L M N O P Q R S T

U V W X Y Z

etc

making sure that there are spaces between all the characters. Then save the screen as an IFF file to disk.

Next you load up SpriteX and cut out the characters as Sprites, using the built-in sprite grabber. Once you have cut them out, you go through the bank with Auto scrunch on to eliminate any waste space. (Newer versions of SpriteX allow you to press the Z key to do this automatically.) Once you've done this and you're with the font, hit the SWAP button on the top row, so that the sprite bank becomes an icon bank.

After that you need to use the Fontsetter program. This utility is used to assign icons to ASCII characters as well as widths and baselines. By clicking on any of the ASCII characters listed, the image used for it will appear in the lefthand editing box at the bottom of the screen. You can use the left mouse button to drag the baseline/width lines around this character, or click with the right button to automatically set the width as the width of the icon + 2 pixels and the baseline to the bottom of the icon. Clicking on the ASCII characters with the Right button will store the icon shown in the righthand box to that character.

Multifonts are a CText font with more than one character set in them. This means you can have a number of designs in your program all at once, rather than just one set which might get a bit boring after a short while. The creation of multiple font types in a single bank is handled quite amply by the Fontsetter program. Using Fontsetter you can create fonts from scratch, but with the Font Converter program you can convert directly from a regular AmigaDOS font to a CText font. This means that you can use the wealth of *colorfonts* available in the Public Domain and commercial fields, like the epic Karafonts set. Whichever route you take to generating your CText fonts you won't regret it as this is the best way to handle fonts for games in AMOS.

To make life even easier there's a tutorial program included on the disk, which takes you through all the different aspects of using the program, and making sure that you grasp all the basic concepts.

CText, How Easy it is

As you can see it's all a piece of cake, and I can highly recommend this program to anyone who's serious about AMOS programming. The flexibility and speed of the system is such that I can't see anyone using those stupid old IFF font routines ever again. But to get the most out of CText, you really need to use SpriteX, and as luck would have it there's a new revision of that out by the time you read this. See Chapter 21 for more details about SpriteX 2.0. But first it's time for TOME.

20:
AMOS TOME

TOME is a super extension to the AMOS system which enables you to create mapped games with ease. In fact anything that requires screens linked in a certain order is more easily done with TOME installed.

TOME began life as a small utility program on the Atari ST version of AMOS (called STOS as you probably gather by now), which allowed the user to produce game backgrounds that were much larger than the actual physical screen. Over a period of the last few years the product has improved until, when AMOS was finished, an Amiga version of TOME was created. AMOS TOtal Map Editor, or AMOS TOME, is the ultimate MAP designer for use not just with AMOS but with any language on any computer!

This chapter is designed as an in-depth introduction to TOME and all its important bits and pieces, as this is the biggest extension to the system besides the Compiler or AMOS 3D, and as such is something you really need to know about.

TOMEing About

The program comprises of the TOME Editor, where all your bits of map are patched together and saved as a file, and the TOME extension, which is added to the AMOS system to do various map type commands for you.

The latest versions are fully AMOS 1.3 upwards and Compiler compatible and new versions are supplied free to all previously registered AMOS TOME users. At the time of going to press version 4 was about to be completed which has up to 60 commands for creating the largest and most detailed maps on *any* computer.

The best reason for using TOME in your AMOS programs rather than creating the routines from scratch is that TOME does it *all* for you. It allows you to create giant screens in memory using a series of simple building blocks. These areas of memory are called MAPs, for obvious reasons, and you can design a giant MAP the height of many screens and it will not take up nearly as much memory as drawing a picture that big (a super-bitmap). TOME works a little bit like a jigsaw or collage in that first you create the basic building blocks called Tiles, you then use the editor to paste these building blocks onto your MAP area thereby creating a giant background for your games.

Tiles are simply square blocks of a picture cut out using the utility supplied with TOME. This utility cuts up a picture into 16*16 or 32*32 pixel blocks and stores them as AMOS Icons in an AMOS Icon bank. So your Tiles are initially created by drawing them on a paint program like Deluxe Paint and saving them off as IFF screens. The Tiles are drawn on the screen starting from the top left (Tile number 0) and working right, then going to the next line, working right and so on. You then load up the TileMaker program, which converts the picture into AMOS Icons. AMOS Icons are areas of a screen which can be cut out and saved inside a safe area of memory ready for later use. They can be thought of as less-flexible versions of AMOS Bobs. (See Chapter 12 for more details.)

The practical use of TOME can be seen in AMOS games from PD libraries, but also in commercial games which have large scrolling areas. *Rainbow Islands* (Ocean Software) and *Ghouls'N'Ghosts* (US Gold) are two examples that spring to mind.

Installing TOME

You can't just pick up a copy of the TOME disks and run them. TOME is an extension to the language, and as such has to be installed. Before you can use the TOME commands, or any of the programs on the TOME disk, you need to install the TOME extension onto your copy of AMOS. Extensions are special additions to the AMOS system, and they have to be copied to the right directory and have the config program look for them on bootup.

Once the extension is installed into AMOS, you can use the AMOS TOME commands within your programs or even in direct mode, as they become part of the AMOS Language.

To install the TOME tools, just load the TOME_INSTALL.AMOS program into your AMOS editor and run it. Then you just need to select what version of AMOS you wish to install the extension onto. The program will then look for a disk called AMOS: (if you have ASSIGNed this in your startup-sequence on your hard drive it will also work) and save a program called TOME.Lib into your AMOS_SYSTEM directory. Once this is done, you can quit the TOME_INSTALL program.

The next step is to load in the AMOS configuration program, for example on V1.3 of AMOS it's called CONFIG1_3.AMOS. Next you will have to load the default configuration. Next you have to select the LOADED EXTENSIONS item. This will give you a listing of all the extensions that have been installed into AMOS. You will probably have something like the following installed:

```
1:AMOS_SYSTEM/Music.Lib

2:AMOS_SYSTEM/Compact.Lib

3:AMOS_SYSTEM/Requester.Lib

4:

5:AMOS_SYSTEM/Compiler.Lib

6:AMOS_SYSTEM/Serial.Lib

7:

8:AMOS_SYSTEM/CTEXT.Lib

9:AMOS_SYSTEM/Range.Lib
```

next you have to click on the blank Line 7 and enter:

```
:AMOS_SYSTEM/TOME.Lib
```

then save that configuration as the default.

Now every time you boot your version of AMOS, it should load up with the TOME extension installed, ie. it'll show up on the list of loaded extensions shown on the AMOS startup screen. The extensions to the system have been added and you can now use all the TOME commands in your AMOS program.

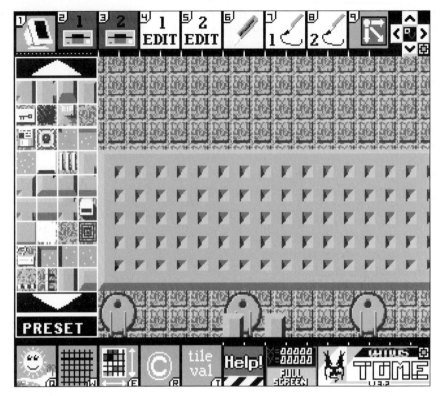

Figure 20.1. The TOME Editor.

The TOME Editor

The heart of the TOME program is the editor. Using this very slickly written program you can create, edit and save all of your game MAPs to disk ready for use in your own programs. Editor is a powerful map editing system which includes simple drawing facilities similar to those found in DPaint, although these should be viewed as strictly touch-up tools rather than for origination of your backgrounds. To get the most out of the system you must have at least 1Mb of memory, but these days I reckon everyone must have 1Mb at the very least. (What, you haven't? Run out and buy some more memory at once! What do you think you're playing at?)

When you load the editor you see that the screen is divided into four main parts. The first two are tool bars which run along the top and bottom of the screen and control all of TOME Editor's functions. Each bar is divided up into a number of small buttons, and as you click on a button on the top bar a new selection of options appears on the bottom bar.

The next part of the screen at the far left is the tile selector and contains copies of all the Tiles you created previously with a paint program, and tiled with the TileMaker.AMOS program. Obviously the scroll arrows at the top and bottom of this area allow you to move through the selection of Tiles you have loaded, as most of the time you'll have more tiles loaded than you can view on a single solitary screen sidebar!

You click on the righthand button while positioned over the map to select a Tile for placement. At the bottom of this part of the screen is a button with the word PRESET on it. If you click on this you will see the current range of Tiles replaced with another set, a user defined set.

The last bit of the screen, the largest area on the screen, is of course the current MAP itself, just off centre and to the right of the screen. To navigate around the MAP you can use either the joystick, cursor keys or the little arrows in the far right corner of the top tool bar.

Configuring TOME

The Niceness menu option allows you configure the editor to suit your own tastes. The different options allow you to change the screen from PAL to NTSC, switch on the cursor coordinates, adjust the Tile/tool bar palettes, save the settings exactly how you want them and even return everything back to their default states, the usual config sort of stuff really.

The palette controls are the same as in the AMOS Sprite editor (and SpriteX), and allow you to set either the colours of the control icons (to your own preference) or of the Tiles themselves. Simply click on the colours you want to change, and use the sliders to set the RGB values.

Auto Parts

There are a couple of automatic modes you should know about. First is Maze Mode. By using this and selecting Tiles for corners and junctions etc TOME will follow your mouse movements and will create instant mazes as you draw. This is a really nice feature, but not as nice as Auto Map. Whereas Maze Mode will follow your mouse movements to produce a maze of your own design, this mode goes a step further and does all the work for you. This mode can take a while, especially when used on large maps.

The TOME Command Set

The actual TOME extension only works from within AMOS and on files created with the TOME Editor. As a bit of a taster here are some of the commands you can use from within AMOS when TOME is installed. Obviously these have been augmented and with the new version 4 you'll have a great many more options, but I'll go into those in a minute. TOME is good, not just for map based games, but for all programs where a larger area of screen is required, like city maps, circuit diagrams, medical software, you name it.

MAP DO x,y

Redraws the map to the current screen.

MAP TOP x,y

MAP BOTTOM x,y

MAP LEFT x,y

MAP RIGHT x,y

These four commands are exactly the same as the MAP DO command, except that they only redraw one edge of the display area, very handy for fast scrolling.

MAP VIEW x1,y1 to x2,y2

This command creates a window to which TOME will limit all of the MAP drawing functions. Obviously the window wouldn't be any bigger than the currently defined screen, or you couldn't see it!

TILE SIZE x,y

This sets the size of the Tiles to be used. Normally either 16 or 32, but smaller sizes can be used if necessary.

MAP PLOT t,x,y

Places Tile t at co-ordinates x,y in the map. The same as using the DRAW function within the TOME Editor.

MAP BANK b

Changes the bank used for map storage to bank number b. Normally, the default is bank 6, which you should reserve to the length of the map, and then Bload the map in, like so:

```
Rem * Map Bank.AMOS *

Rem

Open in 1,"Bigmap.map"

L=Lof(1)

Close 1

Reserve as work 6,L

Bload "Bigmap.map",start(6)
```

TILE BANK b

Changes the Tile value list bank from the default of 8 to b. This is very handy if you want to keep multiple Tile value banks in memory at one time, a bit like the multifont aspect of CText.

And the extension also has some new functions like these:

=MAP X

Returns the width of the current map in Tiles.

=MAP Y

Returns the height of the current map in Tiles.

=XTILE(x)

Changes pixel coordinate x into a Tile coordinate.

=YTILE(y)

Changes pixel coordinate y onto a Tile coordinate.

=MAP TILE(x,y)

Returns the Tile number at found at MAP coordinates x,y.

=TILE VAL(x,y,l)

Returns the value from list l of the tile at MAP coordinates x,y.

=MAP CHECK

This function will run through the map data, checking all the Tiles used in the map against those available in the Tile bank. If a Tile is used in the map that isn't available in the Tile bank, then the function will change its Tile number to zero. MAP CHECK returns the number of Tiles that it has had to change.

TOME is very flexible indeed, and the applications for the extension grow with each upgrade. These commands I've explained here are just some of the commands available with the TOME extension installed, there are many more and I'm afraid if you want to know more about them you'll have to buy TOME and find out!

TOME Docs

In the past the docs to the TOME program were featured on the TOME disk as a home built hypertext program (albeit a very good one), but recent versions of the program have had a specially produced paper manual. Hypertext is fun and informative, for sure, as you can click on various text screens and get information about any aspect of the program that interests you, roaming around the text for the manual in an interactive way. This is quite impressive as I say, and fun, but I still prefer paper manuals. Nothing replaces flipping back and forth through a manual to find the information you like, and holding it on your lap while you code. And also the paper manual has one big advantage: you can read it and run the program at the same time! I'm glad that Shadow Software have made the switch, and the new TOME manual is a nice, cleanly written piece of documentation.

More Goodies

The bonuses to the system don't stop there. The AMOS TOME Goodies Disk is only available to registered AMOS TOME Users, and the current disk includes three new games written with AMOS TOME. These are: *Magic Forest II,* a horizontal scrolling platform game, Green Flag, an Isometric 3D scrolling game, and *The Dungeon*, a Dungeon Master style 3D dungeon game. All three are supplied in AMOS source form, so that you can examine the code and use similar routines in your own productions. The TOME Goodies Disk 1 costs £5.00 and is only available to registered TOME users who have sent in their registration card. Goodies Disk 2 is said to be in preparation and will be available soon after the release of TOME Series 4.

TOME Series 4

I've spoken a lot about TOME Series 4, so I asked Aaron what was going to be new in the next version of TOME. Apart from including a better editor (could it be any better?) TOME series 4 includes a lot of very important additions, not least of which is MaPLe, the Map Programming Language. Not only that but it features a Tile Animation page, and a command set now up to 60 commands. The new commands offer a whole new universe of subtlety over the previous versions, but also include such things as Tile Animation control, automatic map updates, and the special Map Fall command which enables you to create your own Boulder Dash type clones. There's even a single command to handle 8 way scrolling of your maps!

Currently on what Aaron calls the "will we put them in for this version" list are map flooding, special commands for drowning your player as well as dropping rocks on his head! Best of all, you will be able to upgrade from TOME v3 to Series 4 very cheaply, with the obvious discounts for AMOS Club members.

Don't Just Sit There

AMOS TOME is just one of those things you *have* to have if you're serious about AMOS. Anyway if you're like me you like to have everything to do with AMOS anyway, and this is one of the sexier add-ons, so it's compulsory really. At present TOME costs just £24.99 (or £19.99 to AMOS Club members) from Shadow Software.

As I said before, the next upgrade is going to be TOME 4, released probably by the time you read this. Install TOME today, and create game maps as big as your ideas.

So, colour text and maps are easily sorted out it seems, but what about Sprites? Is there anything we can add to our AMOS system to make capturing and manipulating Sprites easy? Well, you should know by now I don't ask a question in this book unless the answer is yes. The next chapter is all about that champion of the Sprite Bank, SpriteX.

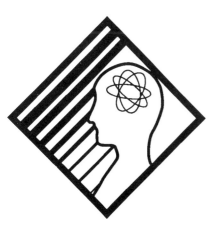

21:
SpriteX

Creating Sprites and Bobs for your AMOS programs has always been a bit of a chore. Either you draw a shape on screen or load an IFF file and grab an area of the screen as a Sprite, or you use the AMOS Sprite Editor program on your AMOS disks. This program was until a short while ago the only convenient way to produce movable objects for your screens. But the author of the AMOS Sprite Editor, Aaron Fothergill of Shadow Software, decided to upgrade the program and make it more powerful. To be honest the original program had some annoying bugs, and being a bit of a perfectionist, Aaron wanted to do a proper job on the program. So SpriteX was born.

Right Tool for the Right Job

SpriteX is a modified version of the original AMOS Sprite Editor, with many more features, and greater amounts of what the Americans would call *functionality*. The main screen looks similar, but you'll find more functions. Whereas the original Sprite Editor was limited as to the type of objects it could create, the SpriteX editor is designed for drawing AMOS Bobs, Sprites and even Icons.

Any images designed in SpriteX are stored in a bank, ready to be saved to disk and used as Sprites, Bobs or Icons by AMOS. To use them as Icons, you use the SWAP button on the top line of buttons to swap them into the Icon bank, and then hit the SAVE as ICONS button. See Figure 21.1 for a look at the SpriteX screen.

The editor is very easy to use, and borrows much of its look and feel from Amiga paint programs. For example two buttons at the top left of the screen allow you to cut out an area from the zoomed sprite, and then paste it elsewhere in the sprite. When Cut is selected, you click on the zoomed area and drag the cut area to size. The program will then use this cut area as a brush. Clicking on Paste will allow you to go back to using this brush while you are in the editor.

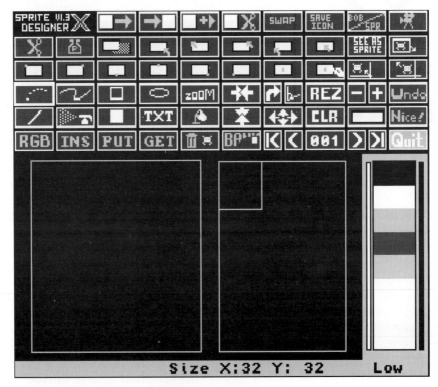

Figure 21.1. SpriteX 1.32.

At the bottom of the screen are tools to help you move Sprites to and from the Sprite bank, and a number of other tools for manipulating banks.

RGB

This button allows you to change the values of the colours being used in the bank, that is to say the palette of the Sprites, Bobs or Icons you are creating.

Insert Sprite, Put Sprite, Get Sprite, Delete Sprite

These buttons put Sprites in and out of the bank, and erase ones you don't want any more.

Erase Bank

Of course this deletes the bank in memory ready for you to get another one from disk or create one from scratch.

As well as being able to draw your Sprites from scratch, you can also grab them from an IFF file, like you would to grab an exciting graphic font for use in CText. To do this you use the extra module called GrabberX.

New Features

A lot of modifications have been made for version 1.23. Load and Save are now on buttons on screen as well as the L and S keys on the keyboard. The 1.23 version can handle Sprite colours as well as Bob colours. Grabber is now built in and is a separate but integrated grabber module. An Animation checker is also included. SpriteX can now hold both a Bob/Sprite bank, as well as an Icon bank in memory and swap between them. A Rotator utility has been added, so that you can rotate images to an accuracy of a tenth of a degree (more about that in a sec). Generally speaking several of the existing functions have been *tuned*. There is an Auto Scrunch facility which automatically scrunches Bobs when *got* from the bank which saves time when working on Bobs grabbed from IFF screens.

New Buttons

Load Sprite/Icon bank

This is the same as the L key on the keyboard. It loads Sprites into bank 1, or Icons into bank 2. To edit Icons, swap them into bank 1 with the SWAP button.

Save Sprite Bank

This saves bank 1 to disk, the same as the S key.

Append Sprite/Icon bank

Loads a new bank and adds it to the current one.

Sprite Grabber

This is the same as the old Sprite grabber program. It allows you to grab Sprites from IFF pictures with ease.

Swap Icons/Sprite banks

This function swaps banks 1 and 2 about, so that you can edit one or the other.

Save Icon Bank

As with Save Sprite bank, but it saves bank 2 (Icons).

Sprite/Bob Palette

Swaps between the normal Bob/screen palette, and the special Sprite palette.

Animator

Allows you to test animations of your Sprites, back and forth and one frame at a time.

Niceness Mods

In SpriteX the NICE button was the internal preferences of SpriteX. The Niceness option has been slightly modified in the current version, with a new function added. The Free memory display now only shows the amount of CHIP memory, as of course this is the only relevant memory for Bobs, Icons and Sprites.

The new button in the NICE menu is the Auto Squash option. When switched on, any Bob got from the bank so that you can edit it, is automatically squashed to the top left, and the size of the Bob automatically reduced. This saves you having to use the squash button on every one of the 128 Sprites you grabbed from your IFF picture.

There is another option to do this job, and that is pressing the Z key when editing, so that SpriteX will go through the whole bank, and squash every Bob for you.

The Rotator

The Rotate Button has now been split into two. The lefthand side will rotate the image by 90 degrees, and the righthand side accesses the Rotator, a powerful utility for rotating images. In the Rotator there are three option buttons, as well as Cancel and OK. Here they are:

Number of Rotations

This can be set from 1-64.

Rotation Angle

This is set in degrees, and can be from 0 to 360.

In 360

This button will take the number of rotations you want, and work out the angle required for that number of rotations in 360 degrees.

For instance, you could have the number of rotations set at 16, and press the In 360 button. The Rotator will then work out that each rotation needs to be 22.5 degrees, and set the rotation angle accordingly. When you press the OK button, the Rotator will calculate all the rotations you will need, and insert them all into the Sprite bank.

It isn't as fast or accurate as the rotation routines in some art packages, but it does just about everything for you. Even the hotspot of the image is rotated to the correct point!

C'mere, there's More

A few other features have been added to make life easier. All functions which move the image, such as Horizontal/Vertical Flip, Rotate (Including the Rotator) and Squash, will automatically adjust the hot spot.

You need to hold the right button down over the Sprite display buttons to be able to view them. Also, when scrolling through the Sprites with the left button, holding down the right button as well (hold the left first then click with the right), will let you scroll through 10 sprites at a time. The two colour Hires mode has been replaced by four colour Lores (for working on mouse pointers). The Alert boxes have been replaced with better ones from AMOS TOME.

How Does that Grabber You?

The Grabber in SpriteX is a development of the original Sprite Grabber, first supplied as a separate program to the main SpriteX, now used as part of the main program. Grabber has had a few modifications, and now has an extra function called Line Grab.

For those of you who haven't used the Sprite Grabber before, GrabberX is for grabbing images from IFF or AMOS style spacked pictures to be used as Bobs or Icons. This is done by loading in the picture, clicking on the scissors or *cut* button, and then marking the area to cut. For most images, it is best to mark an area larger than the area you want, and then optimise it in the main menu, to chop out the unwanted space. For some images, like those that are too large to be edited for instance, you can use the arrow keys to fine tune the grabbing area.

If you press the up/down arrow keys, you can control the icon bar up and down the screen so that you can view and grab different and larger areas. Clicking on the Cut icon will grab a single image and store it in the Sprite bank at the current location, which is changed by the arrow buttons. Clicking on the Cut Line icon will allow you to grab a whole row of images in one go. This is especially useful when using SpriteX in conjunction with CText, as you can grab most of an alphabet on one line. The only rule with this function is that the images must have at least a one pixel gap between them. You simply move the box over the area you want to grab and GrabberX will grab the whole area and split it horizontally into separate images.

Animation Station

Finally, you have a means to test Sprite animations using the ANIMX module. The ANIMX animation tester is designed to enable you to test out your Bobs to make sure that they are animating properly. You can animate up to 16 Bobs over 51 frames. To use ANIMX, you control the Frame Number, Bob Number and Image number for each Bob with the three controllers at the top of the screen. The Button at the bottom left allows you to load in a background screen to animate the Bobs over, and there are four more control buttons, Wipe, INS and some arrow buttons:

Wipe

Clears all the animation, so you can restart.

INS

Inserts a gap in the animation, so that you can insert a frame.

->

<-

A sort of ping pong effect plays the animation to the last frame, and then plays it backwards to the first.

->

Plays the animation to the last frame, and then jumps back to the first. Clicking on either the Ping Pong or Play buttons will also stop the animation.

As with GrabberX, the control bar can be moved up and down with the cursor keys.

Sprite Xtras

On the SpriteX 1.32 disk as well as the world's best AMOS Sprite, Bob and Icon creator, as a bonus are the Rem Maker.AMOS program (to design fancy REM statements to introduce your program), and a pair of *10 Liner* games, *Logger Larry* and *Ping*. Why 10 Liners? Well they're only 10 lines of code, that's why. These 10 Liners crop up quite a lot in the AMOS Club newsletter, and apart from being excellent examples of how to code a game in a concise and clever way, they are great sources of info on how to get the very best games from the minimum of code.

Full details about how to get a copy of SpriteX appear at the end of this chapter. But what's this I hear about a new version coming along soon?

SpriteX 2.0

Coming soon to an AMOS based Amiga system near you, available as an upgrade from the AMOS Club, comes SpriteX 2.0. It's not quite available yet at the time of going to press, but Aaron has been nice enough to give me a sneak preview. Figure 21.2 shows the new screen.

The program is an upgrade, with many new features worthy of note. The program can now edit Bobs, Sprites, AMOS Icons, Workbench Icons and Screens. That's right, you can now create Icons for programs as well as the AMOS kind of Icons for game backgrounds. And anything up to a full screen can be used and edited, so you can grab Bobs from a full screen or have a full screen as your Bob! There are now almost twice as many editing options as there were with the original version I've talked about in this chapter, version 1.32 or thereabouts.

The animation test feature has been expanded to be a full animation page (which may also be an AMAL editor) including path generation for your Sprites along sine or circular waves. (Nice touch that.)

The new version of the Grabber is artificially intelligent, that is to say you can set it going grabbing a screen full of small Sprites while you go off and make a cup of tea. When you come back it's all done and all you have to do is save to disk. The algorithms used are very advanced, and Aaron is quite rightly very proud of them. Fractals come into it somehow, I don't know how it works though. (Join the AMOS Club and they'll doubtless explain it to you.) The Grabber also automagically cuts out any guide spots you used on your images, and fixes a hotspot on the Sprite. In other words "Basically you can go from screen to game without editing anything", according to Shadow Software.

Finally there is a new *image arrangement page* where you can shuffle and swap all the images in the 11 banks that SpriteX 2 can hold in memory at once.

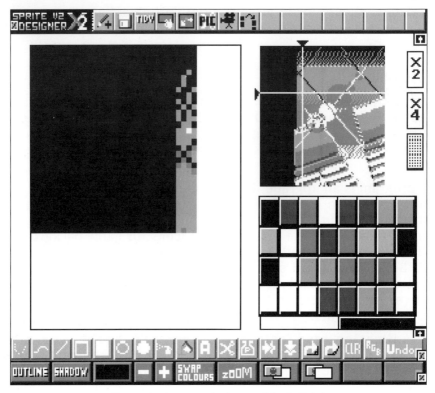

Figure 21.2. An early demo of SpriteX 2.0.

Gotcha!

The original SpriteX 1.32 program is licenseware, and available for very little dosh from Deja Vu Professional Licensed Software. SpriteX 2.0 is available as a £10 upgrade from the AMOS Club, and is only available to club members.

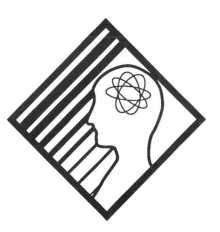

22:
AMOS
Professional

AMOS Professional is a brand new version of AMOS for sophisticated program development in the '90s and, although it is more powerful and more advanced than the classic AMOS v1.34, great pains have been taken to ensure that it remains compatible with existing AMOS products.

You may find yourself asking as I did "What on Earth was wrong with the old AMOS?' The answer is, of course, nothing much really, but the problem was that everyone who used the original program had an idea of how the program could be improved and couldn't stop themselves from telling Europress. Being a go-ahead kind of a firm (pass me that soft soap will you?) Europress decided that the best way forward was to pay attention to some of these suggestions and move AMOS into a new market and new level of programming power.

From the start AMOS was Francois Lionet's personal vision of what a programming language and editor should be like and, although it was revolutionary at the time, there would obviously come a time when people would want to see changes. Tastes change and, although the environment in classic AMOS could be configured to suit, a lot of things about the system were not quite right – to some folk's way of thinking.

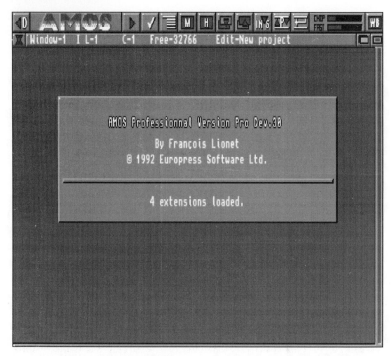

Figure 22.1. AMOS Professional – a new look and feel.

New Kid on the Block

Much has been learned from the development of other AMOS products, like the Easy AMOS system, and so things like new requesters and a tutor have been implemented in AMOS Pro. The tutor is called AMOS Monitor and it enables you to step through your programs a line at a time and see the effects either as a small screen or a full screen preview. To my mind this is the most useful innovation of the AMOS line, because it means you can stamp out the bugs as they arise rather than slaving away trying to track them in a program that's running at full speed. Under normal circumstances most bugs in programs need to be traced by sheer weight of logic, thinking your way through the program and then stomping on them. This way you can see an odd effect in slow motion, and not have to blow your brain up trying to figure out what could be wrong.

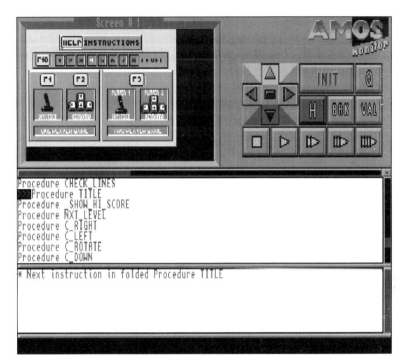

Figure 22.2. AMOS Monitor.

By and large most of what you know from using AMOS in all its many versions will see you all right. AMOS Professional is a more flexible and powerful environment for you to develop software in, rather than a complete change of program. The fundamental principles are the same, it's just the manner in which they are presented and the options open to you that have really changed for the better, I think.

For my money it's the best version of AMOS yet, and no messing. I can't think of a better answer to the question 'What can you add to AMOS to make it better?' than this. The customising options alone kept me busy for weeks and, in a few years time, I might even get around to using some of the new commands (only joking).

You can use AMOS Pro to write AMOS programs like the ones you wrote before, except this time you'll be using an elegant new editor with a new cleaner setup and pull-down menus.

Should you buy AMOS Pro? The answer to that question is that it very much depends on your status now in the world of AMOS. If you are a complete beginner the answer is no, forget it and buy Easy AMOS because it's easier to grasp and you'll get more than adequate results. If you have Easy AMOS and are getting quite proficient, then the regular AMOS would be a better bet for the moment. If you already have regular AMOS, then the only way is up and AMOS Pro is the only way to go. The beauty of the AMOS family is that there are a lot of entry points on the scale and, like a family, the range is growing all the time and almost anything you want to do is possible.

New Features of AMOS Pro

IFF ANIM

The new system now has commands to play IFF ANIM files directly and, it is said, they operate faster than those used in DPaint IV! This is not possible at all in AMOS, except by some very clever programming beyond the scope of normal humans.

Double Precision Support

For floating point operations and, of course, support for any maths coprocessor you might have lying around cluttering up your computer. Those damn accelerator cards get everywhere.

Unlimited Banks

In classic AMOS you had just 16 short memory banks to store all your graphics and sounds in, but now you can have up to 65,000 which is as near to unlimited as you can imagine really _ can you picture keeping track of about 900 banks? Of course there are also some new bank commands to cope with the strain, and these are very powerful.

Speech Mouth

There's nowt so queer as folk, as the Great Bard once said. Some people, when asked what they wanted to see most in the new AMOS said they'd like a little animated mouth movement to match narrator driven speech. What are these people on?

ELSE IF

A new control structure has been added, which is more like switch casing in C than any structure you'd find in BASIC. You can have as many cases as you like and you can hop out of the test with an ENDIF. Very slick, and C programmers will get off on the similarity with switch case.

Error Trapping

The new command TRAP prevents any errors hit by the program from stopping the program dead. This means your compiled programs won't bomb out when they hit a problem.

ASSIGN

An ASSIGN command has been added, which acts just like the AmigaDOS command of the same name. This allows you to assign a device name to a directory or device, like ASSIGN STORE: RAM: or anything like that.

Ports and Libs

About 40 or 50 commands have been added covering the devices like SER: PRT: PAR:, and also advanced commands for libraries like Lib Open, Lib Close. Advanced stuff, and of more use to people who really know what they're doing. Not for the faint hearted.

MED Support

AMOS couldn't play modules from Soundtracker type programs directly. As the most popular and sophisticated tracker of the '90s is MED, AMOS Pro has a method for playing MED modules directly with MIDI support through MED. MED not only supports MIDI and samples but it also allows very sophisticated synthesis. The MED player is a library rather than part of the main AMOS Pro program so it can be updated regularly to keep pace with developments to the MED system without altering the main AMOS Pro program.

Noisetracker Support

The ability to play Noisetracker modules directly has been added. This is bolted into the system so future revisions of the NT program may differ. Noisetracker is pretty much static now, though, so this will not really be a problem. Previously the converter programs for trackers were a little erratic and this fixes a lot of the problems.

ARexx Control

A big selling point in the US, as ARexx has been a major force over there even before it was incorporated into the Amiga system. This interprocess communication language is now becoming very popular over here too, and so ARexx ports can be opened and data sent and received as normal.

EXEC

You can now run any AmigaDOS program from within AMOS using the new EXEC command. This is an enhancement from the previous way of running Amiga programs from AMOS which was a little more involved.

POKE$ and PEEK$

Now you can use these commands to put strings into memory locations as well as numeric data. Exactly why you would want to is a bit of a mystery to me, but there it is if you need it.

AMOS Interface

This is a major part of the revised AMOS, allowing you previously impossible control over the interface of your AMOS system and any other interfaces you might like to design for programs. The system starts humbly by letting you customise the interface using IFF screens containing all the buttons and window graphics. The elements are grabbed using a similar process to a sprite grabber. A resulting resource file is then saved, ready to be loaded by the program when the interface is in use! There is also the AMOS Interface string based language, which is like AMAL only bigger and far more complex. Once again this is not for the faint hearted.

AMOS Monitor

The tutor program from Easy AMOS has been revamped and is now available for full AMOS users. Bug tracing and stomping a speciality. The name change is to lose the tutorial tag, but the program remains largely unchanged.

New Editor

There is a new editor program in AMOS Pro, with a much more workmanlike interface design, pull down menus and the ability to load, edit and run multiple programs. The look is cleaner and more Workbench 2 like, although previous users of AMOS will find many similarities with the system they're used to. The pull down menus replace the old buttons across the top of the AMOS window, although some functions are still allocated buttons on the main window.

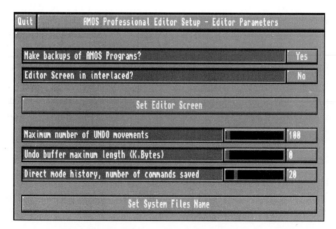

Figure 22.3. The Editor can be customised to suit your own needs.

Configuration

There's a new online configuration program, which lets you alter your settings easily and quickly without having to load and run a separate program. There are also configure editor options like screen sizes, error messages etc, all of which can be changed to suit your needs.

Compatibility

You can load old AMOS and Easy AMOS programs, and run them quite happily, as the basic elements of the system remain unchanged. There's also a auto check facility to test compatibility between AMOS Pro programs and older versions of the interpreter, which automatically traces the areas where you are likely to have problems if you want the program to run on all versions. This means that with AMOS Pro you can still tap in the examples in this book, which were mostly written in AMOS 1.34!

Machine Code

Although it has always been possible to use machine code in AMOS programs, you can now load machine code directly into procedures. Machine code is loaded directly into their own procedures, which then can be called from any part of the AMOS program. If the procedure is full then the code in the proc will be erased and replaced with the machine code block. In most cases it's best to load machine code into a blank proc, and then that machine code program can be accessed using the proc name.

Keyboard Macros

Almost all computer programs these days allow you to assign a series of regularly used commands to a single keystroke or combination of keys to save time. The macro system in AMOS Pro lets you assign any series of commands to single keystrokes making life a lot easier if there are some long repetitive processes you used to do by hand, like block out areas of the program using REM statements. Not only that but any menu option can be reconfigured to be triggered by any key you like.

Mark and Find

Special marks in the source code remember where you've been and using this process you can mark places in the program which you intend to visit often, like the bit where you initialise variables etc.

Undo/Redo System

Using a special new smart undo feature, you can undo and redo any number of lines, up to the limited of your memory.

Cut/Paste

Now you can cut and paste at any position in the text and not just whole lines. The left button is used to mark sections of code, rather than the right button in old versions, and this mode is activated by double-clicking on the character you wish to start from. I must admit I still forget and try to use the right button.

Sound Effects

You can now set up any sound you want to be used by the system, rather than the old built-in sounds. You can have different system sounds, and this makes using your favourite sounds even easier.

Custom Commands

You can replace menu commands with your own AMOS programs.

Autosave

For those of you who don't save often enough, or live in country areas and have power cuts every now and then because a cow bites through a power cable or a tree falls on the lines. Yes, this has happened to me!

Kill Editor

A new command which removes the whole editor from use while a program is running and reloads it after you've finished, saving a complete pile of memory. There are options in the configuration file to stop this happening in programs you get from other people, although why you'd want to do this I'm not sure.

User Menu

A place to store your own programs and run them etc. All accessories run from this menu, as well as any programs you like to have handy for close encounters.

Online Help

A sophisticated Help system is included in the system. This means you have no real excuse for getting lost once the program is running. Any word in a program can be clicked on and help about the keyword is available online by hitting the Help key. Okay so there's a manual too, but this is very handy when you can't really be bothered to hunt around in the manual just a for a single word definition. Besides, what's the point of running computers unless you can use them to save time?

Direct Mode

The Direct Mode was one that I for one used a lot, and I'm overjoyed to see it improved like this. The direct mode window has been enhanced to have window gadgets for certain functions, and a

AmigaDOS Shell style command *history*, using the cursor keys rather than the function keys. This means that you can get the last line you typed back by pressing the up cursor key like you can in the Shell. Once you have the line back you can re-execute it by pressing Return or re-edit it like a line in a wordprocessor. Handy for executing a long stream of similar lines.

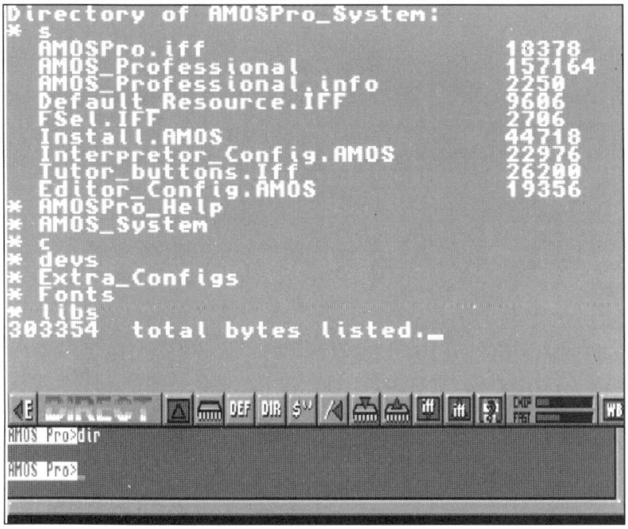

Figure 22.4. The AMOS Pro direct mode of operation.

File Selector

The new file selector has a lot of new features, one of which is the ability to store directories that you visit often and allow you to page back through them rather than hunt about for them every time. It's a much more Workbench 2 kind of affair as well, and enables you to quickly and quietly zip to the exact directory you were looking for without having to noodle about with typing in filenames etc.

Physical Differences

The program now comes on six disks, as many people complained about AMOS that the examples were too few and not very high quality. I thought they were pretty good myself, but I guess the customer is always right! So you now have loads of examples and backup programs and the online help facility for the hard of thinking. In total there are around 200 more commands in AMOS Pro than there was in the latest version of AMOS classic. Your old compiler won't work with the new program, instead you'll need to use the AMOS Professional Compiler.

AMOS Pro works better on hard disk than on floppies by virtue of its size and complexity, but will quite happily sit about on discrete floppies if that's the way you work.

The size of the working area on the screen has been enlarged, so you see more of the program you're working on and less of the on-screen buttons. This has been made possible by transferring a lot of the more complex functions from buttons to pull down menus, which you only see when you press the right mouse button.

The Help function used in Easy AMOS has been enhanced to be much more helpful. Help is available for any command in the AMOS language, simply by clicking the cursor on the word in question and then activating the help function either from a menu or by simply slapping the help button. A window pops up over the main source code giving syntax (a sort of template showing the way the word should be used) and working examples of how the command is used in context. This is invaluable for users who are used to AMOS classic or Easy AMOS. The new editor is, as I said before, able to load more than one program, but there is also the possibility of editing the two programs on a split screen at the same time. Each program window is separate and accessible by simply clicking on the window.

One thing which I particularly approve of is the addition in the new editor of better and more accessible printer functions. I don't know about you, but I really need to debug programs on paper. I can't debug source code or proof read text for that matter on screen. If I have to read a piece of code for mistakes I prefer to have a printout on a sheet of paper and sit down in a comfy chair with a cup of tea and a pen. Regular AMOS can print out but you have to select all as a block and print the block. Printing any area of the program is much more simple with AMOS Pro and, for that little relief, much thanks.

The new block mode is excellent, activated by double-clicking on any area of the text. Now the program is much more Amiga-ised, with proper windows, pull down menus and proper use of the mouse buttons.

Yet another new feature which I've been waiting for since the program began all those years ago, is the ability to adjust the size of the buffer at any time, without having to save the program first. The old system meant that you had to fiddle about a bit to operate on large programs which were saved with PROCs folded when they were saved. Now you can simply whack up the size of the buffer and unfold the PROCs at your leisure. The SET BUFFER command makes this possible, and in Direct mode you can make any adjustments to the buffer size which take you fancy.

AMOS Intelligence

The new editor is not only easy to use it's also very intelligent. Typing into the editor you are checked at every turn. If you mistype anything you can alter it at the time rather than later when you might not recall exactly what it was you were trying to get at.

Movement around the editor has been made even easier by allowing you to hop from procedure to procedure or even label to label. As Labels and procedures are the key elements of any program, this makes moving about in an AMOS program a very easy and convenient routine.

The buttons along the top of the screen are for switching to direct mode, flipping back to Workbench, and buttons for Run, Test, Indent, Amos Monitor, Help, a button for sorting the windows on your Editor screen, a button for folding/unfolding procedures and a button for inserting a return. Editing windows can be compressed to a single line with the title in it, by hitting the compressor button on each editor window. This saves space on a cluttered screen.

Direct mode is more intelligent too. The command line history makes it easy to input a number of similar commands as you can recall the last one, edit and re-execute it, all in a few seconds. But more important than this is the ability of the direct mode screen to redirect output to the AMOS screen above it (as normal) or to the Direct mode window. This means if you've killed the screen, you can still type files to the direct mode window. Or you can list directories to the direct window to save time and make them easier to read. The direct mode screen has a number of its own buttons for the creation of bank lists etc just like the Function key shortcuts in the old AMOS.

The File Selector

One of the enhancements which really makes a big difference is the file selector, which has been enhanced beyond recognition. The new selector is faster, easier to use and a lot better looking too. Just like before, if there isn't enough memory for the file requester then you simply get a single line input bar.

The file list has a slider bar and two buttons down the side, allowing you to pull the bar about with the mouse or click on the two arrows to scroll through the list. The buttons are for OK, Cancel, Parent, Devices, Assigns, Sort, Sizes, Get Dir, and Store. The store button stores up to 10 directories in memory, and this is useful if you have a lot of partitions and want to scan through them quickly.

The selector can be moved around anywhere on the screen simply by dragging it with the mouse.

Another very handy feature is the fact that AMOS prompts you every 30 minutes to save your program, although this can be turned off, I recommend you leave it be! Protext has this feature and many's the time when a few moments after it's made me save the computer has gone down for some reason and I would have lost everything. Autosave is a good thing, capital G, capital T.

Figure 22.5. The AMOS Pro File Selector.

Pull Down Menus

The menus on AMOS Pro take over from the buttons on the old AMOS classic. From the menus you can take a look at loaded extensions, load accessories, run programs, save them, and even check them for compatibility with AMOS 1.3!

This function does a scan of your program and points out if your program will work under the old system, a good idea if you intend releasing your program into the Public Domain. The function obviously tests for any new commands which have been used, and any memory banks above the number 16 allowable in the old system. Then you get a message telling you if the program is 1.3 friendly or not. The program can also save the programs as 1.3 or Pro. Each files has its own type of header, and the Amiga knows which files are compatible with which program by the name in the header. AMOS Pro can save both types of file, to ensure full retro compatibility.

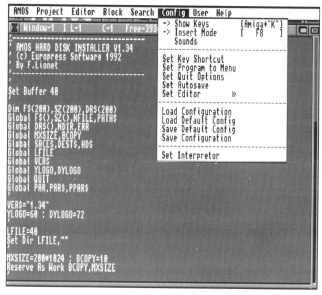

Figure 22.6. Menus are fully implemented in AMOS Pro, including a Config menu.

Macros

The new macro system is really very good indeed. This enables you to store lists of commands to the editor or any facet of AMOS Pro, and repeat that string of moves or commands at the touch of a button. For example you could write a macro which goes through a program and strips out all Rem statements, or a macro which adds an often used line of code. Anything you can do to the editor you can do automatically with macros.

User Menu

Finally, from my point of view, there is the user menu, which lets you insert a program of your own making into the menus of the editor. If you have a favourite sprite editor (SpriteX 2 of course) you can simply add it to the user menu and access it simply and quickly from that menu rather than adding it as an accessory. Accessories also work differently accessing the current program directly. To add a program to the menu you simply use Add Option from the User menu and the dialogue box lets you type in the name of your program. The user menu allows you up to 20 external programs which can be accessed through the menu. These can be anything utilities or even simple games to help relieve a bit of the old hacking tension. Twenty hours at the keyboard every day requires a little bit of a rest every once in a while, you know. All work and no play makes Jack a dull boy. These are my excuses for playing games on my machine, but you can use them if you like!

What Do I Think?

Obviously there's a lot more to AMOS Pro than this, and the evidence of this is the 600 page manual that comes with the package. I'm torn between allegiance to AMOS original version and a nice warm glow of novelty for the new version. I like the AMOS Professional Editor that's for sure, but liking it means I have to spend the next six months of my life learning all the new functions and taking on board all the new concepts that a new language entails. But the beauty of it is that I don't have to learn from scratch. AMOS itself hasn't changed, it's just been added to. The best extended BASIC of all time has itself been extended, which I suppose is only natural.

AMOS Professional is bigger, meatier and more powerful than any other programming language on the Amiga. And this power is not defined in it's efficient code and slim program size. No, the power is the power to grab a person who's barely typed in a few lines of BASIC, and turn them into someone who can produce programs of startling quality almost overnight. That is the best application of computer power that I can think of.

23:
Where to from Here?

Now you've read this book and worked through the examples, what can you do now? Obviously making your own programs based on the examples in this book is the first step to take, but more developments are appearing every day: new extensions, new techniques for optimising AMOS code, and all manner of things like this.

As a *for instance*, these days AMAL is put to use fairly infrequently for any task apart from simple animation, as it has limitations, especially when you intend to compile your programs. Obviously if your programs contain no animation and are not games, you will never use AMAL. This is something that couldn't be predicted when AMAL was introduced, but this is the trend looking at the kind of programs I'm getting through from the country's AMOS programmers and gurus. This is just one example, and there are many more things you need to know about the state of AMOS today.

Whereas many recent AMOS books have been out of date before they even come out, this book is as up to date as it could be. It was written very rapidly and updated all the way along so everything I've said is state of the art, but only for now. What you really need is a really good source of news and updates every once in a while, and one of the best sources of really up to date information is the AMOS Club.

The AMOS Club

The AMOS Club has been going ever since AMOS was created, and they are also programmers of AMOS extensions and technical supporters of the program. They produce a regular newsletter and disk containing all you need to know about the best in current AMOS thinking, and if you have a question about AMOS then joining the AMOS Club is the way you go about solving it.

The AMOS Club is also the home of Shadow Software, an AMOS based software company run by Aaron Fothergill, the author of CText, SpriteX, and TOME. Support for these programs is obviously very up to date to all AMOS Club members, and you are also kept abreast of any future programs which Shadow Software are working on. Basically if you really want to know what is happening with AMOS, you need to talk to the AMOS Club.

Totally AMOS

There's a new disk magazine in town, and this time it's totally dedicated to AMOS. The Totally AMOS disk magazine is produced by AMOS gurus Len and Anne Tucker and this is the first and indeed only AMOS magazine on disk. This first edition, number 0, was distributed via the Public Domain so that everyone could see what TA is doing. The magazine is organised and programmed using AMOS, and the articles and pieces of code/art/music are spooled together using a specially written reader program, which gives you access to all areas of the magazine using a nice original hypertext type format. You can read the articles, play music, look at nice graphics and animations, simply by clicking the mouse.

As a magazine TA is being aimed mostly at the beginners end of things, although there are enough skilled contributors to the mag to make it interesting for everyone whatever the level. There are articles from many well known names on the AMOS scene: Sandra Sharkey has written articles about Licenseware in her column *Sandra's Space*, and future issues will include contributions from AMOS heads like Peter Hickman, Aaron Fothergill, and of course the readers as well. There are articles on programming, reviews of programs, hints & tips, for sale, program routines, graphics, music files, sound samples, graphics, all manner of good things, and all on disk too!

AMOS Columns

As well as the AMOS magazines, there are a few AMOS columns in a number of the popular Amiga magazines, and obviously I would tell you that my own in Amiga Computing is the best. It's more tutorial based than the others, and it also has the benefit of having the programs on disk.

That bit of outrageous ego massage aside, there are similar columns in other magazines like Amiga Shopper, Amiga User International and CU Amiga. Check out the columns for tutorials, up to date news and information on everything AMOS.

Contacts

AMOS The Creator, AMOS Compiler, Easy AMOS and AMOS 3-D can be obtained from your local stockist or from:

Europress Software
Europa House
Adlington Park
Macclesfield
SK10 4NP

Tel: (0625) 859333

Details about the AMOS Club are available from:

The AMOS Club
1 Lower Moor
Whiddon Valley
Barnstaple
North Devon
EX32 8NW

Totally AMOS is available from:

Totally AMOS
1 Penmynydd Road
Penlan
Swansea
SA5 7EH.

AMOS licenseware can be obtained from:

Deja Vu Software
7 Holling Brook
Beech Hill
Wigan
WN6 7SG.

Tel: (0942) 495261

AMOS PD can be obtained from:

AMOS PD Library
1 Penmynydd Road
Penlan
Swansea
SA5 7EH.

17 Bit Software
PO Box 97,
Wakefield,
WF1 1XX.

Tel: (0924) 366982

A:
AMOS
Error
Messages

Sometimes you'll get an error message in AMOS. Usually it's just that you've forgotten to type something in, or AMOS can't figure out what it is you are trying to do. AMOS is a fairly forgiving language on the whole, as you know, for example when you type in a load of rubbish like this:

screenopen1,320,200,16,lowres

AMOS will *automagically* tidy it up to read:

Screen Open 1,320,200,16,Lowres

so a lot of problems are nipped in the bud when you type the commands in at first. But this smart sensing of commands sometimes leads to problems in itself. If the command you type in turns up in capital letters instead of having a leading capital and then lower case like all AMOS commands, that is to say:

THIS

instead of:

This

AMOS has interpreted the word as a label rather than a command. There are a few potential reasons for this. Either you're using the command in the wrong way or you've typed it incorrectly. Or perhaps you don't have the appropriate extension installed, if for example the command you typed is for a particular extension like CText.

But sometimes you get an error (you know how it is) and you just can't make the thing go away. What do you do? Turn to this appendix of course.

Most of the messages are pretty much descriptive in themselves, but here I've just explained basically what it means in English and given a suggestion about why it happened and what you can do about it.

Note: most of the references to disks in AMOS are spelled *disc.* I always use the spelling *disk,* to distinguish a floppy disk from a Compact Disc. I've left the spellings of error messages as is, but in my definitions a disk is a disk.

AMOS Error Messages

256 characters for a wave

You've tried to define a WAVE and you've either fed the command too few or too many numbers. Look at your definition and see where the numbers are going.

Address error

An address used in a DOKE, DEEK, LOKE or LEEK command is wrong. Check your data.

Animation string too long

Your AMAL program on a particular channel is more than 65536 bytes. Split the AMAL program into two programs and run on different channels.

Array already dimensioned

A DIM command is trying to dimension an array which you've already opened. Perhaps the loop in your program is going back too far towards the start of the program, and perhaps you ought to move it to miss the DIM.

Autotest already opened

You've tried to run Autotest again, so either you've looped back to the original Autotest command or you've put it in twice.

BAD IFF format

That IFF file is either corrupted or not in a format that AMOS can understand. IFF ILBM images are the only kind of IFF file that AMOS likes to load.

Bad structure

You've not nested your loops together properly. FOR NEXT, or DO LOOPs must always be one inside the other, so you can't do this:

```
Do
For I=1 To 10
Loop
Next I
```

Check your loops to see which ones are crossed.

Bank already reserved

Clearly you've tried to reserve a bank which is already reserved. Banks 1-4 are usually already taken with the music and graphics for your program, for example.

Bank not reserved

You tried to access a bank which hasn't been created with the RESERVE command. Also happens if you try to use a bank like Icon or Sprite banks which have nothing in them.

Block not found

This block has not been created with GET BLOCK.

Bob not defined

You have tried to use a Bob which has not been defined at any point.

Bordered windows not on edge of screen

You have tried to position a window right next to the edge of the screen. Windows need eight pixels space for their borders.

Bottom of text

In the editor you are pushing the cursor against the bottom of the window and there's no more code to look at.

Can't fit picture into current screen

You've tried to load an IFF picture to a screen which isn't the same format. Tag a ,n (where n is a new screen number 0-7) to the command and AMOS will open an appropriately sized screen.

Can't fit program into editor buffer

The space allocated for source code in the editor is set to a certain value. If a program is loaded which is bigger than the editor buffer you have to increase the buffer size in the Config.AMOS file.

Can't open narrator

The device governing speech production on the Amiga isn't present or cannot be found for some reason. Check the boot disk to see if the narrator.device is in the devs directory.

Can't resume to a label

You can't use the RESUME label in an error procedure.

Can't set dual playfield

You've tried to employ dual playfield mode with a pair of screens which are not appropriate to that mode. Look more carefully at the instructions in the AMOS manual about dual playfield.

Copper list too long

The normal sized copper list is 12K, and you've made a bigger list than that. You can expand it using the Config.AMOS accessory.

Copper not disabled

Before using COP MOVE or COP SWAP you must turn off the Copper with COPPER OFF.

DATA must start at the beginning of a line

Any DATA statements you have in your program must be the first text on any program line, excluding labels.

Device not available

You have tried to refer to a device (disk or other logical device name) which isn't currently mounted. Is the disk in the drive?

Directory not empty

You have tried to erase or KILL a directory which is not empty.

Directory not found

The directory you have asked for isn't anywhere to be found. Is the disk in the drive? Have you typed the name of the directory incorrectly?

Disc full

Yep, you can't fit anything else on this disk. Either erase something from the disk or format a fresh one.

Disc is not validated

Some kind of error has corrupted the data temporarily on this disk, and the disk-validater can't get to it or isn't on the boot disk for some reason.

Disc is write protected

Adjust the little tab in the corner of the disk and you can write to it. Or perhaps you write protected the disk for a reason? Check which disk you are writing to, it might be important.

Division by zero

Divide by zero? That's a mathematical no-no. One of your variables has dropped unexpectedly below zero so check your loops.

DO without LOOP

You forgot to type a LOOP command at the end to seal up your loop.

ELSE without ENDIF

Another loop which isn't closed.

ELSE without IF

Another loop which isn't closed.

End of file

A file ended before expected during a disk operation, a situation you can test for in your programs using EOF function.

End of program

This is the message you get if your program finishes, that is to say the last instruction is executed and the program comes to a close.

ENDIF without IF

Another loop which isn't closed.

Error not resumed

The program has exited without resetting the error with RESUME.

Error procedure must RESUME to end

You must not exit from an error with END PROC, you must reset the error with RESUME.

Extension not loaded

The command you've used is only available with a certain AMOS extension installed. CText, AMOS 3D, AMOS Compiler, TOME, all need to be installed before the commands can be used.

File already exists

If you try to rename a file on disk to a name which already exists on the disk you'll get this message. Save the file as TEMPORARY or something like that, and then get back to AmigaDOS and sort out the file names.

File already opened

You are using OPEN or APPEND on a file which has already been opened.

File format not recognised

This happens when you try to LOAD something which isn't an AMOS memory bank. If you are wanting to load an IFF picture use LOAD IFF.

File is protected against deletion

The protection bits have been set on this file, protecting it from deletion.

File is protected against reading

The protection bits have been set on this file, protecting it from being read. Stupid idea, but there you go!

File is write protected

The protection bits have been set on this file, protecting it from being written to.

File not found

The file you've asked for cannot be found on the current path. Either the disk with the file in it isn't mounted or the path you specified is wrong. Check it.

File not opened

You've tried to action a file or change a file which hasn't yet been opened.

File type mismatch

A command has been used which is not allowed for the file you've specified. Check the type of file you are working on and look up which commands are appropriate to work with it.

Flash declaration error

The animation for the FLASH command is wrong. Check the values and redefine.

Fonts not examined

Before you use the SET FONT command you must first use GET FONTS, GET ROM FONTS or GET DISC FONTS.

FOR without matching NEXT

You have constructed a loop containing a FOR but not a NEXT.

I/O Error

One of the files you are trying to use is corrupted for some reason. Check the file and if necessary use another copy of it. You may be able to salvage some files using a PD program called DiskSalv.

Icon not defined

The Icon you are trying to use is not in the current Icon bank (usually bank 2). Either you have the wrong Icon bank loaded, or you've moved it to another location.

IF without ENDIF

An IF ENDIF loop in your program has no terminating ENDIF.

IFF compression not recognised

The form of compression used on this file is non-standard. Load it into the program in which it was created and save it as a standard IFF file. If you can't do that then load the file into the program and grab it with either a software screen grabber like ScreenX or a hardware device like Action Replay.

Illegal block parameters

You have made a mistake with the figures you've fed to a PUT BLOCK or GET BLOCK command. Check them, and whichever variable is responsible.

Illegal copper parameter

The values in a COP MOVE or COP MOVEL are out of the range of the command. Check them and retype.

Illegal file name

You have tried to use a filename which is not legal in AmigaDOS. Try another one, and check you AmigaDOS guide for details about proper filenames.

Illegal function call

A popular error this one. Basically if you put too few or too many parameters into an AMOS command, you'll get this message. Check the manual for the correct number of parameters for the command.

Illegal instruction during autotest

You've used a regular AMAL command in an Autotest, probably you've placed your brackets wrongly.

Illegal number of colours

You've selected the wrong amount of colours when opening a screen. Remember that you can use up to 4096 in HAM, 32 in Lowres, 16 in Hires and Laced, and only 2-4 in some of the new Super-Hires and productivity modes which aren't quite implemented yet!

Illegal number of parameters

You've fed the wrong number of parameters to a function or procedure. Check any variables you might be running to see what values they're holding. You might be going around a loop one too many times.

Illegal screen parameter

A screen size has been defined which is outside the minimum or maximum allowed. Check your SCREEN OPEN command for size. The minimum is 32x8 and the maximum is governed by the amount of memory you have.

Illegal window parameter

You've fed the wrong numbers to a window command. Check your loops and variables to see if you're accidentally looping too much or sending the wrong variables to the wrong command.

Input too long

An input string is too long, over 1000 characters.

Instruction only valid in autotest

Direct or Exit are only valid inside AMAL as part of an Autotest routine.

Jump to/within autotest in animation string

Your AMAL program has jumped into an Autotest routine, which isn't allowed. Autotests shouldn't be connected to your main AMAL programs.

Label already defined in animation string

You've accidentally defined the same label twice in an AMAL program. Not to be confused with the following case.

Label defined twice

Different from the last error. You've accidentally defined the same label twice in an AMOS program.

Label not defined in animation string

In order to use a label you first have to define it. This is the AMAL version of the error.

Label not defined

The label you have used has not been defined. Either you typed it in wrongly or you forgot to create the label. This is the AMOS version of the error.

Line too long

The editor can only handle lines of 255 characters in length.

LOOP without DO

The reverse of the DO without LOOP error. You've put a LOOP in the program with no DO to close the loop.

Menu item not defined

The menu you've chosen has not been defined with MENU$.

Menu not opened

You called a menu with MENU ON, but no menu exists. You need to define a menu with MENU$ or MAKE MENU BANK.

Music bank not defined

You've tried to access a music bank which is empty. Either the music is in another bank or you've forgotten to load the bank.

Music bank not found

The music can't be played with MUSIC because you have no tunes in the banks.

NEXT without FOR

Like FOR without NEXT, except this time you've forgotten to put a FOR at the beginning of the loop.

Next without For in animation string

Same as the last error, only this time you've forgotten to put a FOR before a NEXT in an AMAL program.

No data after this label

The RESTORE command has tried to get data from a set of lines which don't contain DATA statements.

No disc in drive

Either the disk in question isn't mounted in a drive or you didn't wait a few seconds for the disk to be recognised. Try again now the disk has settled down.

No errors

This is not so much an error message as an alert. You test your program and this is usually the result unless you get an error. Mind you, simply just because there is no error of syntax doesn't mean the program will work, you have to find the bugs and fix them yourself. Sorry about that.

No jumps allowed into the middle of a loop

You can't jump into the middle of loop, using for example a GOSUB or GOTO.

No ON ERROR PROC before this instruction

You can only use RESUME LABEL after an ON ERROR PROC.

No programs below current program

The program you are running is not installed as an accessory, and you've attempted to use BGRAB. Reload the program as an Acc.

No THEN in a structured test

IF but no THEN in a structured test. Similar problem to other loop errors. Check your structure.

No zone defined

You've tried to act upon a Zone which has not been defined. Define it properly and try again.

Non dimensioned array

A variable is either wrongly typed to look a bit like an array, or you've forgotten to dimension the array in question.

Not a packed bitmap

You've tried to unpack a bitmap file to a screen and the file you are trying to unpack isn't in a packed bitmap format.

Not a packed screen

The data you are trying to unpack is not a packed screen format.

Not a procedure

You've tried to UNFOLD a procedure but the cursor isn't on a procedure. Reposition the cursor and try again. Either that or the procedure is locked!

Not an AmigaDOS disc

The disk you have tried to access is either corrupted or not an Amiga disk.

Not enough loops to exit

The loop count in an EXIT or EXIT IF loop is greater than the number of active loops in the program.

Not found

The search you just carried out did not find the characters you specified. Either they aren't there or you need to be more specific. Have you set upper and lower case?

Not marked

You can't move to a mark until you've set some markers.

Out of buffer space

You've run out of space in the editor. Save your program, and use S.BUFFER in the Search menu.

Out of data

The READ command has run out of bits of DATA to read. Count the amount of data you have in the DATA statement, and start again.

Out of memory

Just what it says. You haven't got enough memory to do what you're doing, loading big pictures in Hires Lace, whatever. Go and buy some more memory or run a smaller program. You can CLOSE WORKBENCH, or CLOSE EDITOR to save a good bit of space. During a test the AMOS interpreter may run out of variable space.

Out of stack space

This error is due to nesting too many PROCs together. Spread them out a bit and it should go away. You'll have to rethink the structure of your program.

Out of variable space

The variable buffer is set to 8K by default, and if you get this error you need to use SET BUFFER to increase it.

Overflow

A calculation has exceeded the maximum size of a variable. Check the calculation to see how high it's going and why.

POP without GOSUB

POP can only be used to exit from a routine entered by GOSUB. To exit from a PROC use the POP PROC command.

Procedure not closed

You've created a PROC but not terminated it with END PROC.

Procedure not opened

You've used END PROC but not opened the PROC with a PROCEDURE command.

Procedure's limits must be alone on a line

You can't have anything else on the line. Break it up.

Program interrupted

This is the message you get when you end a program with a BREAK or <Ctrl-C>.

Program not found

The program you've tried to run with PRUN has not been loaded with LOAD OTHER.

Rainbow not defined

Before you use RAINBOW you must first use SET RAINBOW to define the rainbow.

REPEAT without matching UNTIL

A loop error with a REPEAT at the start of your routine but no corresponding UNTIL.

Resume label not defined

You have tried to RESUME to a label that doesn't exist.

Resume without error

You can't use RESUME without an error. That's to say you can't fake an error with it, one has to have actually happened.

RETURN without GOSUB

You've somehow ended up at a RETURN without having got there with a GOSUB. Check back and see what's happened to your GOSUB and you'll probably find you either forgot to put it in or you deleted it and forgot to delete the RETURN.

Sample bank not defined

You can't play a sample unless it exists in the sample bank.

Sample bank not found

There is no sample bank in memory.

Screen already in double buffering

You've clearly tried to set up DOUBLE BUFFER twice for some reason. Perhaps a loop has sent you around to the same command twice.

Screen not in dual playfield mode

The DUAL PRIORITY command can only be used once the screen is in DUAL PLAYFIELD mode.

Screen not opened

You can only go to a screen and do something with it if it has actually been opened with SCREEN OPEN.

Screens can't be ANIMated

You can move or scroll screens but you can't animate them with AMAL.

Scrolling zone not defined

Before using SCROLL, you must first define the area you wish to scroll with SET SCROLL.

Shared must be alone on a line

Shared variable definitions must be on a line on their own.

Shift declaration error

This error tells you there has been a mistake with the SHIFT UP or SHIFT DOWN statements.

Sprite error

You've fed the wrong figures into a sprite definition.

String too long

You have exceeded the limits for the length of a string which is 65000.

Syntax error in animation string

Your AMAL program has a syntax error.

Syntax Error

There is a syntax error in your program. The command specified is not an AMOS keyword or you've used the wrong number or type of parameters.

This array is not defined in the main program

The array in the procedure has not been dimensioned in the main body of the program.

This instruction must be used within a procedure

The SHARED command can only be used inside a procedure definition.

This variable is already defined as SHARED

You have tried to define a variable as shared twice.

This window has no border

You have tried to employ the BORDER command on a window which has no border.

Too many colours in flash

The maximum number of colours in a flash command is 16.

Too many direct mode variables

Direct mode allows you to create up to 64 variables, but this is restricted if memory is low.

Top of text

In the editor you are pushing the cursor against the top of the window and there's no more code to look at.

Type mismatch

The wrong kind of data has been assigned to a variable, for example a string has been assigned to a variable lacking the $ symbol.

Undefined label

You've tried to go to a label which does not exist. In order to move to a label you must first create it.

Undefined procedure

You've tried to use a procedure which has not been defined.

UNTIL without REPEAT

Another loop error, this time you've left off the REPEAT or deleted it in error.

Use empty brackets when defining a shared array

The definition of a shared array should be followed by a pair of empty brackets.

Valid screen numbers range from 0 to 7

You've tried to open a screen with a number greater than 7.

Variable buffer can't be changed in the middle of a program

I think that says it all. Why aren't AmigaDOS errors that descriptive?

Variable buffer too small

Use the SET BUFFER command to alter the amount of variable space.

Variable name buffer too small

Use Config.AMOS to change this.

Wave 0 and 1 are reserved

These two waves are reserved by AMOS for the BELL and NOISE commands and cannot be changed.

WEND without WHILE

Loop error. You've added a WEND to your program without a WHILE to start it off.

What block?

You've tried to perform some kind of block operation and there is no marked block.

WHILE without matching WEND

Loop error. You've got a WHILE in your program but have not closed the loop with WEND.

Window already opened

You've tried to open a window which is already open.

Window not opened

You've tried to do something to a window which isn't open or hasn't been defined.

Window too large

The window size you've specified is too large for the current screen, and this isn't allowed.

Window too small

The current window is too small. The smallest size you can define a window to is 3x3.

B:
Some
Useful
Programs

This appendix is all about programs and routines, and also some hints and tips to keep get you back on the road when something's going wrong and you can't figure it all out. It's a bit of a grab bag, but then I think that makes it more fun, don't you? These programs are some of my own work, and part unattributed guff off bulletin boards, and part code that people have sent me for publication in my AMOS columns which never made it in full or even at all. My thanks to all the contributors who ever sent me programs to print, and I'm only sorry I can't print them all. Especially thanks to the likes of Steve Bennett for his Lazerzone game, which although very good was very long, even for inclusion here. People produce some very nice stuff on AMOS these days. If you'd like to submit super programs for the next edition of this book, why not send mail to me at Bruce Smith Books?

How about this neat routine for getting a vertically scrolling centred text? The text in the DATA statements is centred and scrolled up the screen, and it's also faded in and out at the top and bottom by a Rainbow.

```
Rem * Vertscroll.AMOS *
Rem
Rainbow Del : Auto View Off : Hide
Restore TEKST : Read N : Dim TE$(N)
For X=1 To N : Read TE$(X) : Next
'
Screen Open 0,640,N*8+256,2,Hires : Curs Off : Cls 0
Colour 0,$0 : Colour 1,$0
SPEED=0
'
For I=1 To N : Centre TE$(I) : Print : Next
Set Rainbow 0,1,3000,"(16,1,16)","(16,1,16)","(16,1,16)"
EFX
Rainbow 0,,0,256
Screen Display 0,128,300,320,255
Auto View On
'
Repeat
   Screen Display 0,,280,,
   Screen Offset 0,0,0
   For Y=280 To 40 Step -1
      If SPEED>0 Then Wait SPEED
      Wait Vbl
      Screen Display 0,128,Y,320,258
   Next
   For Y=0 To N*8
      If SPEED>0 Then Wait SPEED
      Screen Offset 0,0,Y
      Wait Vbl
   Next
   Wait 100
Until Inkey$<>""
End
```

```
TEKST:
Data 64-36
Data "-ooOOOoo--"
Data ""
Data "Hello there!"
Data ""
Data "Welcome to the Vertscroller"
Data ""
Data "Specially made by KV"
Data ""
Data "and freshly baked by Phil Snout."
Data ""
Data "AMOS allows you to do many things..."
Data ""
Data "...and this is one of them!"
Data ""
Data "And using only simple AMOS Basic instructions."
Data ""
Data "-oO*Oo-"
Data ""
Data "Original code by KV                    "
Data "   '92 version by Phil South           "
Data "       Produced by Bruce Smith         "
Data ""
Data "That's all we have time for now. See you later..."
Data ""
Data "Okie dokie artichokie!"
Data ""
Data "-oOo-"
Data "-o-"
Procedure EFX
   C=0
   For L=0 To 127 Step 8
```

```
            For X=0 To 7
                Rain(0,L+X)=C
            Next
            C=C+$111
        Next
        C=$FFF
        For L=128 To 255 Step 8
            For X=0 To 20
                Rain(0,L+X)=C
            Next
            C=C-$111
        Next
    End Proc
```

AMOS has the remarkable ability to store items of code (like sounds and screens and music) as part of the AMOS program itself, so rather than loading in IFF sounds or pictures you can load and save them as special format .abk files, and this is an especially good method for using IFF screens in your own programs. But the screens have to be packed with the SPACK command, and this means writing your own program to do this. Yes, packing and unpacking screens can be such a bore, so why not use this utility program to take all the slog out of it? Why not, indeed.

```
Rem * Spack me.AMOS *
Rem
Screen Open 0,320,16,2,Lowres
Curs Off
Flash Off
Colour 1,$FF
Screen Display 0,,40,,8
    '
TEN:
Screen Open 1,320,200,2,Lowres : Screen Hide 1
    '
TWENTY:
```

```
F$=Fsel$("","","Load IFF Picture To SPACK") : If F$=""
Then Goto TWENTY

If Exist(F$) Then Screen 0 : Centre "Loading IFF Picture"
: Print : Load Iff F$,1 : Else Goto TWENTY

Screen 0 : Centre "Spacking Current Picture..." : Print :
Spack 1 To 6 : Screen Close 1

'

THIRTY:

F$=Fsel$("","","Save Spacked Bank") : If F$="" Then Goto
THIRTY

Screen 0 : Centre "Saving Spack bank to disk" : Print :
Save F$,6 : Erase 6 : Centre "Press Key To Continue..." :
Print : Wait Key : Goto TEN
```

Then all you have to do is load thc .abk bank in direct mode, and the screen will be in a memory bank in the AMOS program ready for you to unpack to the screen of your choice. Simple and yet very effective.

In the AMOS manual it tells you that LLIST will give you a hard copy of the program currently in memory. This turns out not to be the case, so how can you get a hard copy of your programs, for debugging? Well, first mark the whole program text with the <Ctrl-A> short-cut keystroke, then hit <Ctrl-F10> to print your program out to your connected Prefs printer.

If you're directing your own science fiction movie (and why not? Steven Spielberg had to start somewhere) some special effects are very easy to do. Like this one, which does a fair impression of a radar screen, with the sweeping green scan line rotating around the screen. The program keeps going until you press a mouse button. Can you alter the program to give an occasional green trace which fades after being revealed by the scan line? Of course you can.

```
Rem * RadarLove.AMOS *

Rem

Degree

Screen Open 0,320,256,2,Lowres : Curs Off : Colour 1,$F0
: Colour 0,0 : Ink 1 : Cls 0

Double Buffer : Autoback 0

D=180

S=3

Repeat
```

```
       For ANGLE=359 To 0 Step -S
          XP=D*Sin(ANGLE)
          YP=D*Cos(ANGLE)
          Cls
          Draw 160,128 To 160+XP,128+YP
          Screen Swap : Wait Vbl
       Next
    Until Mouse Key
```

There are some built-in patterns in AMOS, which can enhance your programs if used properly. This program helps you to try out the pattern types, and lets you display them in all manner of different colour combinations. You are prompted at all stages of the operation, so no further explanation is necessary. Can you alter the program to display a pattern and let you try different colours on the pattern more interactively than this? All you need is an extra routine and a couple more keys to stab.

```
Rem * GeneralPattern.AMOS *
Rem
Screen Open 2,350,350,32,Lowres
Colour 0,$0 : Colour 1,$FFF : Colour 2,$F
Pen 0 : Paper 1
Curs Off : Flash Off
ST:
Cls 1
Locate 2,2 : Print Space$(30)
Locate 2,2 : Input "Select Pattern 0 to 34 ";P$
P=Val(P$)
Locate 27,3 : Print "Pattern ";P
Locate 2,2 : Print Space$(30)
Locate 2,2 : Input "Enter colour 0 to 31 ";C$
C=Val(C$)
Locate 27,5 : Print "Colour ";C
Ink C : Box 50,50 To 200,200
Locate 2,2 : Print Space$(30)
```

```
Locate 2,2 : Input "Ink ";I$
I=Val(I$)
Locate 27,7 : Print "Ink ";I
Locate 2,2 : Print Space$(30)
Locate 2,2 : Input "Paper ";O$
O=Val(O$)
Locate 27,9 : Print "Paper ";O
Locate 2,2 : Print Space$(30)
Locate 2,2 : Input "Border ";B$
B=Val(B$)
Locate 27,11 : Print "Border ";B
Ink I,0,B
Set Pattern P : Set Paint 1
Bar 50,50 To 200,200
Locate 2,28 : Input "Press Return to Continue or E to
Exit";A$
If A$="E" Then Cls 0 : Edit
If A$="e" Then Cls 0 : Edit
Goto ST
```

This is a simple but effective colour selector program which appears on the current screen after saving its background colour. It waits for you to select a colour and returns the colour's number as a parameter. Original program written by Gary Fearn.

```
Rem * ColourSelect.AMOS *
Rem
Flash Off : Curs Off
RGBWINDOW[120,20,12]
_COL=Param
Print " You have selected colour ";
Pen _COL
Print _COL
Wait Key
Edit
'
```

```
Procedure RGBWINDOW[X,Y,SIZE]

   NCOLS=Screen Colour

   Get Cblock 1,X-10,Y-
10,X+(SIZE*2)+10,Y+(SIZE*NCOLS/2)+10

   Bar X-8,Y-8 To X+(SIZE*2)+8,Y+(SIZE*NCOLS/2)+8

   Reserve Zone NCOLS+1

   For B=0 To NCOLS/2 Step NCOLS/2

      For A=0 To(NCOLS/2)-1

         Ink A+B : Bar X,Y To X+SIZE,Y+SIZE

         Set Zone A+B+1,X,Y To X+SIZE,Y+SIZE

         Add Y,SIZE

      Next A

      Add X,SIZE

      Add Y,-(SIZE*(NCOLS/2))

   Next B

AGAIN:

   While M=0

      X=Mouse Zone

      M=Mouse Key

   Wend

   If X=0 Then Goto AGAIN

   Put Cblock 1

   Reset Zone

   RGB=X-1 : Rem RGB = selected colour

End Proc[RGB]
```

You'll often find that you need a Bob or Sprite to appear at a specific location. Also since you sometimes need to flash or change colours, you need to know which colour is at which location in the current palette. For this reason Terry Aston wrote this short tool, which loads up the background scene, and picks up your Bob/Sprite so you can position it exactly on the screen while showing the hardware coords. Click the Sprite in place, and it gives you the screen coords. Now you can use the two menus to select the screen and Sprite palettes. Highlight the colour you want to alter and the program prints the hex number of the colour to the screen. Now you have a record of all you need. To change the sprite you position, simply alter the Sprite number in the XMouse/YMouse Do Loop.

This is a very neat and quick programming utility, which I suppose you could program as an accessory, if you really wanted to. What about writing a way of saving the data in a meaningful form to a file or the printer? Any ideas how that could be done? Thanks anyway to Tony. This is an excellent example of what hackers call a *hamster*. A short program, which is neatly and logically written and which does something useful. Brilliant.

```
Rem * XSpriteYSprite.AMOS *
Rem
Cls
Erase 1
F$=Fsel$("DF0:",""," Load Background Picture ")
If F$="" Then Edit
Load Iff F$,0
'
SPR$=Fsel$("*.Abk",""," Load Related Sprite Bank ")
If SPR$="" Then Edit
Load SPR$,0
'
Get Sprite Palette
Curs Off : Paper 22 : Pen 15 : Rem - or whatever !
'
Locate 0,0 : Print " X Hard is  ";
Locate 0,1 : Print " Y Hard is  ";
'
Do
Sprite 9,X Mouse,Y Mouse,1
Locate 20,0 : Print X Sprite(9);"   ";
Locate 20,1 : Print Y Sprite(9);"   ";
If Mouse Key=1 Then Goto LABEL
Loop
'
```

```
LABEL:
Locate 28,4 : Print "Sprite";
Locate 28,5 : Print "Register";
For C=16 To 31
Locate 28,C-9
Print Hex$(Colour(C),3)
Next C
'

Locate 0,4 : Print "Screen";
Locate 0,5 : Print "Register";
Locate 0,7
For C=1 To 15
Print Hex$(Colour(C),3)
Next C
'

Locate 0,0 : Print " X Screen is  ";
Locate 0,1 : Print " Y Screen is  ";
'

Locate 25,0 : Print X Screen(1);"  ";
Locate 25,1 : Print Y Screen(1);"  ";
'

Menu$(1)="    0 to 15 "
Menu$(2)="              16 to 31 "
'

For D=1 To 15
Menu$(1,D)="(IN 1,"+Str$(D)-""+")(BA 30,12)"
Menu$(1,D,1)=Hex$(Colour(D),3)
Next D
'

For C=16 To 31
Menu$(2,C)="(IN 1,"+Str$(C)-""+")(BA 30,12)"
Menu$(2,C,1)=Hex$(Colour(C),3)
Next C
```

```
'

Menu On
'

Do

If Choice

Locate 28,25 : Pen 24 : Inverse On : Print
Hex$(Colour(Choice(2)),3)

End If
'

Loop
```

Tony's excellent program gave me an idea, and so recently I whipped up this next little program to show up mouse coords. I know the thing which flummoxed me about limiting the mouse and reading the mouse over certain points on the screen was positioning. And this program enables you to do this very accurately. Load an IFF picture, preferably the one you want to locate the mouse over, and then just read the figures (and write them down) as you move the mouse over the screen.

```
Rem * MouseMeUp.AMOS *

Rem

Paper 0 : Clw

Curs Off

F$=Fsel$("*.IFF",""," Load Background IFF Pic ")

If F$="" Then Edit

Load Iff F$,0

Locate 0,0

Print "Mouse Co-ords Tool v1.1"

Locate 0,1 : Print "X=    " : Print "Y=    "

Locate 0,20 : Print "CTRL-C to stop"

Do

    Y1=Y Mouse

    X1=X Mouse

    Y1$=Str$(Y1) : X1$=Str$(X1)

    Locate 6-Len(X1$),1 : Print X1 : Locate 6-Len(Y1$),2 :
Print Y1

Loop
```

This is a replacement for the Sort routine on page 59 of the original AMOS manual. Graham Jones invented this routine as part of an excellent program he wrote called *Natcodes,* which is currently available as licenseware from Deja Vu. Natcodes takes the STD codes you would dial to get a call placed to a certain part of the country, and it tells you where that place is. In the phone book it tells you the place and then the number. This way you can type in a code you've dialled and find out where it was you were calling. This nice string sort is the part of that program of which Graham was so proud he sent it to me in isolation, and he's right, it is a very good sort.

```
Rem * Stringsort.AMOS *
Rem
Screen Open 0,640,256,4,Hires
Paper 0 : Clw
Locate 0,0
Print "This routine replaces that given in the "
Print "AMOS manual for the Sort command."
Print "It can also be modyfied to use variables."
Print
Print "<Press a key>" : Wait Key : Cls
   '
Input "Enter max No. of Array values   ";N
Print : Inc N
Dim A$(N)
P=1
Repeat
    Input "Enter string (Null to stop) ";A$(P)
    Inc P
Until A$(P-1)="" or P=N
Sort A$(0)
For I=N-(P-2) To N
    C=I-(N-P+1)
    A$(C)=A$(I)
    A$(I)=""
Next I
```

```
Cls

Print "Sorted array in ascending order." : Print

For J=1 To N

    Print A$(J)

Next J

Wait Key
```

One of the biggest criticisms of AMOS from so called *serious* programmers, is that you can't leave a blank line between sections of the program. As you know AMOS always closes up spaces automatically, and so the common solution from AMOSsers is to type a ' for a REM statement in the line. But real programmers can't cope with this. (You'd have thought they'd have better things to do than whine on about things like this!) In fact you can fit a space in an AMOS program if you really want to, and it's very simple. All you do is press the tilde key, the ~ symbol, and voila! The tilde symbol vanishes when you press Return, and the line stays blank. This doesn't affect the functioning of your programs at all, and if it keeps the serious programmers happy, it keeps me happy. Not!

You may have been browsing your AMOS manual and tried to use what it says are two useful functions, namely:

Window Font

and:

Llist

which, so the book has it, are used in AMOS. Well, if you've tried to use these commands you'll know they don't work, and there's a good reason for this. The commands aren't part of the AMOS language. The reason behind this is that the original AMOS manual was being written at the same time as the program, and the program continued to be rewritten in fact, even after the manual was finished. So perhaps these commands were intended to be in the program, but not included at the last minute. So it's not your fault that these commands don't work, they don't work on *anyone's* machine!

And finally Big Text, a large text printing program, which will print up a big scrolling text message across the screen from the text in LET$. There are ways to make this program smoother, and alter the way it prints up its text. See if you can alter the program for more impressive big text.

```
Rem * Big Text.AMOS *
Rem
LET$=" Let's hear it for AMOS!!!   "
LET$=LET$+".  It's a brilliant programming language, and
now with AMOS 3D and the Compiler..."
LET$=LET$+"  AMOS is the best program in the WORLD!!!
That's all folks.....        "
LETOFF=0
Screen Open 1,416,256,4,Lowres
Def Scroll 1,0,0 To 416,256,-58,0
'Curs Off : Flash Off
Do
_SCROLLIT
If Mouse Key=1 Then Exit
Loop
Edit
'
Procedure _SCROLLIT
   Shared LET$,LETOFF
   If LETOFF=Len(LET$) Then LETOFF=0
   Screen 0 : Locate 0,0 : Print Mid$(LET$,LETOFF+1,1)
   Zoom 0,0,0,8,8 To 1,352,0,400,256
   Screen 1
   Scroll 1
   Inc LETOFF
End Proc
```

Book Order Form

Please rush me the following *Mastering Amiga* book(s):

Mastering Amiga Beginners @ £19.95 with PD WP/Games Disk*   £.........·......

Mastering AmigaDOS Vol. One Rev Ed @ £21.95 with Disk   £.........·......

Mastering AmigaDOS Vol. Two Revised Edition @ £19.95   £.........·......

Mastering Amiga C @ £19.95 with Scripts & PD NorthC Disk   £.........·......

Mastering Amiga Printers @ £19.95 with PD Disk   £.........·......

Mastering Amiga System @ £29.95 with Programs Disk   £.........·......

Mastering Amiga Workbench 2 @ £19.95   £.........·......

Mastering Amiga Assembler with disk @ £24.95   £.........·......

Postage (International Orders Only): £.........·......

Total: £.........·......

I enclose a Cheque/Postal Order* for £   .   p.

I wish to pay by Access/Visa/Mastercard*

Card number:.. Expiry Date: ....

Name. ....

Address. ....

....

.... Post Code.....................

Contact phone number. ....

Signed ....

*Delete as appropriate.

Cheques payable to Bruce Smith Books Ltd. E&OE

Send your order to:

Bruce Smith Books Ltd, FREEPOST 242, PO Box 382, St. Albans, Herts, AL2 3BR.

Telephone: (0923) 894355 – Fax: (0923) 894366

C:
Program
Entry

You look at the program you have entered time and time again but for the life of you, you simply cannot work out what the problem is – the program simply throws up some sort of error every time you try to run it. Frustrating simply isn't the word – but this is a situation that every single programmer, beginner or experienced, has encountered and will continue to encounter for the rest of their programming life!

Jump up and down and pull what hair you may have left out by the roots but if the program won't run as expected or throws up an error, there is a mistake and you have to track it down.

Of course, as you become a more experienced programmer you will learn the various pitfalls and problems that can occur and know what to look for. This short appendix might help you along the way. Let's hope!

Entering Book Listings

OK, hands in the air. The listings given in this book (and in magazines etc) should work, certainly the ones herein because they have been lifted from the original AMOS files and inserted smack bang right into the text. That's the theory but life isn't always as it should be and the odd gremlin can creep in.

So the first thing to look for when you have entered a listing that won't work is what I would call obvious errors – for example have two lines become concatenated, ie joined together? For example, look at the program fragment below:

```
Rainbow Del : Auto View Off : Hide Restore TEKST : Read N
```

This should be:

```
Rainbow Del : Auto View Off : Hide
```

```
Restore TEKST : Read N
```

The two lines have become one and AMOS would not recognise:

```
Hide Restore TEKST
```

as a legitimate command. The converse is also true in that a line might have become split into two at a point which makes no sense to the AMOS interpreter when it tries to use it. For example:

```
Rainbow Del : Auto :
```

```
View Off : Hide
```

```
Restore TEKST : Read N
```

These examples are a bit exaggerated perhaps but they illustrate the point.

Another point to bear in mind is that listing lines are quite often much longer than the available width of the page on which they are printed – therefore wrap around will take place and this might confuse you into thinking that there are two lines when in reality there is only one. In other words you whack the Return key when there isn't the need to.

In such instances you must be guided by the style employed by the book or listing. In Mastering Amiga AMOS there is always a very clear line space between each line of listing. Look at this listing segment:

```
Screen Open 1,320,200,2,Lowres : Screen Hide 1
'
TWENTY:
F$=Fsel$("","","Load IFF Picture To SPACK") : If F$=""
Then Goto TWENTY
If Exist(F$) Then Screen 0 : Centre "Loading IFF Picture"
: Print : Load Iff F$,1 : Else Goto TWENTY
Screen 0 : Centre "Spacking Current Picture..." : Print :
Spack 1 To 6 : Screen Close 1
'
```

Although the listing takes ten lines in the book, it is in fact only seven lines in length. The first three lines are clear and obvious, but the next three lines are all too long to fit on a single line width of the printed page and therefore wrap around. However, if you examine the listing you will see that there is almost a full line space between each actual listing line and this should be your guide.

Visual Errors

Apart from the obvious errors such as the misspelling of commands and so forth the other major players under this heading are the misinterpretation of Zero and Oh, One and El and colons and semi-colons. Here is how each one appears in our printed listings:

    0   0

    1   1

    :   ;

Another character that can cause problems is the space character. Spaces are invariably important – or more specifically the lack of a space can be a problem.

The listings in this book are all produced in what is known as a mono spaced font, which means that a space will occupy the same amount of the line as an i or e. Watch out for them and treat them with respect.

Brackets can create problems – ensure you have the right number of them, ie for every left bracket there must be a matching right bracket and so forth.

D:
The ASCII
Character
Set

ASCII (an acronym for The American Standard Code for Information Interchange) consists of a set of 96 displayable and 32 non-displayable characters based on a seven bit character code. Direct ASCII code values are sometimes needed within a program, yet very few people bother to remember more than a handful of values (space, carriage return, linefeed, tab etc).

Since most programmers look up ASCII values, rather than going to the trouble of learning them parrot fashion, we thought it would be useful to include the necessary details. Hopefully we have gone one better than that because three equivalents – decimal, hexadecimal and binary – have been provided. This means, incidentally that, as well as having the ASCII data itself, you have also acquired a reasonably useful (0-127 decimal) binary-hex-decimal conversion table.

Decimal	Hex	Binary	ASCII	Decimal	Hex	Binary	ASCII
00	00	000 0000	NUL	33	21	010 0001	!
01	01	000 0001	SOH	34	22	010 0010	"
02	02	000 0010	STX	35	23	010 0011	#
03	03	000 0011	ETX	36	24	010 0100	$
04	04	000 0100	EOT	37	25	010 0101	%
05	05	000 0101	ENQ	38	26	010 0110	&
06	06	000 0110	ACK	39	27	010 0111	'
07	07	000 0111	BEL	40	28	010 1000	(
08	08	000 1000	BS	41	29	010 1001	)
09	09	000 1001	HT	42	2A	010 1010	*
10	0A	000 1010	LF	43	2B	010 1011	+
11	0B	000 1011	VT	44	2C	010 1100	,
12	0C	000 1100	FF	45	2D	010 1101	-
13	0D	000 1101	CR	46	2E	010 1110	.
14	0E	000 1110	SO	47	2F	010 1111	/
15	0F	000 1111	SI	48	30	011 0000	0
16	10	001 0000	DLE	49	31	011 0001	1
17	11	001 0001	DC1	50	32	011 0010	2
18	12	001 0010	DC2	51	33	011 0011	3
19	13	001 0011	DC3	52	34	011 0100	4
20	14	001 0100	DC4	53	35	011 0101	5
21	15	001 0101	NAK	54	36	011 0110	6
22	16	001 0110	SYN	55	37	011 0111	7
23	17	001 0111	ETB	56	38	011 1000	8
24	18	001 1000	CAN	57	39	011 1001	9
25	19	001 1001	EM	58	3A	011 1010	:
26	1A	001 1010	SUB	59	3B	011 1011	;
27	1B	001 1011	ESC	60	3C	011 1100	<
28	1C	001 1100	FS	61	3D	011 1101	=
29	1D	001 1101	GS	62	3E	011 1110	>
30	1E	001 1110	RS	63	3F	011 1111	?
31	1F	001 1111	US	64	40	100 0000	@
32	20	010 0000	SP	65	41	100 0001	A

Decimal	Hex	Binary	ASCII	Decimal	Hex	Binary	ASCII
66	42	100 0010	B	99	63	110 0011	c
67	43	100 0011	C	100	64	110 0100	d
68	44	100 0100	D	101	65	110 0101	e
69	45	100 0101	E	102	66	110 0110	f
70	46	100 0110	F	103	67	110 0111	g
71	47	100 0111	G	104	68	110 1000	h
72	48	100 1000	H	105	69	110 1001	i
73	49	100 1001	I	106	6A	110 1010	j
74	4A	100 1010	J	107	6B	110 1011	k
75	4B	100 1011	K	108	6C	110 1100	l
76	4C	100 1100	L	109	6D	110 1101	m
77	4D	100 1101	M	110	6E	110 1110	n
78	4E	100 1110	N	111	6F	110 1111	o
79	4F	100 1111	O	112	70	111 0000	p
80	50	101 0000	P	113	71	111 0001	q
81	51	101 0001	Q	114	72	111 0010	r
82	52	101 0010	R	115	73	111 0011	s
83	53	101 0011	S	116	74	111 0100	t
84	54	101 0100	T	117	75	111 0101	u
85	55	101 0101	U	118	76	111 0110	v
86	56	101 0110	V	119	77	111 0111	w
87	57	101 0111	W	120	78	111 1000	x
88	58	101 1000	X	121	79	111 1001	y
89	59	101 1001	Y	122	7A	111 1010	z
90	5A	101 1010	Z	123	7B	111 1011	{
91	5B	101 1011	[	124	7C	111 1100		
92	5C	101 1100	\	125	7D	111 1101	}
93	5D	101 1101	]	126	7E	111 1110	~
94	5E	101 1110	^	127	7F	111 1111	DEL
95	5F	101 1111	_				
96	60	110 0000	'				
97	61	110 0001	a				
98	62	110 0010	b				

E:
Mastering
Amiga
Guides

Bruce Smith Books are dedicated to producing quality Amiga publications which are both comprehensive and easy to read. Our Amiga titles are being written by some of the best known names in the marvellous world of Amiga computing. Below you will find details of eight books in the Mastering Amiga range that are currently available.

Titles Currently Available

- Mastering Amiga Beginners
- Mastering AmigaDOS Vol. 1
- Mastering AmigaDOS Vol. 2
- Mastering Amiga C
- Mastering Amiga Printers
- Mastering Amiga Workbench2
- Mastering Amiga System
- Mastering Amiga Assembler

Titles Coming Soon

- Mastering Amiga AREXX
- Amiga A600 Insider Guide

Brief details of these guides along with review segments are given below. If you would like a free copy of our catalogue *Mastering Amiga News* and to be placed on our mailing list then phone or write to the address below.

Our mailing list is used exclusively to inform readers of forthcoming Bruce Smith Books publications along with special introductory offers which normally take the form of a free software disk when ordering the publication direct from us.

Bruce Smith Books,
PO Box 382,
St. Albans, Herts, AL2 3JD
Telephone: (0923) 894355
Fax: (0923) 894366

Note that we offer a 24-hour telephone answer system so that you can place your order direct by 'phone at a time to suit yourself. When ordering by 'phone please:

- Speak clearly and slowly
- Leave your full name and full address
- Leave a day-time contact phone number
- Give your credit card number and expiry date
- Spell out any unusual names

Note that we do not charge for P&P in the UK and we endeavour to dispatch all books within 24-hours.

Buying at your Bookshop

All our books can be obtainbed via your local bookshops – this includes WH Smiths which will be keeping a stock of some of our titles – just enquire at their counter. If you wish to order via your local High Street bookshop you wil need to supply the book name, author, publisher, price and ISBN number – these are all sumarised at the very end of this Appendix.

Overseas Orders

Please add £3 per book (Europe) or £6 per book (outside Europe) to cover postage and packing. Pay by sterling cheque or by Access, Visa or Mastercard. Post, Fax or Phone your order to us.

Dealer Enquiries

Our distributor is Computer Bookshops Ltd who keep a good stock of all our titles. Call their Customer Services Department for best terms on 021-706-1188.

Compatibility

We endeavour to ensure that all *Mastering Amiga* books are fully compatible with all Amiga models and all releases of AmigaDOS and Workbench.

Mastering Amiga Beginners

The Amiga has enjoyed a phenomenal success over recent years and is now recognised as one of the most powerful and sophisticated computers available. The appeal of the Amiga along with the vast range of programs available for it has made it the ideal machine for the beginner.

If you have recently purchased an Amiga of any type, or have had one for some time but now feel you are still not getting to grips with what lies behind that keyboard then this is definitely the book for you!

Written by Phil South, recognised as one of the most prolific and knowledgeable of Amiga authors, this book will take you step by step through every aspect of its use, from disks and disk drives to AmigaDOS and the extras available to it. It does so in a logical manner, introducing items as and when they are needed so as to become a powerful torchlight through the fog of computer jargon.

This book will not make you an expert in any one particular subject but it will provide you with a solid grounding to allow you to investigate those areas which appeal to you, either on your own or with another book from the growing *Mastering Amiga* series of publications.

But you don't have to take our word for it, here's a snippet or two from a review of the book that appeared in CU Amiga under the headline *Beginners Bible*.

"...this book is both a highly readable and entertaining introduction to the Amiga.....the book gives useful hints and tips rather than detailed instruction, and this works very well.....An excellent introduction to the Amiga, and even at £20 it's an extremely worthwhile investment for the beginner."

Added to this if you order direct from us you can choose to receive a free disk of PD software. Choose from a Wordprocessor (including spell check) or a Games Compendium. State which when you order.

Mastering AmigaDOS 2

Our 700-page plus dual volume set covers all versions of AmigaDOS from 1.2, including 1.2, 1.3, 1.3.2 and 2.x. Volume One is a complete tutorial for AmigaDOS users, both beginners and experts alike. Volume Two is a detailed and comprehensive reference to all AmigaDOS commands.

Here's what the press said:

"If you're a complete beginner or unsure of a few areas, this book is an amazingly informative read." Amiga Format on Volume One

"As a reference book it's very useful. So far as I know there isn't any similar book...If you need to know how every AmigaDOS command works get this book...it is a definitive reference" Amiga Format on Volume Two.

"The Reference book that Commodore forgot to commission" Keith Pomfret of New Computer Express on Volume Two.

"The book can be strongly recommended....and even more strongly to those having difficulty getting to grips with its various commands. You won't find a better guide to, or a more useful book on, the Amiga than this" Micronet AmigaBASE.

"No other authors have investigated AmigaDOS with the thoroughness of Smith and Smiddy and every page provides useful information. Put off getting that new game, and buy this instead. You won't regret it." Micronet AmigaBASE.

And if you don't know if you need either or both books here is what Amiga Format suggested: *"If Volume 1 is so good what is the point of having Volume 2? Volume 1 is a tutorial, it teaches you how to use AmigaDOS. Volume 2 is more of a manual."*

Mastering Amiga C

C is without doubt one of the most powerful programming languages ever created, and it has a very special relationship with the Commodore Amiga. Much of the Amiga's operating system software was written using C and almost all of the Amiga technical reference books assume some proficiency in the language.

Paul Overaa has been writing about C and the Amiga for as long as the machine has been in existence. He knows the Amiga-specific pitfalls that can plague the beginner, knows how to avoid them, and above all he knows about C. Best of all he's prepared to share that experience. The result is a book which is guaranteed to get the Amiga owner programming in C as quickly and as painlessly as possible.

This introductory text assumes no prior knowledge of C and covers all the major compilers, including Lattice/SAS and Aztec. What is more it also covers NorthC – the Charityware compiler – so that anyone who is interested in learning C can do so for just a few pounds. This book assumes no prior knowledge of C and features:

- Easy to follow tutorials
- All major C compilers
- Explanations of special Amiga C features
- Amiga problem areas
- Debugging and testing

Here's what CU Amiga thought of Mastering Amiga C: *"This book has been written with the absolute novice in mind. It doesn't baffle with jargon and slang"*.

Writing in Amiga User International, Mike Nelson called Mastering Amiga C: *"Very thorough, Paul Overaa has gone to considerable lengths to keep up to date with developments the in real world of C and the ANSI Standards......this book will go a long way to help you master C on your Amiga"*.

Mastering Amiga Printers

Next to the Amiga itself, your printer is the largest and most important purchase you're likely to make. It's surprising then, that so little help is available for those about to take this step, whether it be for the first time, or for the purpose of upgrading from an old, trusted but limited model to one of today's much more versatile and complex machines. The problem of course is that you can't take one home on trial to find out what it does.

Today's printers are extremely sophisticated and complex devices, with a wide range of capabilities, so it's all too easy to make a mistake at the stage of buying if you don't know what to look for, the right questions to ask and the sort of comparisons to make between similarly priced models from different manufacturers. Since a printer is such a large investment, quite possibly more expensive than the micro itself, choosing the right type and model for your needs is doubly important, because you'll have to live with your decision for a long time.

Unfortunately for the user, neither computer nor printer manufacturers see it as their responsibility to offer guidance or assistance to users in this important purchase.

Mastering Amiga Printers fills this gap perfectly. Making no assumptions about previous printer experience, the explanations begin with the basic principles of how printers work, including a run-down of the different types most commonly used with home and business micros.

After a comprehensive grounding in the abilities and methods of the different types of printer hardware you'll then learn how to install them in the Amiga. Preference selections and printer drivers are thoroughly explained for both Workbench one and two, so you'll know not only which choices to make, but what they mean. There's also a thorough grounding in the direct use of printers from the command line, which you'll need if you want to write your own programs.

Additional chapters take a logical approach to trouble-shooting and routine maintenance, vital to the newcomer. These chapters include the sort of information and knowledge which is normally only available after long experience, the very thing the new user lacks. *Mastering Amiga Printers* is a must for every user who wants to the best out of their Amiga and its printer.

Mastering Amiga Workbench 2

The Workbench is one of the most important aspects of the Amiga, yet so few users really understand how to use it to its full potential. From it you can access virtually all of the Amiga's functions and determine how your computer will operate from the moment it is switched on. With the advent of Workbench 2, running under the much enhanced AmigaDOS 2, the options open to the Workbench users are greater than ever before.

In this book Bruce Smith explains everything you will want to know about the Workbench version 2.x,using screen illustrations throughout for ease of reference. The book is geared towards all types of users, whether you have a single floppy disk or a hard disk to operate from.

Starting from first steps the book explains the philosophy of the Workbench and how it ties in with your Amiga. It then moves on to describe the best way to perform basic housekeeping tasks such as disk copying, file transfer and how to customise your own Workbench disks for different occasions and requirements.

The author works his way through each of the menu options with full descriptions of their use, providing many hints, tips and tricks *en-route*. By this stage you will already be an accomplished Workbench user, but as the books enters its final stages you will make the transition to expert status as areas such as Preferences, Tools and Commodities are fully explained.

In effect *Mastering Amiga Workbench 2* provides you with a complete guide to your Workbench and Extras disks in an easy to read style guaranteed to upgrade you to full proficiency on your Amiga.

Mastering Amiga System

A complete tutorial to Amiga System programming with copious examples. A basic knowledge of C is required but the book begins with short examples which only later build into full-scale programs, all of which are on the accompanying disk.

In dealing with a difficult subject, the author has avoided merely duplicating standard documentation. Instead he has entered on a journey through the different aspects of the Amiga's system, finding the safest and most effective routes to practical programs. Mastering Amiga System is an invaluable purchase for the Amiga programmer who wants to master the system software. Free disk.

Mastering Amiga Assembler

Although the 68000 processor series is well-documented, the use of assembly language to write efficient code within the unique environment of the Amiga is only now explained in this *hands-on* tutorial. Working with the Amiga's custom chips and system software are only two of the areas which will be appreciated by programmers wanting to generate machine code from the popular Amiga Assemblers, all of which are supported by the many code examples in this 416 page book.

Mastering Amiga AREXX

Another massive tome from the wordprocessor of Paul Overaa – this book is a complete programming guide to the AREXX language. Packed full of examples for you to type in and try. Due for publication early 1993.

Amiga A600 Insider Guide

A perfect companion for all A600 and A600HD owners and users. This book provides you with a unique insight into the use of Workbench and AmigaDOS on all versions of the Amiga A600.

Assuming no prior knowldge it shows you how to get the very best from your machine in a friendly manner and using it's unique Insider Guide steps. Available November 1992.

Contents Lists

The pages list the chapter headings for each of our published books. This should give you a better indication as to their full content.

Mastering Amiga Beginners

Introduction, Workbench, Workbench 2, AmigaDOS, The Ram Disk, Amiga Fonts, Utility Drawers, State Your Preferences, Making Icons, Introducing AmigaBASIC, Making Your Amiga Speak, Text Editors, Sound and Graphics, Good Software Guide, Good Hardware Guide, Using Printers, Comms and Modems, Doing Business, Virus Attack, Public Domain, Emulation, introducing C, Where to from Here?, A Sort of AmiGlossary, AmigaDOS Commands, AmigaBASIC Commands, AmigaDOSError Numbers.

Mastering AmigaDOS 2 Volume One Revised Edition

Introduction, AmigaDOS and Workbench, About Directories, AmigaDOS Command, Formatting and Copying, The Shell, The RAM Disk, Wildcards and Pattern Matching, File Protection and Assigning, ED – The Screen Editor, Multi-tasking Amiga, Environmental Variables, Command Bits and Pieces, The Bootable RAM Disk, Devices, More About LIST, Introduction to Scripts, Structured AmigaDOS, Evaluating and Manipulating, Startup-sequences, AmigaDOS 1.2 Startup-sequence, AmigaDOS 1.3 Startup-sequence, AmigaDOS 2.04 Startup-sequences, Customising Disks, Practical Scripts, Scripts That Write Scripts!, Recursive Scripts, Commodities Exchange, Fountain, MEMACS, Backing Up with BRU, Multi-User Machine, Pipes, Original AmigaDOS2 Startup-sequence.

Mastering AmigaDOS 2 Volume Two

AmigaDOS Command Reference Section, ADDBUFFERS, ADDMONITOR, ALIAS, ASK, ASSIGN, AUTOPOINT, AVAIL, BINDDRIVERS, BINDMONITOR, BLANKER, BREAK, BRU, CD, CHANGETASKPRI, CLICKTOFRONT, CLOCK, CMD, COLORS, CONCLIP, COPY, CPU, DATE , DELETE, DIR, DISKCHANGE, DISKCOPY, DISKDOCTOR, DISPLAY, DPAT, ECHO, ED, EDIT, ELSE, ENDCLI, ENDSHELL, ENDIF, ENDSKIP, EVAL, EXCHANGE, EXECUTE, FAILAT, FASTMEMFIRST, FAULT, FF, FILENOTE, FIXFONTS, FKEY, FONT, FORMAT, GET, GETENV,. GRAPHICDUMP, ICONTROL, ICONX, IF, IHELP, INFO, INITPRINTER, INPUT, INSTALL, JOIN, LAB, LIST, LOADWB, LOCK, MAGTAPE, MAKEDIR, MAKELINK , MEMACS, MERGEMEM , MORE, MOUNT, NEWCLI, NEWSHELL, NOCAPSLOCK, NOFASTMEM, OVERSCAN, PALETTE, PARK, PATH, PCD, POINTER, PREFERENCES, PRINTER, PRINTERGFX, PRINTFILES, PROMPT, PROTECT, QUIT, RELABEL,REMRAD, RENAME, RESIDENT, REXXMAST, RUN, SAY, SCREENMODE, SEARCH, SERIAL, SET, SETCLOCK , SETDATE, SETENV, SETFONT, SETMAP, SETPATCH, SKIP,

SORT , SPAT, STACK, STATUS, TIME, TYPE, UNALIAS, UNSET, UNSETENV, VERSION , WAIT, WBPATTERN, WHICH, WHY, Wildcards, ;,? ,<, >, >> ,*,"",*,',CTRL+\ ,ALT+' , AmigaDOS Error Codes, The Virus Menace, The Interchange File Format, The Mountlist, Telling FIBs.

Mastering Amiga C

Introduction, Making a Start, Types, Operators and Expressions, Functions, Program Documentation and Portability, Flow Control, The C Preprocessor, Arrays and Pointers, Input and Output, Structures and Bitfields, Character Strings, Storage Classes, Data Types Revisited, Files, Special C Features, The Real Problem, Some Amiga Specifics, Resource Allocation, Intuition and the Graphics Library, Making the Most of C's Modularity, Debugging and Testing, Last Words, Glossary, Bibliography, The Lattice/SAS C Compiler, The Manx Aztec C Compiler, The NorthC Compiler, Bits and Bytes, ANSI C Summary, ASCII Character Set, Useful Programming Tools.

Mastering Amiga Printers

Consider the Printer!, Types of Printer, Connected Matters,   Initial Setting-up, Controlling Printers, Printer Commands, Graphics Commands, Printer Peculiarities, Elements of a System, Printer Installation, Printer Preferences, Printer Driver Facilities, Taking Control, Command Line Control, BASIC Control, Graphicus Horizontalis, Graphicus Verticalis, Graphics Preferences, Graphics Options, Screen Dumping, Deluxe Paint, Problems, Problems... Printer Driver Commands, Decimal-hexadecimal-binary-ASCII Conversions, Glossary.

Mastering Amiga Workbench 2

Take Off, The Workbench, Drawers and Directories, Disks and Drawers, Copying Files, The Menus, The Ram Disk, The Utilities Drawer, The Tools Drawer, The Shell, The System Drawer, Commodities Exchange, The Preferences Editors, The Recoverable Ram Disk, Icons and IconEdit, Information and Tool Types, Printer Installation, Graphics Printing, Fonts, Useful AmigaDOS, ED – The Text Editor, Customising Workbench Disks, MEmacs, Tool Types Revisited, The Virus Factor, Hard Disks, Goings On, Creating a Text File, Tool Type Summaries, File Location Guide

Mastering Amiga System

An Overview, Preliminary Style and Programming Notes, Exec Memory Management, Tasks and Processes, Lists and Nodes, Libraries, Libraries and More Libraries, Intuition's Screens and Windows, Resource Allocation, Talking to Intuition, Exec Messages and Ports, Intuition's Text, Line Drawing and Image Facilities, Intuition's Gadgets, Intuition's Menu System, Devices: An

Introduction, The Amiga's Serial Device, Interrupts: Making a Start, The Amiga's Co-Processor, Blitter First Steps, Troubleshooting Software Problems, Last Words.

Mastering Amiga Assembler

Contents, Fundamental Concepts, The 68000 Chip and its Assembly Language, Solving Simple Problems, Subroutines and Parameter Passing, Program Design Issues, Program Documentation, An Introduction to the Amiga Environment, The Amiga System Include Files, Macro Programming and its Benefits, Libraries and the Amiga, An Overview Of Some Important Rules, Some Introductory Shell/CLI Programs, Exec Messages and Ports, Making a Start With Intuition, A Complete Intuition Example, Where To Go From Here, The 68000 Instruction Set, The C Language, Library Function Tables, The 68K Assembler, Bibliography

Summary Book Details

Mastering Amiga Beginners
by Phil South
ISBN: 1-873308-03-5 – Price £19.95   320 pages. Now available.
FREE Wordprocessor or Games disk when ordered direct – please state preference.

Mastering AmigaDOS 2 Volume One – Revised Edition
by Bruce Smith and Mark Smiddy
ISBN: 1-873308-10-8 – Price £21.95   416 pages Now available.
FREE Utilities disk when ordered direct – £1.50 to cover p&p otherwise.

Mastering AmigaDOS 2 Volume Two –Revised Edition
by Bruce Smith and Mark Smiddy
Foreword by Barry Thurston, Technical Director, Commodore Business Machines (UK) Ltd.
ISBN: 1-873308-09-4 – Price £19.95   368 pages. Now Available.

Mastering Amiga C
by Paul Overaa
ISBN: 1-873308-04-6 – Price £19.95   320 pages Now available.
FREE Programs Disk and NorthC Public Domain compiler when ordered direct from Bruce Smith Books.

Mastering Amiga Printers
by Robin Burton
ISBN: 1-873308-05-1 – Price £19.95   336 pages. Now Available.
FREE Programs disk when ordered direct from Bruce Smith Books.

Mastering Amiga Workbench
by Bruce Smith
ISBN: 1-873308-08-6 – Price £19.95   320 pages. Now Available

Mastering Amiga System
by Paul Overaa
ISBN: 1-873308-06-X – Price £29.95   398 pages. Now Available.
FREE Utilities PD Disk when ordered direct from Bruce Smith Books.

Mastering Amiga Assembler
by Paul Overaa
ISBN: 1-873308-11-6 – Price £24.95   416 pages. Now Available.
FREE Utilities PD Disk when ordered direct from Bruce Smith Books.

Mastering Amiga AREXX
by Paul Overaa
ISBN: 1-873308-13-2 – Price £tba 400 pages approx.
Available early 1993

Amiga A600 Insider Guide
by Bruce Smith
ISBN: 1-873308-14-0 – Price £14.95   288 pages approx.
Available November 1992

E&OE.

Index

B

C

S